FLAGS OF THE WORLD

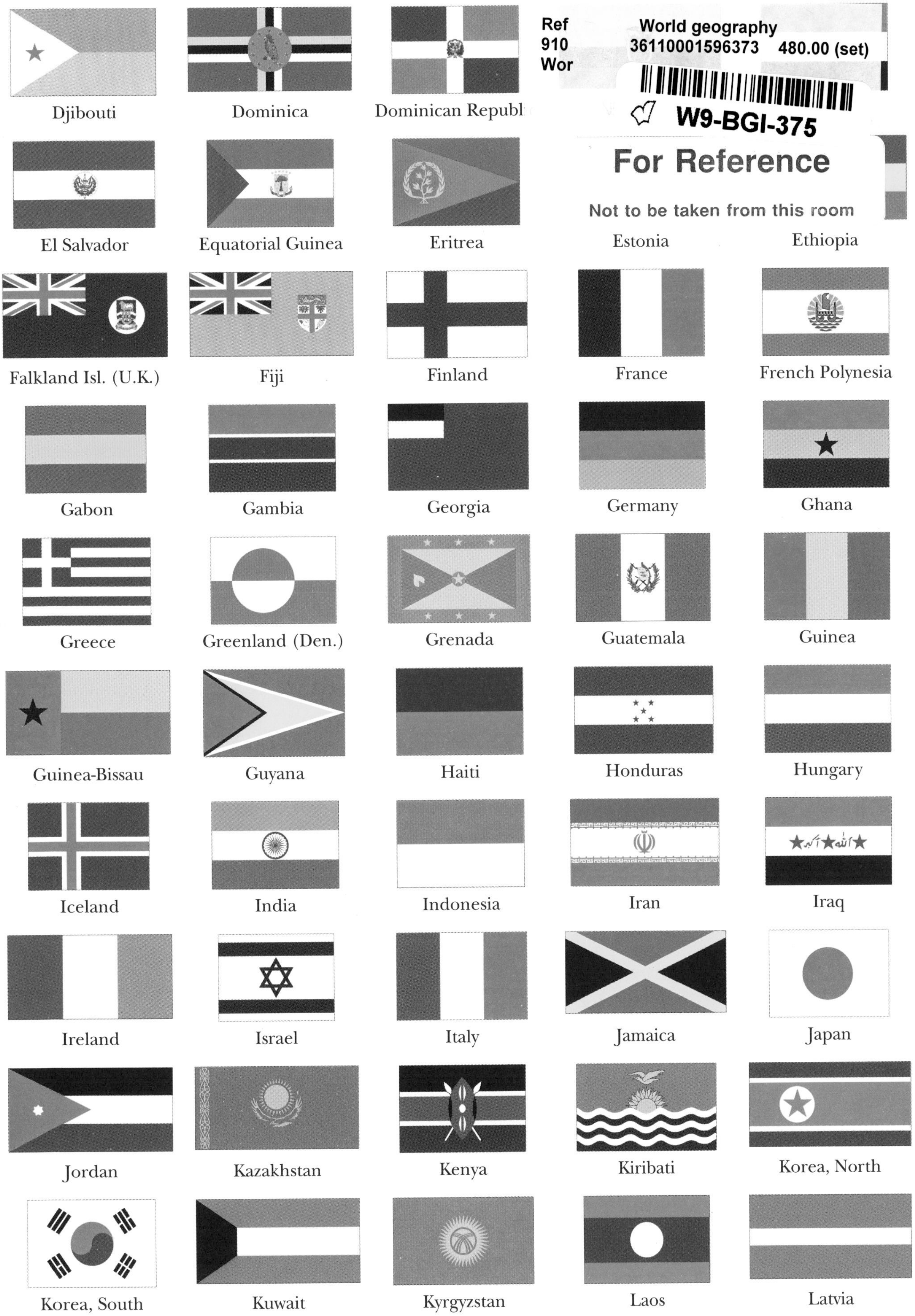

Djibouti

Dominica

Dominican Republ

El Salvador

Equatorial Guinea

Eritrea

Estonia

Ethiopia

Falkland Isl. (U.K.)

Fiji

Finland

France

French Polynesia

Gabon

Gambia

Georgia

Germany

Ghana

Greece

Greenland (Den.)

Grenada

Guatemala

Guinea

Guinea-Bissau

Guyana

Haiti

Honduras

Hungary

Iceland

India

Indonesia

Iran

Iraq

Ireland

Israel

Italy

Jamaica

Japan

Jordan

Kazakhstan

Kenya

Kiribati

Korea, North

Korea, South

Kuwait

Kyrgyzstan

Laos

Latvia

WORLD GEOGRAPHY

WORLD GEOGRAPHY

Volume 5

Europe

Editor

Ray Sumner

Long Beach City College

Managing Editor

R. Kent Rasmussen

SALEM PRESS, INC.

Pasadena, California   Hackensack, New Jersey

Editor in Chief: Dawn P. Dawson

Managing Editor: R. Kent Rasmussen   *Research Supervisor:* Jeffry Jensen

Manuscript Editor: Irene Struthers Rush   *Acquisitions Editor:* Mark Rehn

Production Editor: Cynthia Beres   *Page Design and Layout:* James Hutson

Photograph Editor: Philip Bader   *Additional Layout:* William Zimmerman

Assistant Editors: Andrea Miller, Heather Stratton   *Graphics:* Electronic Illustrators Group

Cover Design: Moritz Design, Los Angeles, Calif.

Frontispiece: Malta, Sicily, and Southern Italy from space. *(Corbis)*

Library of Congress Cataloging-in-Publication Data

World geography / editor, Ray Sumner ; managing editor, R. Kent Rasmussen.

    p. cm.

    Contents: v. 1. The World. — v. 2. North America and the Caribbean. — v. 3. Central and South America. — v. 4. Africa. — v. 5. Asia. — v. 6. Europe. — v. 7. Antarctica, Australia, and the Pacific. — v. 8. Glossary and Appendices.

    Includes bibliographical references (p.   ).

    ISBN 0-89356-024-3 (set : alk. paper) — ISBN 0-89356-276-9 (v. 1 : alk. paper) — ISBN 0-89356-277-7 (v. 2 : alk. paper) — ISBN 0-89356-335-8 (v. 3 : alk. paper) — ISBN 0-89356-336-6 (v. 4 : alk. paper) — ISBN 0-89356-399-4 (v. 5 : alk. paper) — ISBN 0-89356-650-0 (v. 6 : alk. paper) — ISBN 0-89356-699-3 (v. 7 : alk. paper) — ISBN 0-89356-723-X (v. 8 : alk. paper)

    1. Geography—Encyclopedias. I. Sumner, Ray.

G133.W88 2001

910′.3—dc21

2001020281

First Printing

PRINTED IN THE UNITED STATES OF AMERICA

CONTENTS

EUROPE

REGIONS

PHYSICAL GEOGRAPHY

BIOGEOGRAPHY AND NATURAL RESOURCES

HUMAN GEOGRAPHY

Eᴄᴏɴᴏᴍɪᴄ Gᴇᴏɢʀᴀᴘʜʏ

Gᴀᴢᴇᴛᴛᴇᴇʀ   1423

WORLD GEOGRAPHY

REGIONS

WESTERN EUROPE

*Map
Page 1239*

Western Europe extends from the western edge of the Atlantic Ocean and the Bay of Biscay, its seaboard there consisting of the French Maritime provinces, Spanish Galicia and Asturias, the Basque provinces, and Portugal's Atlantic islands. To the south, Western Europe is bounded by the Straits of Gibraltar and the Mediterranean Sea and its subsidiary bodies of water (the Balearic, Ligurian, Tyrrhenian, Adriatic, and Ionian Seas, and the Gulfs of Lion, Genoa, Taranto, and Venice), and includes the islands of Corsica, Sardinia, Sicily, Capri, Elba, Majorca, Menorca, Ibiza, Formentera, and the smaller islands.

The northern portion of Europe is rimmed to the northwest by the English Channel and its subsidiary bodies of water, including the Gulf of St. Malo, the Bay of the Seine, and the Strait of Dover. In the central portion is the North Sea, with the Waddenze, the German Bight and the Helgolander Bight. To the northeast lies the German-Danish border, a boundary set by the Treaty of Versailles in 1919, and the western sector of the Baltic Sea to the mouth of the River Oder, including the Kieler and Meckleburger bights. Eastward, the regional frontiers run along the Oder River Valley (generally, the present German-Polish border) and along the current Eastern borders of Germany and Austria.

PHYSICAL CHARACTERISTICS. The western and northern littorals are the extreme westernmost extension of the Great European Plain, which runs to the Central Russian uplands. The Western European portion of the plain stretches about 1,000 miles (1,600 km.) and is divided into the French and North German plains. The French Plain spans the area from the Pyrenees Mountains to the mouth of the River Meuse (Maas) and is drained by the Rivers Garonne and Dordogne (which form the Aquitaine basin), the Loire, the Seine, and the Scheldt. The North German Plain includes the Netherlands and northern Germany and extends into Poland, being watered by the Rhine/Meuse River system, the Weser, the Elbe, and the Oder.

The Iberian Peninsula is set apart physically from France and the rest of Western Europe by the Pyrenees Range and is, in the main, composed of uplands and plateaus—the Cantabrican Range along the northeastern coastal rim of the Bay of Biscay and, from north to south, the Sistema Central, Sierra Morena, and the Sistema Beltior. These highlands are punctuated by the river valleys of the Duero, Tagus, and Guadalquivir.

Bay of Biscay Page 1377

The Massif Centrale Plateau in France is bordered by the valleys of the Garonne, Loire, and Rhone Rivers. East of the Rhone Valley the Alps, Europe's most spectacular mountain range, begins. Its highest peak, Mont Blanc reaches to 15,781 feet (4,810 meters) in France. The Alps cover the greater portion of Switzerland, southwestern France, northern Italy, southern Germany, and Austria. Their northern spurs, or extensions, include the Jura, the Rhenish Slate Mountains, and the Harz Mountains.

Versailles Page 1239

The Apennine Mountains run north-south along the central spine of the Italian peninsula. The major lowland area there is the valley of the Po River, which flows below the line of the Italian Alps near Turin, eastward into the Gulf of Venice.

The vegetation over most of Western Europe's northern portion—the part bounded to the south by northern Portugal, the coast of the Bay of Biscay, French Provence, and the Alpine rim of northern Italy—is broadleaf forest; Mediterranean shrub and woodland predominate south of this general line. Alfisol soil is present in much of the northern littorals, the Italian peninsula, and central Iberia; but entisoils and mountain soils are found in adjoining regions.

Western Europe's rough dimensions are 1,400 miles (2,250 km.) east to west and 1,300 miles (2,090 km.) north to south, with Switzerland as the approximate geographic center.

POLITICAL COMPOSITION. The political map of Western Europe includes fifteen sovereign states, twelve republics, and eight monarchies: France (republic), Spain (kingdom), Portugal (republic), Andorra (dually administered autonomous principality), Italy (republic), Monaco (principality), San Marino (republic), Vatican City (papal principality), Switzerland (republic), Liechtenstein (principality), Austria (republic), Germany (republic), Luxembourg (grand duchy), Belgium (kingdom), and the Netherlands (kingdom).

A nonsovereign area, the Territory of Gibraltar, has been administered as a British crown colony since 1713. Other areas have agitated to varying degrees for separate sovereignty or complete separation

Early seventeenth century map of Europe based on the work of Gerardus Mercator. (Corbis)

A UNITED STATES OF EUROPE?

European nations in the twentieth century sought to break their centuries-old cycle of violence and to integrate their diverse cultures and ethnicities into a New Europe to be unified economically and, eventually, politically. This plan was gradually implemented after World War II, when Winston Churchill envisioned "a kind of United States of Europe," in stages:

1948:   Benelux, a free trade zone between Belgium, Luxembourg and the Netherlands, is established.

1948:   Organization for Economic Cooperation (OEEC) is created to coordinate the Marshall Plan.

1952:   European Coal and Steel Community (ECSC), between Belgium, France, Germany, Italy, Luxembourg, Netherlands is established.

1957:   European Economic Community (EEC), between Belgium, France, Germany, Italy, Luxembourg, and the Netherlands is established.

1973:   European Community expands the EEC to nine, adding Great Britain, Denmark, and Ireland.

1981:   Greece joins the European Community.

1986:   Spain and Portugal join the European Community.

1993:   European Union (EU) is established, using the existing framework of the European Community, to implement greater integration among its members.

1995:   Austria, Sweden, and Finland join the EU.

1999:   EU begins monetary integration with a common currency, the euro.

from the states under which they are currently administered: the Basque region (Euskadi) in northern Spain and southwestern France, Brittany, Catalonia, the island of Corsica, West Frisia in the Netherlands, Wallonia and Flanders in Belgium, and South Tyrol in Italy.

LANGUAGES. The languages of Western Europe, with the exception of Euskara, spoken in the Basque region, are of the Indo-European language family. Euskara has not been classified, because it bears no relationship to or affinity with any known language family. Within the Indo-European family, certain Western European languages fall into larger groupings. Romance tongues, deriving mainly from the

Latin of the Roman Empire, include French, Spanish, Portuguese, Italian, Romansch (eastern Switzerland), and Catalan (northeastern Spain). Celtic languages include Irish and Scottish Gaelic, Welsh, Breton (Brittany in northwestern France) and Galician (extreme northwestern Spain). Germanic tongues include German, Dutch, Flemish (spoken in Flanders in northern Belgium), Frisian (northeastern Netherlands), and English.

There are pockets of Slavic speakers in the southern border region of the Austrian Alps (Slovenian and Croatian in Carinthia and Burgenland, respectively). French is also spoken in Monaco, the southern portion of Belgium (Wallonia),

Roman ruins Page 1240

western Switzerland, and—along with German—in Luxembourg. German is spoken in Liechtenstein, the greater portion of the Swiss cantons, Austria, small areas in eastern Belgium, and in scattered communities in the southern Tyrolean region of the Italian Alps. Italian is spoken in San Marino, some parts of Corsica, and in certain southern Swiss cantons. In Andorra, both French and Spanish are spoken, although Catalan is the language of common usage. Significant patois—which some argue constitute separate linguistic entities—exist in many provincial areas throughout Western Europe, especially in Alsace (eastern France), Languedoc and Provence (southern France), Luxem-

bourg, Corsica, and South Schleswig in Germany.

RELIGIONS. The vast majority of Western Europe's population adheres to one or another Christian denomination. Roman Catholicism is the predominant Christian variant in Spain, Portugal, most areas of France, Italy, Belgium, Luxembourg, Monaco, Andorra, Liechtenstein, Austria, a portion of the Swiss cantons, and Southern Germany (mainly Bavaria, Wurtemberg, Baden, and the Rhineland).

The Lutheran Protestant faith holds sway in northern Germany, while varying offshoots of Calvinism are in the majority in the Cevennes, Vivarais, and other parts of French Languedoc, most of the Swiss

Innsbruck, the site of two Winter Olympic Games. (PhotoDisc)

cantons, and the greater part of the Netherlands. Many urban centers contain Jewish communities, the highest proportion residing in France, and an increasingly significant number of Islamic worshippers. This is largely a result of the immigration of unskilled workers from North Africa, West Africa, the Middle East, and the Balkans. France has the largest number, because its colonial empire included many countries in Muslim regions.

CLIMATE. Western Europe spans two major humid midlatitude climatic regions. A Mediterranean climate prevails in the south, along a line extending 50 miles (80 km.) below the Bay of Biscay through France to a line below the Alps, and including the bulk of the Italian peninsula. It is distinguished by warm, dry summers, cool winters, moderate precipitation, and low humidity; vegetation is Mediterranean chaparral.

From this line north to the English Channel, North Sea, and Baltic Sea coasts, the climate is marine west coast, notable for deciduous forest vegetation, mild winters and summers, and prevailing westerly rainfall during the cooler season.

The Alpine region is in a class by itself—typically having a high-altitude climate with coniferous forestation and generally cooler highlands temperatures.

DEMOGRAPHY. Western Europe is one of the world's most densely populated areas. The Parisian basin, the Benelux countries, the portion of Germany along the North German Plain, and northern and central Italy average 300 or more people per square mile. Maritime France, maritime Portugal, the area around the Rhone basin, most of the remainder of northern Germany and southern Italy, and easternmost Austria average 150-300 individuals per square mile.

Less-densely populated areas include the French Massif Centrale, the Iberian plateau (except for the Madrid metropolitan area), the interior Pyrenees, and the more remote Alpine areas. Major urban centers include Oporto and Lisbon in Portugal; Paris, Marseilles, Lyons, Bordeaux, and Toulouse in France; Turin, Milan, Rome, Naples, and Venice in Italy; Madrid and Barcelona in Spain; Brussels and Antwerp in Belgium; Amsterdam, Rotterdam, and The Hague in the Netherlands; Berlin, Hamburg, Dortmund-Essen, Munich, and Frankfurt-am-Main in Germany; Zurich, Basel, and Geneva in Switzerland; and Vienna and Linz in Austria.

ECONOMY. Although Western Europe is one of the world's most intensely industrialized regions, agriculture still plays a major role. In the south, Mediterranean agriculture geared heavily toward the export market is most common. The main products there are grains, grapes and wine, olives and olive oil, figs, fruit, vegetables, beef, and sheep. The northern lowlands produce such cooler-weather crops as grains, cabbage, potatoes, sugar beets, and turnips. Cattle, hog, and sheep farming are also widespread. Among the nonmanufacturing and nontechnological industries, fishing, tourism, and services are the most significant.

The main industrial concentrations are found along the Catalan coast of northeastern Spain, including the city of Barcelona; the lower Seine from the coast to Paris, France; most of the Benelux countries; in a belt extending from the coast through Liege into Germany to the Ruhr, Lower Saxony, Brandenburg (Berlin) and the Bohemian basin; and through the Saar coal-mining area into northern Lorraine as far as Nancy in France (the *Pays de ferre* or "Land of iron"); the region around the city of Lille in northern France; central eastern France through Belfort and Sochaux-Montbelliard and into northern Switzerland; and northern Italy with major

Lisbon
Page 1432

Spanish
farms
Page 1249

Barcelona
Page 1375

concentrations around Turin, Milan, and Venice-Mestre. Western Europe is resource-poor in oil fuel, having to import the bulk of its crude, but significant coal deposits are found in Eastern France and Western Germany.

Coal
Page 1318

Industry is highly diversified and includes heavy machinery, optical and surgical instruments, chemicals, technology, building materials, automobile manufacturing, shipbuilding, food processing, pharmaceuticals, electronics, and printing and publishing.

Raymond Pierre Hylton

FOR FURTHER STUDY

Abercrombie, Thomas J. "The Basques: Europe's First Family." *National Geographic* (November, 1995): 74-97.

Durbin, Chris. *The European Community.* New York: Watts, 1994.

Knox, Paul J. *A Geography of Western Europe: A Socio-Economic Survey.* Totowa, N.J.: Barnes & Noble, 1984.

Krause, Axel. *Inside the New Europe.* New York: HarperCollins, 1991.

Mazower, Mark. *Dark Continent: Europe's Twentieth Century.* New York: Knopf, 1999.

Panayi, Panikos. *An Ethnic History of Europe Since 1945: Nation-States and Minorities.* Harlow, England: Longmans, 2000.

Roberts, Elizabeth. *The New Europe: Maastricht and Beyond.* New York: Gloucester Press, 1993.

Unwin, Derek W. *The Community of Europe: A History of European Integration Since 1945.* New York: Longmans, 1995.

Wallace, William. *Regional Integration: The West European Experience.* Washington, D.C.: Brookings Institution, 1994.

THE BRITISH ISLES

Map
Page 1242

The British Isles are located off the northwest coast of mainland Europe. At the nearest point across the Strait of Dover, they are only 22 miles (35 km.) from the French coast. They stand on the continental shelf; even so, the surrounding waters can be stormy and uncertain. The prevailing current is the southwesterly Gulf Stream, which gives a yearlong temperate climate.

The British Isles consist of two main islands, Great Britain and Ireland; numerous small island clusters, such as the Orkneys and Shetlands; and individual islands, such as the Isle of Man. The Irish Sea separates the two main islands, narrowing to the North Channel 13 miles (21 km.) wide at its narrowest, and to the south, to the St. George's Channel, 48.5 miles (78 km.) at its narrowest. They lie between 49°90′ north latitude (the Scilly Isles) and 60°90′ north latitude (the Shetlands). Longitudinally, they lie between 10°50′ west and 1°70′ east. The longest uninterrupted land distance lies between John o'Groats in the north and Land's End in the south of mainland Britain, a distance of some 1,000 miles (1,600 km.).

PHYSICAL FEATURES: GREAT BRITAIN. Britain is bounded to the east by the North Sea; to the south by the English Channel, one of Europe's busiest sea lanes; and to the west by the Irish and Celtic Seas. The north and west of Britain are typified by ranges of hills and mountains running variously southwest to northeast, or north to south. The mountains of Wales, northwest England, and northern Scotland are particularly old (granites) and suitable only for light grazing and recreational purposes. Lowland areas lie to the east, south, and southeast, in small coastal areas in northwest England and southern Wales, and in the east-west midland valley of Scotland.

Stonehenge
Page 1243

Glaciation from the last ice age affects all but southern England. The most fertile areas are the English Midlands and East Anglia, where the traditional agricultural wealth has lain. The chief crops are cereals, oil seed, vegetables, and potatoes. Cattle, sheep, and poultry are plentiful.

Britain contains few navigable rivers and its extensive canal system now is used only recreationally. However, its many large estuaries and natural harborage have traditionally provided an abundance of ports all round the coast except in northwest Scotland. Numerous lakes are situated in the mountains, many of which are used as reservoirs and, in Scotland, for hydroelectric projects. There is a declining fish stock in the seas, now strictly controlled by fishing quotas. Rainfall is plentiful, especially on the western side of the island.

Land's End
Page 1379

Coal production peaked in 1913 and now is largely confined to output for coal-burning electricity-generating plants. Iron ore production has declined also. However, oil and natural gas were discovered in the North Sea in 1970, and later in the Irish Sea, and these are now Britain's main fossil fuel resource. There are twelve nuclear power stations, which have not proved popular. There are plentiful supplies of salt, but most other mineral resources are imported.

Welsh village Page 1245

Scottish hills Page 1242

PHYSICAL FEATURES: IRELAND. The island of Ireland is bounded on the east by the Irish Sea; on the south by the Celtic Sea; and by the Atlantic Ocean in all other directions. It could be described as saucerlike in physical projection. Mountains of up to 3,250 feet (1,000 meters) lie around the perimeter, except the central east coast around Dublin; in the center lies a plain full of rivers, lakes, and peat bogs. The geological formations run southwest to northeast and are continuous with those of Wales and Scotland. The western mountains particularly are treeless, suitable only for light grazing. Some of these areas are uninhabited. Much of the underlying rock is sandstone and limestone, being overlaid by glacial and other deposits in the center.

Various types of farming use about 83 percent of the country, and 23 percent of Irish exports are agricultural. Forestry is limited; fishing is small scale but plentiful, both in inland waters and the seas. Lough Neagh in Northern Ireland is the largest lake in the British Isles. The heavy rainfall, often 100 inches (254 centimeters) annually in the west, has led to the term "the Emerald Isle" and the green of the Irish tricolor.

Ireland has few mineral resources. In the absence of coal and timber, peat has been the traditional fuel, and several electric power stations are peat-fired. Hydroelectric projects along the River Shannon provide much of the island's electricity. A small natural gas field lies off Kinsale on the south coast. Ireland's many areas of

Fishing boats in Dublin. (PhotoDisc)

London's famous black taxi cabs help form one of the world's busiest public transportation systems. (PhotoDisc)

outstanding natural beauty on the Atlantic coast and in the southeast form the basis of a thriving tourist industry.

ECONOMIC DEVELOPMENT IN GREAT BRITAIN. Historically, Great Britain was the first country to become industrialized, moving toward an urbanized society at the beginning of the nineteenth century. Areas particularly affected were those situated near iron and coal deposits and ports. Those were mainly located in the midland valley of Scotland; the North and the west and north Midlands of England; and South Wales. Because of the political and economic predominance of London, all new forms of communication still led there, and it drew secondary industrial and commercial growth to itself.

Although the nature of such industry has largely changed over the last 150 years,

urban patterns have remained. As older industries such as cotton and woollen mills or shipbuilding yards have shut down, new industries usually have been attracted to replace them, often through government subsidies. In South Wales, for example, coal mining and iron manufacture have been replaced by consumer electronics and fiber-optics. New roads have increased accessibility for foreign investment, and the adaptability of the local workforce and its successful use of Japanese work practices in particular have led to new growth and business confidence. Cardiff, Wales, has again become a thriving city. New industrial wealth from oil and natural gas have not influenced these patterns, since these resources are out at sea.

New towns have been created as one means of urban renewal; slum clearance

Thatched-roof house Page 1244

schemes have been less successful. Strict zoning laws exist throughout the United Kingdom. One area, southeast England, has been an exception. Largely rural until the end of the twentieth century, the unprecedented growth of London as a national and international cultural, financial, and political center and a major port with a well-developed commuter railroad network has continued to pull population and service industries into its peripheries. The metropolitan area of London has extended beyond its immediate Home Counties into the whole of the southeast. Special greenbelt zoning to protect rural areas has only been partially successfully applied. London's growth underlined the rapid shift from manufacturing industries to service ones.

ECONOMIC DEVELOPMENT IN IRELAND. By contrast, Ireland has remained largely rural, having no mineral resources to be exploited in the industrialization of Western Europe. Only the Belfast area in the predominantly pro-British (unionist) northeast of the island developed, first through the manufacture of textiles (particularly linen) and shipbuilding, then through the aircraft industry. At the 1921 partition, the republic was left without this industrial base and fell back into its traditional role of exporter of foodstuffs and unskilled labor, particularly to Britain. The postrevolutionary Irish governments wanted to keep a traditional rural and Roman Catholic set of values and urbanization was not encouraged. Consequently, Dublin stayed the only major Irish city.

In 1959 the Irish government instituted a program of modernization. The fruit of this was membership in the European Union and rapid economic growth in the 1970's, largely fuelled by foreign capital. Ireland became one of the world's most indebted nations per head of population. When a recession came in the 1980's, the government reluctantly reined in the expansion. However, Ireland had kept a trade surplus, but the measures, as in Britain under Margaret Thatcher, brought social divisiveness although they were successful economically.

Not until 1971 did more than 50 percent of Ireland's population live in towns or cities. It is still one of the least urbanized countries in Western Europe. While Dublin has attracted most growth, it has perhaps been least able to solve those urban problems of slums, high unemployment among the unskilled, and faceless housing projects that breed crime.

LOCAL ISSUES. Typically, large industrialized cities and conurbations have drawn migrants from rural areas and small towns and from other countries, as economic migrants or political refugees. The United Kingdom's former headship of a large overseas empire drew significant numbers

---

Chunnel Page 1369

THE CHUNNEL

Although a tunnel under the Strait of Dover had been discussed since the time of Napoleon, it was only in 1994 that plans for a rail link under the sea were carried out. Financed by France and Great Britain at a cost of $16 billion, the tunnel is 31 miles (50 km.) long. Trains carry cars and trucks and passengers straight from London to Brussels or Paris. Britain's strict quarantine laws still apply, however: Although a non-British pet owner can cross the channel in thirty-five minutes, a non-British pet must be held for six months.

of migrants from its former colonies, especially from the West Indies and the Indian subcontinent between 1954 and 1962, to service the economic growth of the 1950's and 1960's. Recessions in the 1970's and 1980's caused significant social problems among such groups, and racial tensions grew. Ethnic groups have continued to remain somewhat ghettoized in the larger cities of the British Isles. Dublin is an exception—its social problems are largely indigenous, reflecting the less advanced nature of welfare and town-planning in Ireland.

The United Kingdom reorganized its local government several times over the last half of the twentieth century to reflect its growing population and to attempt to create larger and more efficient units. The former county of London as part of a two-tier system of local government was reformed first into Greater London and then into one-tier metropolitan districts. Boundaries of cities have been extended, and counties have been reorganized similarly. By contrast, the Republic of Ireland has kept its original allocation of 26 of Ireland's 32 counties, adding only five county boroughs. Again, this reflects the more conservative nature of the Irish political system, and the depopulation of many areas.

More significant, the growing centralization of government in the Thatcher era (1979-1996) was reversed by the recreation of the Scottish Parliament situated in Edinburgh and a Welsh Assembly in Cardiff. Powers have been devolved from the central government sitting in

Canterbury Cathedral, in southeastern England, is the seat of the archbishop of Canterbury, the head of the church of England. The cathedral site's history stretched back to Saxon times. The present cathedral was built in the late twelfth century, after the previous cathedral was nearly destroyed by fire. The cathedral is famous as the destination of the pilgrims in Geoffrey Chaucer's Canterbury Tales *(1387-1400). (PhotoDisc)*

Westminster, London. A Northern Ireland Assembly was also restored in 1999 as part of the peace accord there. No plans exist for creation of regional assemblies for England or the Irish Republic. The Isle of Man and the Channel Islands have always been self-governing.

David Barratt

Edinburgh
Page 1380

1211

FOR FURTHER STUDY

Brunt, Barry. *The Republic of Ireland.* London: Paul Chapman, 1988.

Central Office of Information. *Britain 2000: An Official Handbook.* London: H.M.S.O., 1999.

Hudson, Ray, and Allan Williams. *The United Kingdom.* London: Harper & Row, 1986.

Panton, Kenneth J., and Keith A. Cowlard. *Historical Dictionary of the United Kingdom.* Landham, Md.: Scarecrow Press, 1998.

Stamp, Dudley, and Stanley H. Beaver. *The British Isles: A Geographic and Economic Survey.* 6th ed. London: Longman, 1971.

Thomas, Colin, and Avril Thomas. *Historical Dictionary of Ireland.* Landham, Md.: Scarecrow Press, 1997.

SCANDINAVIA

*Map
Page 1245*

*Balstad,
Norway
Page 1246*

*Stockholm
Page 1443*

The Scandinavian Peninsula in northern Europe extends south from the northwestern corner of Russia and includes the countries of Sweden and Norway. Scandinavia, as a region, also includes Denmark, Iceland, and Finland. Denmark is located on the Jutland Peninsula, north of Germany and west of Sweden, and includes more than 450 islands. Iceland, the westernmost country of Europe, is an island in the Atlantic Ocean, just below the Arctic Circle. Finland is located across the Gulf of Bothnia from the Scandinavia Peninsula and adjacent to Russia. The term Norden is sometimes used to refer to all five of these countries; Fenno-scandia refers only to Sweden, Norway, and Finland.

Scandinavian countries extend from the plains of Germany in the south to the Arctic Circle in the north. They are unified by a challenging physical environment and the history of the region. The Viking explorers came from this area, which was a single country for a long period of history. Today, the separate countries have small populations but enjoy much prosperity and have some of the world's highest levels of living.

POPULATION. The population of the region is small, with a low population density. In all countries, the highest populations are found in the southern parts of the country. In Finland, the majority of population is found around the capital of Helsinki, with some 1.5 million people in the metropolitan area. Other large cities in Finland include Tampere and Turku, and Rovaniemi on the Arctic Circle. Other

geographic locations of interest are the Åland Islands and Lapland. In Norway, the Oslo region in the south has the majority of the country's population, with about 1 million residents. Other locations of interest include Bergen, Trondheim, Hammerfest, and the North Cape.

In Sweden, the corridor from Stockholm to Göteborg via Lake Vänern has a high population density, which expands to the south where Malmö is located. Further north, centers such as Kiruna are of interest. Denmark's capital, Copenhagen, and the surrounding area has well over 1 million people, and Odense, Åarhus, and Allberg follow. The population of Iceland is concentrated on the western side of the island, with Reykjavik being the only significant city of the country.

CULTURES. Except for the Finns, the people of these countries share linguistic, cultural, and religious ties, which help people in the region to relate to one another. The Evangelical Lutheran Church is the major Scandinavian religion, with at least 90 percent of the population as adherents. This Protestant faith has influenced the lives of the people and their attitudes toward work and social life. Recently, the combination of affluence and materialism has broken many of these cultural links and loosened the control exercised by the churches in many activities.

The languages of Denmark, Norway, Sweden, and Iceland are all Germanic in origin, and people from these four countries can often speak to and understand each other without much difficulty. The Finnish language is distinct and unique in

THE SAUNA: FROM THE WOODS OF FINLAND TO THE HOTELS OF THE WORLD

A feature of Scandinavian life that has become popular worldwide is the sauna. Originally used for bathing by Finns and other Scandinavians, the practice of sweating in a small, heated room and throwing water on the rocks to make steam dates back over a thousand years. The sauna also was used as a birthing place before hospitals became common. Early Finnish homesteaders in North America built saunas before completing their main dwelling quarters. Often people and animals lived in the sauna together before other farm buildings were built.

First observed by the Russian missionary Saint Andrew in the year 1100, the sauna has not changed much since. Men and women, children and entire families sit together, sweating in air temperatures ranging from 140 to 203 degrees Fahrenheit (60 to 95 degrees Celsius). Beating the body with birch whisks encourages perspiration. The whisks are made of birch branches with leaves tied together to form what looks like a small whisk with a handle. In the summer, one cools down by jumping into a lake for a swim. In the winter, a dive into a snowbank or a quick dip into a hole made in a frozen lake does the trick. Although most North Americans are unaware of the sauna's traditional use, the sauna has become a popular amenity in hotels and health facilities. Its use in the United States developed partly as a result of the 1960 Winter Olympics held in California, where Finnish athletes introduced the sauna to others. Of the three million saunas that exist worldwide, two million are found in Finland. *Sauna* is perhaps the only Finnish word commonly used in the English language.

---

the region, being part of the Finno-Ugric family, which is related to Hungarian and Estonian.

ECONOMIES. The economic development of Scandinavian countries has been relatively recent. Sweden has the longest history of industrialization, beginning in the mid-ninteenth century, and is the most industrialized. Farming has been important in the southern half of the country, where there are dairy farms and some grain farms. The center of the southern part of the country is the city of Malmö. Sweden has large deposits of iron ore and other minerals in the northern parts of the country, the most important location being in Kiruna. Forests are also used, and with good management they provide a continually renewable natural resource. Much iron and wood is exported, but there is diverse manufacturing in the central part of Sweden, extending from Stockholm to Göteborg. This region produces stainless steel products, ships, automobiles, electronics, furniture, and glassware. Sweden also has developed and maintained a strong social support system for the country's population.

Denmark's economy is based on agriculture and high-tech manufacturing. Seventy-five percent of its lowland area on the Jutland Peninsula and the islands of Fyn and Zealand are farmed, with an emphasis on dairy and livestock products. Danish cheeses and butter cookies are popular worldwide. Copenhagen, located on the largest Danish island, grew as a port controlling the entrance to the Baltic Sea, acting as a center of trade and transshipment of goods. It is now a major service and

Copenhagen
Page 1378

manufacturing center with government offices and financial services.

Norway, because of its mountainous physical landscapes, has little arable land. Farming is only possible around the southeastern corner of the country, near Oslo and Trondheim. Until the 1970's, Norway's economy was based on fishing and the smelting of metals using hydroelectricity. With the discovery and exploitation of oil and natural gas in the North Sea, Norway found a new resource base, which has helped improve its fortunes. More than half the country's wealth comes directly from the North Sea resources. Many of the profits obtained from this industry have gone to improve the infrastructure of the country, which has encouraged and increased tourism there. The success of the 1994 Winter Olympics also has promoted tourist growth. Some Norwegian products include canned fish and thin bread.

Finland is a northern country with short summers and thin soils. It has a few mineral resources and, for a long period, was inhibited from economic development because its position next to the Soviet Union forced it to trade with that country and avoid external political ties. Until recently, the forests were the biggest natural re-

source, with timber and pulp making up half of Finland's annual exports. In the late 1990's, the export of high-tech equipment such as cellular phones made up more than half its exports. Most people live in the southern part of the country, in or around the capital of Helsinki. Well-known products obtained from Finland include metal manufactured goods, machinery, ships, glassware, and mobile phones.

Iceland is the smallest of the Scandinavian countries, and was linked to Denmark until it gained its independence in 1918. Along with Greenland, which also was part of the Danish Kingdom until 1979, it is much influenced by Denmark. Fishing, the biggest industry of the country, was threatened by foreign fishermen who obtained many fish from waters near Iceland, until an international agreement extended the offshore fishing limit to 200 miles. Foreign fishing vessels can no longer fish inside this limit. Iceland also has developed and improved its attraction as a tourist destination. Ecotourism and such natural features as the volcanoes of Mount Hekla, geysers, hot thermal pools, and glaciers have brought more tourists to the island.

Mika Roinila

Norwegian farms Page 1247

INFORMATION ON THE WORLD WIDE WEB

There are numerous Web sites featuring information about Scandinavian countries. The following sites are good starting places on each country:

Virtual Finland, a Web site maintained by the Ministry of Foreign Affairs of Finland, features current articles and news about Finland. (virtual.finland.fi/)

Guide to Sweden is an on-line guide for tourists and visitors. (www.swedenguide.com/)

A Web site called Norwegian Scenery features information about Norwegian cultures, economy, geography, government, and history. (www.norwegian-scenery.com/)

Explore Denmark is a site collecting links to Denmark-related topics. (www.geocities .com/TheTropics/4597/)

A Web site sponsored by the Icelandic Tourist Board gives information about the history, geology, and cultures of Iceland. (www.goiceland.org/main.htm)

FOR FURTHER STUDY

Brown, Jules, and Mick Sinclair. *Scandinavia: The Rough Guide.* 4th ed. London: Rough Guides, 1997.

Eskola, Matti. *Facts about Finland.* 4th ed. Helsinki, Finland: Otava, 1996.

Halfdanarson, Gudmundur. *Historical Dictionary of Iceland.* Landham, Md.: Scarecrow Press, 1997.

"Happy Family? A Survey of the Nordic Countries." *The Economist,* January 23, 1999. Special Insert, 16 pages.

Hintz, Martin. *Sweden.* Chicago: Childrens Press, 1985.

John, Brian S. *Scandinavia: A New Geography.* New York: Longman Publishing, 1984.

Maude, George. *Historical Dictionary of Finland.* Landham, Md.: Scarecrow Press, 1995.

Scobbie, Irene. *Historical Dictionary of Sweden.* Landham, Md.: Scarecrow Press, 1995.

Taylor-Wilkie, Doreen. *Insight Guides: Norway.* 2d ed. Boston: Houghton Mifflin, 1998.

Thomas, Alastair H., and Stewart P. Oakley. *Historical Dictionary of Denmark.* Landham, Md.: Scarecrow Press, 1998.

MEDITERRANEAN EUROPE

*Map
Page 1247*

The location of Mediterranean Europe may be considered in absolute and relative terms. The absolute location is about 35 degrees to 45 degrees north latitude and about longitude 10 degrees west to 27 degrees east. The relative location or situation has changed throughout history.

In ancient times, the eastern Mediterranean was the center of Western civilization. From about 1600 to 1400 B.C.E., the Minoan people of Crete, the oldest of the Aegean civilizations, had interests extending from Egypt to Sicily and north to Athens and probably Troy. The focus shifted between 264 and 133 B.C.E. as Rome extended its control from the Italian peninsula to the entire Mediterranean Sea. In the fifteenth and sixteenth centuries, the focal point was the Iberian Peninsula, as Portugal and Spain reigned as great sea powers. The region then declined in importance until the opening of the Suez Canal, which linked the Mediterranean and Red Seas and allowed Europe much quicker access to South and East Asia.

Boundaries change according to the criteria selected to define a region. If one considers nation-states, Mediterranean Europe has traditionally included Greece, Italy, Portugal (although it has no Mediterranean coastline), Spain, and the island countries of Cyprus and Malta. Using natural phenomena, an inner or "true" Mediterranean Europe can be identified whose limit is that of the Mediterranean climate, roughly coextensive with the olive tree. The young fold mountains to the north—the Pyrenees, Alps, and Dinaric Alps—mark the limits of a larger Mediterranean Europe.

Wherever the boundaries are drawn, Mediterranean Europe is a cohesive region. The most unifying factor is the Mediterranean Sea. There is a great interpenetration of land and sea, most notable in Greece. The proximity to the sea, along with an absence of strong surface currents in most parts, a small tidal range, and frequently clear skies, has favored participation in navigation, fishing, and maritime trade. The sea also offered easier routes of communication than the surrounding lands.

PHYSIOGRAPHY. A basic similarity of relief exists throughout Mediterranean Europe. The proximity of the relatively young fold mountains to the sea has led to the formation of mountains and hills close to or even abutting the coasts. East and west of the Alps lay arcuate ridges that enclose many plateaus and depressions. The main plateau is the Meseta Central of Spain. The most significant depressions are the Plain of Lombardy and Po Valley in northern Italy. The coastal plains are small, discontinuous, and isolated, but occasionally are linked to the interior by easily traveled corridors such as the Carcassone Gap and the Rhone Corridor in France.

*Po Valley
Page 1438*

CLIMATE. The inner or "true" Mediterranean Europe shares the Mediterranean climate, which has hot, dry summers and cool, moist winters. This unusual climate results from the region's location in a transition zone between high- and low-pressure belts and between trade and westerly winds. In the summer, high pressure,

*Southern
Spain
Pages
1248,
1249, 1305*

THE MEDITERRANEAN REGION'S NATURAL HAZARDS

Structurally young and in the contact zone between two of the world's great crustal plates—the Eurasian and African—most of Mediterranean Europe is subject to volcanism and earthquakes as mountain-building continues. Earthquake disasters have struck Greece, Italy, Portugal, and elsewhere in the region: Dubrovnik, in what is now Croatia, was shattered in 1667; Lisbon, Portugal, was destroyed in 1775; numerous villages in northeastern Italy were leveled in 1976; and thousands were left homeless in Greece in 1999. The most destructive quakes have been along the coasts, where resulting tidal waves have swept over the lowlands.

Although volcanic activity was once widespread, Italy is now the center of such activity. Etna, on the east coast of Sicily, is Europe's largest active volcano. It has claimed many lives over the last twenty-five centuries and has extended the island's shoreline with its lava flows. Vesuvius, to the southeast of Naples, is the only active volcano on the European mainland. In 79 C.E., its eruption destroyed the Roman cities of Pompeii, Herculaneum, and Stabiae. As recently as 1906, Vesuvius erupted for ten days, killing two thousand people.

northerly winds, and North African air masses prevail over the region. The average temperatures in July range from about 70 to 85 degrees Fahrenheit (21 to 29 degrees Celsius). During the sunny days, the temperatures can soar beyond 104 degrees Fahrenheit (40 degrees Celsius).

In the winter, low pressure and westerly winds allow Atlantic storms to penetrate into the region. As the lows approach, southerly winds such as the sirocco can bring hot North African air northward. As the lows retreat eastward, cold northerly winds such as the mistral can move southward along corridors tied to central Europe. Föhn winds may move south over the mountains and warm as they descend leeward slopes. Annual rainfall typically ranges from 15 to 35 inches (38 to 89 centimeters), although mountainous areas may receive considerably more precipitation.

BIOGEOGRAPHY. This region was once covered by a Mediterranean open forest of broadleaf evergreen trees and woody shrubs with interspersed grasses, but frequent cutting for timber and repeated burning to create pastureland prevented the forest from reestablishing itself. Today, there are small open woodlands of holm oak, wild olive, and other trees, all of which tend to be short and are broad-leaved, evergreen, and gnarled. The fruit may be small and thick (like the olive) and the bark may be thick (like the cork oak). All these characteristics help to reduce the evaporation of water.

Relatively common are thickets of tangled evergreen bushes and shrubs such as brooms and common myrtle; they are called *maquis* in French and *matorral* in Spanish. In areas of dry, shallow soil, especially over limestone, there is often garigue, which consists of highly scattered bushes such as broom and low-growing aromatic plants such as lavender, sage, and thyme. Two American desert plants, the century plant and prickly pear, were introduced by the Spaniards in the sixteenth century, and they are now common in garigue.

Wildlife has largely been relegated to marginal lands such as the mountains and deserts. The domesticated animals are similar to those found elsewhere in Europe, but sheep and goats are particularly well adapted to the dry conditions and scanty herbage. They are supplemented by cattle, pigs, fowls, bees, and the silkworm.

MEDITERRANEAN SOCIETY. Since Greco-Roman times, a degree of similarity has existed in the languages, religions, and lifestyles of the Mediterranean Europeans. Romance languages prevail from France through Italy; even the unique Basque language, Euskara, is written in the Roman alphabet, and Maltese, a Semitic language, is written with an alphabet and grammar derived from Latin. Roman Catholicism, which traditionally used Latin in its services, predominates in the same subregion. Hellenic languages, represented today by modern Greek, prevail east of Italy. Greek orthodoxy predominates in Greece and Cyprus.

About 119 million people lived in Mediterranean Europe in the year 2000. More than fourteen cities had more than 1 million inhabitants. This number is modest compared to those for western and central Europe. Farmers usually live in villages or small towns, often located on hilltops, and commute to farms in the valleys and lowlands. Even where there appears to be an isolated farmstead, the owner typically resides in town. Thus, although Mediterranean Europe is not full of cities, the urban way of life is central to the culture.

ECONOMIC GEOGRAPHY. The European Mediterranean region, except for northern Italy and part

of northern Spain, is outside Europe's urban-industrial core. Its relative economic backwardness is a consequence of the limited resource base available for industrialization.

The first impediment to development is the scarcity of water. Winter precipitation must be stored for irrigation during the summer growing season. Although the Arabs built extensive irrigation works in Spain, Sicily, and southern Italy, many of

*Sheep
Page 1249*

*Roman
ruins
Page 1240*

Olives in a shop in Athens, Greece. (PhotoDisc)

THE EUROPEAN UNION GOES SOUTH

Although France and Italy were among the six original members of the European Community (EC) when it formed in 1957, Greece was not admitted until 1981 and Spain and Portugal not until 1986. The late admissions of these countries reflected the EC's displeasure with their dictatorial governments, which existed until the mid-1970's, as well as the EC's concern over how the largely agricultural economies of Greece, Spain, and Portugal could be absorbed into a union already well supplied with Mediterranean products such as olives and wine.

Membership in the European Union (the name for the EC since 1994) will force Greece, Spain, and Portugal to adapt quickly to a common market in which goods, labor, and capital move freely across national borders. Spain and Portugal adopted the euro, the EU's new common currency, with Greece following suit. Economic union with states to the north should raise the three countries' standards of living. However, the union also requires that Mediterranean countries conform to the work schedules of the rest of the Europe. The large afternoon meal and siesta, a traditional three-hour break in Spain, is disappearing.

Barcelona
Page 1375

which are still in use, only in the twentieth century did the area under irrigation increase significantly. Before then, small-scale, unirrigated farming prevailed except in southern Spain and southern Italy, where equally unproductive *latifundia* (large estates), owned by absentee landlords, were the norm. The crops grown included wheat, barley, olives, and grapevines, and the productivity was so low that the Mediterranean countries could not compete in their own markets, let alone abroad. Today it is not uncommon to find modern irrigation works supporting a more competitive, specialized agriculture: citrus fruits, olives, cork oak, high-quality grapevines, vegetables, flowers, cotton, and rice. Wheat, barley, corn, and other

grains also are grown, usually without irrigation.

The separation of animal husbandry from crop cultivation also has impeded the development of agriculture. Livestock management has traditionally emphasized the herding of sheep and goats in dry or mountainous regions. Swine have been herded around the remnant open forests, and cattle have been common only in the few wetter locations. Their dung was not traditionally used to fertilize the fields.

Mediterranean Europe has been a latecomer to industrialization not only because of its agriculture, but also because of the scarcity of key resources. The region has a serious deficiency of coal and petroleum. However, commercial deposits of iron, the principal industrial mineral, occur in many locations, the most important of which is at Bilbao, Spain, where an important iron and steel industry has existed since the nineteenth century. The region is also well endowed with ferroalloys such as manganese and tungsten and with nonferrous metals such as lead and mercury. Bauxite, the source of aluminum, is found in commercial deposits in southern France and Greece.

The only extensively industrialized subregion is the Plain of Lombardy in northern Italy. More localized industries may be found in port cities such as Barcelona, Genoa, and Naples, or near important supplies of energy or raw materials (for example, coal in Oviedo and hydroelectricity in Turin).

The service sector is now the most important part of the region's economy. The Mediterranean basin is the most-visited region on earth, accounting for 35 percent of the total world tourism market. The tourist bonanza, however, has come with a price: Many coastal destinations are overwhelmed with visitors in July and August, and the European Mediterranean coastal waters have been polluted with sewage and industrial wastes.

Steven L. Driever

FOR FURTHER STUDY

Gilbert, Mark F., and K. Robert Nilsson. *Historical Dictionary of Modern Italy.* Landham, Md.: Scarecrow Press, 1999.

Jordan, Terry G. *The European Culture Area: A Systematic Geography.* 3d ed. New York: HarperCollins, 1996.

King, Russel, et al. *The Mediterranean: Environment and Society.* New York: John Wiley & Sons, 1997.

McDonald, James R. *The European Scene: A Geographic Perspective.* 2d ed. Upper Saddle River, N.J.: Prentice Hall, 1997.

Matvejevic, Predag. *The Mediterranean: A Cultural Landscape.* Translated by Michael H. Heim. Berkeley: University of California Press, 1999.

Panteli, Stavros. *Historical Dictionary of Cyprus.* Landham, Md.: Scarecrow Press, 1995.

Robinson, Harry. *The Mediterranean Lands.* London: University Tutorial Press, 1965.

Veremis, Thanos M., and Mark Dragoumis. *Historical Dictionary of Greece.* Landham, Md.: Scarecrow Press, 1995.

Zwingle, Erla. "Olive Oil, Elixir of the Gods." *National Geographic* (September, 1999): 66-81.

INFORMATION ON THE WORLD WIDE WEB

The World Factbook 2000 Web site, maintained by the U.S. Central Intelligence Agency (CIA), features profiles of individual European Mediterranean countries. (www.odci.gov/cia/publications/factbook/es.html#geo)

THE BALKANS

Map
Page 1250

The Balkan countries lie on a wide triangular peninsula in southeastern Europe. The triangle points south into Greece; to its west is the Adriatic Sea; to its east, the Black Sea. The northern boundary is harder to define, but can be placed to the north of the Dinaric Alps and west of the Transylvanian Alps, where mountains grade into the plains of Central-Eastern Europe.

The Balkan countries are Albania, Bosnia-Herzegovina, Bulgaria, Macedonia, and Yugoslavia (including Montenegro and Serbia). Croatia, Romania, Slovenia, and the European part of Turkey are usually regarded as Balkan also. Greece belongs to the Mediterranean region, and Hungary and Moldova also fit best into other regions.

PHYSIOGRAPHY. Mountains define the Balkans: *Balkan* means "forested mountain range" in Turkish. Most extensive are the Dinaric Alps, running from Slovenia in the northwest down to the Pindus Mountains in Greece to the south, and the Transylvanian Alps in Romania in the northeast. All are part of the great Alpine system that arches from Morocco through southern Europe into Turkey.

In the west lie the long, dry islands and infrequent coastal plains of the Adriatic Sea. Moving inland, the coast abruptly gives way to the Dinaric ranges, dense masses of interlocking ridges largely unbroken by passes. The northwestern parts of these mountains are famous for karst landforms: subterranean caves, sinkholes, and vanishing rivers caused by groundwater dissolving the underlying limestone.

Still moving eastward, the Dinaric Alps gradually give way to masses of lower mountains and basins, the sources of important rivers. In the south, the Vardar, Struma, and Maritsa flow southward to the Aegean Sea. In the north, the Sava, Drava, Drina, and Morava Rivers flow northward to join the Danube, the mightiest of Balkan rivers. These northern river valleys spread out into the Pannonian Basin, a flat, fertile plain of loess soils (glacial rock dust deposited by wind) that forms the northern border of the Balkans.

From there, the Danube flows eastward and splits the eastern Balkans into three subregions. The middle one is the rich Danube valley where Romania and Bulgaria meet, a broad, well-populated area much like the Pannonian Basin. To its north lie the massive and isolated Transylvanian Alps. The southern subregion of the eastern Balkans is made up of mountain ranges that parallel the east-west direction of the Danube: the Balkan or Stara Planina range and the Rhodope Mountains. At the easternmost edge of the Balkans, the Danube winds through marshy islands and low-lying sandy beaches to empty into the Black Sea.

CLIMATE. Most of the Balkan countries have a humid continental climate, with moderate summer temperatures and winter temperatures around freezing, much like central Europe. Temperature ranges are greater to the north and east under the influence of the Asian landmass. Precipitation is variable in this mountainous terrain, but is greatest in the east (about 60 inches/152 centimeters) and least in the west (about 25 inches/64 centimeters). A narrow band of warm Mediterranean climate spans the Adriatic coast, with hot summers and warm, dry winters.

FLORA AND FAUNA. Temperate broadleaf and conifer forests cover most of the Balkans, varying with altitude. Centuries ago, oak forests stretched for hundreds of miles in the central Balkans; humans have altered the ecosystem greatly, but forests remain, although their use is carefully rationed. Broad grasslands in the north and along the eastern Danube valley have been converted into farmland, as with prairies elsewhere in the world. The isolation of the mountains has protected bear, deer, and wolf populations. Lake Ohrid in Macedonia (the third-oldest in the world) is home to fish species found nowhere else.

HUMAN GEOGRAPHY. The Balkans have always been a region of ethnic diversity. One reason is that the region is a two-way route between Europe and western Asia, a passage for traders and soldiers. Second, the Balkans have always been on the borderland between opposing empires and religions, and the lands have changed fortunes repeatedly. Third, its mountains isolate local groups from contact with invaders.

The Illyrians, who inhabited the western Balkans at the time of the ancient Greeks, left their language in the form of Albanian. The Roman Empire in the west ruled only briefly, but their colonists preserved the Latin language in Romania. Slavic farmers came from the northern plains and settled in the river valleys as far

Dubrovnik, a Croatian port on the Adriatic, was leveled by an earthquake in the seventeenth century. (Charles F. Bahmueller)

south as central Greece; Slavic languages are spoken by the majority populations in most of the Balkans except for Romania and Albania. The Bulgars, a central Asian group, conquered what is now Bulgaria and blended into the Slavic population they ruled.

To this variety was added religious diversity. From the south and east, the Byzantine Empire spread Eastern Orthodox Christianity, while Roman Catholicism came from the west and northwest, creating a fault line that still runs through Bosnia-Herzegovina and Croatia. The Turks brought most of the Balkans under the Ottoman Empire and drew converts to Islam.

Later, Germans and Hungarians from the north migrated into the Balkans, especially Transylvania. Large numbers of Rom (Gypsies) migrated from India. The Austro-Hungarian Empire moved whole villages of soldier-farmers onto its southern frontier in Croatia and northern Serbia to protect against the Ottoman Empire, which accounts for Slovak, Hungarian, and Ukrainian minorities there.

POPULATION. National boundaries do not match ethnic boundaries in the Balkans. Every country has large minority populations, many of whom want to be reunited with their fellows in neighboring countries, a phenomenon called irredentism. In Bosnia-Herzegovina, for example, the near-majority is Muslim (49 percent), but some of the 31 percent Serb minority have split off into a self-described state called Republika Srpska, and many Croats (17 percent) want reunification with neighboring Croatia. Majorities may react oppressively: informal discrimination (for example, in hiring), assimilation (forcing name changes, for example), legalized discrimination (such as laws forbidding minority political parties), population transfer (evicting a minority from a country), ethnic warfare, and genocide (the systematic destruction of a people). These last three policies are called ethnic cleansing.

Ethnic rivalry has led to population shifts. For example, 300,000 ethnic Turks left Bulgaria for Turkey in 1989 because of discrimination, and Serbs drove out eth-

"THE SHATTER BELT" AND "BALKANIZATION"

Geographers have described the Balkans as a "shatter belt," an area of long-term political fracturing. The word coined to describe this breakup into small and often hostile countries was "balkanization." These terms evoke narrow ethnic rivalries, small nations with dreams of grandeur, and a sense that ethnic conflict has always existed there and always will. The use of these terms can distort people's observations. For many centuries the Balkans were no less stable than the rest of Europe, and outsiders did not view the Balkans as "balkanized."

The change in perception of the Balkans as particularly fractured came with the collapse of the Ottoman and Austro-Hungarian Empires at the end of the nineteenth century. The search for nationhood that followed was sometimes bloody, but other European nations, such as Great Britain, Germany, and Spain, already had endured equally bloody struggles of ethnic rivalry and nation-building. Overuse of the terms "shatter belt" and "balkanization" overemphasize the twentieth-century political instability in the Balkans, implying that it can never be changed. In actuality, geography shapes—but does not determine—human events.

nic Albanians from the Kosovo region in 1998.

Other population shifts have been economic. For decades, men have become temporary workers in the prosperous countries of the European core, North America, and Australia. In the poorest regions, whole villages of women and children depended on the money sent back by these men, who might be gone for decades. In another shift, young people have left the most rural regions to get training in large cities, leaving villages with elderly populations and leading to a marked cultural difference between the modern cities and traditional village lifestyles.

Birth rates vary among groups and nations. In northern Albania and Kosovo, the Albanians have the highest birth rate in Europe, largely because their poverty and isolation require children to help with the work. Their Serb neighbors in Kosovo have been losing ground because their birth rate is less, which is one cause of conflict there. Romania, on the other hand, has a negative birth rate—fewer children are born than are needed to replace people who die—because of a dictator who destroyed the economy during the 1980's, plunging people into such extreme poverty that few could afford to have children.

Population densities vary tremendously. They are highest in the Pannonian basin and the eastern Danube River valley, where land is flat and fertile, and least in mountain areas. Populations are generally densest in the river valleys because of alluvial soil, trade routes, and cities.

URBANIZATION. The Balkans are rural. The population is least urbanized in Albania (37 percent) and Bosnia-Herzegovina (40 percent)—both resource-poor, soil-poor countries with mountainous terrains. Elsewhere, urbanization ranges from 50 percent in Slovenia to 68 percent in Bulgaria, compared to 77 percent for the United States and around 80 percent for Western Europe.

Balkan cities are small. Bucharest is the largest with 2,300,000 inhabitants in the 1990's, but that is only about as big as metropolitan Pittsburgh. Belgrade and Sofia are about the size of New Orleans and Kansas City respectively, not large compared to major cities elsewhere in Europe, and most other cities have fewer than 500,000 people. Cities tend to be located in river valleys and in plains; the largest cities—Bucharest and Belgrade—are located where these physical features meet. An exception is Sofia, which was set in hilly western Bulgaria as a "forward capital," one that would be geographically central to a state which, it was hoped, would include both Macedonia and Bulgaria.

AGRICULTURE, RESOURCES, AND INDUSTRIES. Other than Romania, the Balkans are rich in minerals. Albania has major world deposits of chromite, Serbia has Europe's largest copper reserves, and other metals are found particularly in the mountainous regions. The soils are not rich, and the rugged terrain does not favor large farms except in the north, but agriculture is successful in producing grains, potatoes, and livestock; the Balkans' southern situation in Europe allows fruit and vine culture in many places.

The mountains of the western Balkan nations provide good hydroelectric power, though only a quarter has been developed, compared to three-quarters in Western Europe. Romania and Albania have petroleum and gas reserves, and low-grade coal is burned in Serbia and Romania (leading to major air pollution), but most Balkan nations need to import mineral energy. Bulgaria has developed thermal power.

The majority of people work in manufacturing, which ranges from heavy machinery to textiles and light manufacturing, and most goods are exported within

Europe. Years of inefficiency under Soviet-dominated governments held back economic development, especially in Albania, and the region is slowly reemerging economically.

TRANSPORTATION. The easiest routes into the Balkans are across the flat terrain of the north, especially along the Danube River and its tributaries, which bisect the region from north to east. Another bisecting route, although mountainous, runs north-south from Belgrade to the Aegean Sea along the river valleys of the Morava and Vardar. In the west, the Black Sea ports of Bulgaria and Romania allow trade with the former Soviet nations and indirect access to the Mediterranean Sea. The eastern ports of the Adriatic are well situated but small, and separated by massive mountains from the goods they might export. For internal transportation, ground routes along river valleys are important, as are the rivers themselves.

Christopher Marshall

FOR FURTHER STUDY

Andric, Ivo. *The Bridge on the Drina.* Chicago: University of Chicago Press, 1984.

Cuvalo, Ante. *Historical Dictionary of Bosnia and Herzegovina.* Landham, Md.: Scarecrow Press, 1997.

Detrez, Raymond. *Historical Dictionary of Bulgaria.* Landham, Md.: Scarecrow Press, 1997.

Georgieva, Valentina, and Sasha Konechni. *Historical Dictionary of the Republic of Macedonia.* Landham, Md.: Scarecrow Press, 1998.

Hutchings, Raymond. *Historical Dictionary of Albania.* Landham, Md.: Scarecrow Press, 1996.

Kaplan, Robert D. *Balkan Ghosts: A Journey Through History.* New York: Vintage, 1994.

Suster, Zeljan. *Historical Dictionary of the Federal Republic of Yugoslavia.* Landham, Md.: Scarecrow Press, 1999.

Todorova, Maria. *Imagining the Balkans.* New York: Oxford University Press, 1997.

INFORMATION ON THE WORLD WIDE WEB

The Web site of the University of Pittsburgh's Center for Russian and East European Studies contains a comprehensive index of information on the Balkans. (www.ucis.pitt.edu/reesweb)

CENTRAL-EASTERN EUROPE

*Map
Page 1251*

Central-Eastern Europe is an area of transition, instability, and diversity. It has often been called the Shatter Belt, or the Devil's Belt, because of the traditional instability of its political units and the fragmentation of its cultural units. The densely settled region has played an important role throughout history. With an area only slightly larger than Texas, Central-Eastern Europe has a population more than four times greater than that state's population. In the year 2000 there were five countries in the region: the Czech Republic, Hungary, Poland, Slovakia, and Romania.

PHYSICAL GEOGRAPHY. Central-Eastern Europe lies between the Baltic Sea on the north and the Black Sea on the southeast. It is located at high latitudes: Gdánsk, in northern Poland, is at about the same latitude as the southern part of Hudson Bay; Budapest, the capital of Hungary, is at about the same latitude as Quebec; and Bucharest, the capital of Romania, is at a latitude comparable to that of northern Vermont.

The region is divided by the Carpathian Mountains and their extensions into the uplands of Moravia and Bohemia. The Carpathians extend about 900 miles (1,450 km.) in the shape of a semicircle, both ends of which touch the Danube River. The mountains arise near Bratislava, Slovakia, ending at the Iron Gate in Romania. The range is not high: Gerlachovsky Stit in Slovakia is its highest point, rising to 8,710 feet (2,655 meters) above sea level. Although the mountains bisect the region, they have not been a barrier to invading armies. Throughout history, numerous passes have provided intruders with penetrable routes through the Carpathians. The Carpathian Mountains are subject to earthquakes. In 1977 an earthquake killed more than 1,500 people and caused serious damage in Bucharest.

To the north of the Carpathian Mountains lies the North European Plain, also called the North European Lowlands. This plain provided invaders from both east and west with easy passage through the region. The vast plain has been covered with eroded sediments over millions of years. Some of these sediments include plant remains that, under pressure of later sedimentary deposits, were converted to coal. The harnessing of this energy source was a basis for the industrial revolution in Europe. Even today, there are few industrial centers in the region that are not located near coal-bearing deposits. Most of the lowlands originally were covered by forests. However, the forests were cleared and swampy valleys were drained to make room for settlements and agricultural lands. The Oder and Vistula Rivers, both navigable, flow south to north through broad lowland valleys.

To the south of the Carpathians, other easy invasion routes appear between the mountains and the Black Sea. The Wallachian Plain, wedged between the Transylvanian Alps and Dobruja, is also a low-land area.

CLIMATE. Most of the Central-Eastern European region has a humid continental climate. However, there are variations within the region. For example, the Czech Republic tends to be humid with cold winters and warm summers, while Hungary, which also has cold winters and warm summers, tends to be dry, and eastern Poland has a humid continental climate with cool summers. Unlike other areas in Central-Eastern Europe, the western portion of Poland has a marine, west coast climate.

Vegetation varies by both elevation and latitude. In the higher areas to the north, fir and spruce trees are more common. To the south in high elevations, spruce and pine are the most common trees. At lower elevations, deciduous trees such as oak, birch, poplar, willow, beech, and linden are found.

While much of the region was forested in the past, throughout history, forests have been cleared for use as agricultural fields. More recently, air pollution has brought about acid rain, damaging the remaining forests, particularly those with coniferous vegetation. Today, forested lands range from less than 20 percent of the land use in Hungary to about 40 percent in Slovakia.

HUMAN GEOGRAPHY. Because of its geographical location between Western Europe, Scandinavia, Russia, and Asia, Central-Eastern Europe has been a place where peoples, armies, and empires have met over the centuries.

The population there in the twentieth century had ancestors who arrived from all directions to settle. By the time that Roman legions entered Central-Eastern Europe early in the second century, numerous small groups had already established themselves in the area. The origins of

these early people are not known with certainty, but they are believed to have come from at least three source regions: the grasslands of west central Asia; lowland areas between the Oder and Vistula Rivers; and the plateaus and basins of the Polish uplands. During the third and fourth centuries, Huns and Avars from the central Asian steppes crossed into the Carpathian basin.

The Slavs began to leave their original homelands to the north and east to move into the area in the second and third centuries. Magyars (Hungarians), originally a herding people, came into the Pannonian basin from central Asia in the ninth century, dividing the Slavs into a northern group (Poles, Czechs, and Slovaks) and a southern group (Slovenes, Croats, Serbs, Macedonians, and Bulgars). The origins of the Romanians are more controversial. While many Romanians consider themselves to be descendants of the Roman settlers, some think that they are descended from invaders who entered the Carpathian basin between the ninth and thirteenth centuries.

Other settlers came later. Germans moved eastward for a number of reasons: military conquest, territorial increase, and missionary and trading activities. In addition, some Slav and Magyar rulers encouraged German craftsmen and artisans to settle in their territories. In the thirteenth century, the Magyars encouraged German settlement on the eastern edge of their territory in Transylvania to protect against Mongols and other invaders from the east. In the north, Germans moved into Central-Eastern Europe along the Baltic coast. The Teutonic Order, a German Christian fraternity of knights, entered the region along the Baltic Coast. Other migrants were Swedes from the north and Jews from the west, who migrated hoping for freedom from religious persecution.

Into this virtual stew of differing peoples came the armies of empires, both eastern and western. These included the Romans (second and third centuries); the Avars (sixth to ninth centuries); the Byzantine Empire (fifth to fifteenth centuries); Ottoman Turks (fifteenth to twentieth centuries); the Holy Roman Empire (ninth to nineteenth centuries); the Habsburg Empire (thirteenth to nineteenth centuries); the Austro-Hungarian Empire (nineteenth and twentieth centuries); the Prussian Empire (seventeenth to twentieth centuries); the Russian Empire (ninth to twentieth centuries); and Nazi Germany and the Soviets (in the twentieth century).

The armies and leaders of the various empires carved and recarved international boundaries, often leaving political boundaries that did not match traditional population patterns. Poland even disappeared from the map in the late eighteenth century, divided up among the Russian, Prussian, and Austro-Hungarian Empires; it did not reappear as a nation until after World War I. The imperial powers introduced new languages, foods, governmental systems, and customs. Using religion as an example, the Roman Empire brought Catholicism, the Byzantine Empire brought Orthodox Christianity, the Ottoman Empire brought Islam, and the Prussian Empire brought Protestantism.

TWENTIETH CENTURY CENTRAL-EASTERN EUROPE. After World War I, international boundaries in the region changed dramatically. As part of the peace settlement, Poland and Czechoslovakia appeared as new countries, Romania's territory and population almost doubled in size, and Hungary lost about two-thirds of its territory and about 60 percent of its population.

After World War II, Central-Eastern Europe fell under the influence of the Soviet Union, and communist governments were installed in each nation. While the countries were still independent in name, many policies and decisions were dictated by the Soviet Union. They became part of what was called the Eastern Bloc, a group of nations in the eastern part of Europe that came under Soviet domination after World War II.

Centralized economic planning was imposed. This means that decisions about the economy were made by governments rather than by individuals or companies. The government owned most major factories and businesses. Government five-year plans focused on developing heavy industry at the expense of agriculture and goods and services for ordinary people. Steel production was especially important. The Soviets planned, financed, and built huge new steel plants such as the Lenin Plant in Nowa Huta, Poland.

In order to be able to impose the economic plans, have enough workers for the new factories, and control the rural population, agriculture was collectivized. Collectivization is the creation of large, state-controlled farms to replace the smaller, privately held farms. When farmers did not voluntarily give up their land to the collective farms, financial pressures and intimidation were used. By the end of the Soviet era, about 75 percent of the farmland in Czechoslovakia, Hungary, and Romania had been collectivized. The program met more resistance from small landholders in Poland; less than 25 percent of Polish farmland was collectivized.

After Joseph Stalin, the leader of the Soviet Union, died in 1953, the Eastern Bloc thought the Soviets might loosen control over their countries. This did not happen to a great extent, however, and uprisings in Hungary (1956) and Czechoslovakia (1968) followed. A new Polish labor movement called Solidarity began a strike to improve working conditions in 1980-1981. Armies were called in to put an end to these rebellions. While these protests were unsuccessful, they helped to lay the groundwork for massive changes that were soon to take place.

In 1989 Mikhail Gorbachev, the head of the Soviet Union, declared that the Soviets would not intervene in the affairs of the independent countries of the Eastern Bloc. Change came rapidly. In 1989 Hungary's communist party was taken apart and the country opened its borders to Western Europe, the Solidarity movement reappeared in Poland and its leader won a national election, and the "Velvet Revolution" ended communist rule in Czechoslo-

vakia. Only in Romania was there a violent end to the communist regime: dictator Nicolae Ceausescu was forced from power and executed.

Central-Eastern Europe turned from communism to democracy, from centralized economic planning to a free-market economy, in which decisions are made by companies, people, and marketplaces rather than governments. However, the transitions have not been without problems.

The drive to increase industrial production at almost any cost during the communist years caused widespread, intense environmental degradation. Air pollution is pervasive. Water pollution affects many

Visible reminders of the years of Soviet domination in Eastern Europe are these Prague apartment buildings used by the families of occupying Soviet troops. (PhotoDisc)

TRENDS IN CENTRAL-EASTERN EUROPEAN BIRTHS AND DEATHS

Geographers evaluate fertility (births) and mortality (deaths) using measures called the crude birthrate and crude death rate. These rates show the number of births or deaths per one thousand people in the population and help to explain population growth and decline among nations. In many European countries, a population trend has emerged that has potentially disturbing long-term social, economic, and political consequences: The population is growing older, death rates are rising, and birthrates have fallen. If these trends continue, there could be future problems replacing workers, caring for the elderly, and supporting social programs such as old-age pensions or medical care.

The nation of Hungary provides a good example of this trend. In 1999 for every one thousand people in the population, ten babies were born, but fourteen people died. This means that the population—assuming that no one moved into or out of the country—experienced a decrease in population of 0.4 percent. In fact, Hungary's population has declined in size every year from 1980 to the present.

lakes and rivers in the region. Nuclear power plants constructed under the communist regimes were not built to Western European or U.S. standards.

Before the transition, life was not easy for many of the people in Central-Eastern Europe. However, most basic needs (such as housing and health care) were paid for by the government. With the transition to a free-market economy, people have to pay for services that previously were free. This has caused not only some hardship, but also some resentment against the new governments and the new economic system.

In 1993 Czechoslovakia ceased to exist, replaced by two countries: the western, more urban and industrial, Czech Republic and the eastern, more agricultural, Slovakia.

THE FUTURE. After years of being strongly tied to Soviet interests in the east, the Central-Eastern European nations are once again looking westward. In 1999 the Czech Republic, Hungary, and Poland joined the North Atlantic Treaty Organization (NATO), a defense organization primarily composed of Western European nations, the United States, and Canada. Poland, Hungary, and the Czech Republic also are among the first of the former Eastern Bloc nations being considered for membership in the European Union (EU), a powerful economic and governmental organization of Western European nations. Full membership was not expected to occur until at least 2004. Romania and Slovakia were also hoping to join this influential organization, though farther in the future.

Michelle Behr

FOR FURTHER STUDY

Bachman, Ronald D., and Eugene K. Keefe. *Romania: A Country Study.* 2d ed. Washington, D.C.: U.S. Government Printing Office, 1991.

Beck, Paul, Edward Mast, and Perry Tapper. *The History of Eastern Europe for Beginners.* New York: Writers and Readers Publishing, 1997.

Burant, Stephen R., and Eugene K. Keefe. *Hungary: A Country Study.* 2d ed. Washington, D.C.: U.S. Government Printing Office, 1991.

Chelminski, Rudolph. "Warsaw: The City that Would Not Die." *Smithsonian* 28, no. 8 (November, 1997): 108-120.

Crampton, Richard, and Ben Crampton. *Atlas of Eastern Europe in the Twentieth Century.* New York: Routledge, 1996.

Curtis, Glenn E. *Poland: A Country Study.* 3d ed. Washington, D.C.: U.S. Government Printing Office, 1994.

Hochman, Jiri. *Historical Dictionary of the Czech State.* Landham, Md.: Scarecrow Press, 1998.

Johnson, Lonnie R. *Central Europe: Enemies, Neighbors, Friends.* New York: Oxford University Press, 1996.

Kirschbaum, Stanislav J. *Historical Dictionary of Slovakia.* Landham, Md.: Scarecrow Press, 1998.

INFORMATION ON THE WORLD WIDE WEB

Specific to the Central European region are the following sources of news, events, and trends: Central Europe Online (centraleurope.com/), Transitions Online (www.tol.cz/), and the Central European Review (www.ce-review.org/).

EUROPEAN NATIONS OF FORMER SOVIET UNION

Map
Page 1252

Seven European nations were formerly part of the Soviet Union: Russia, Estonia, Latvia, Lithuania, Belarus, Moldova, and the Ukraine. These nations cover approximately 2.3 million square miles (5.96 sq. km.)— nearly 4 percent of the earth's surface and 75 percent as large as the contiguous forty-eight states of the United States. The region's width, from the Hungarian border to the Ural Mountains, is more than 1,400 miles (2,250 km.), and its maximum north-south extent, from the shores of the Barents Sea to the beaches of Dagistan along the western shore of the Caspian Sea, is about 2,200 miles (3,540 km.). The European nations of the former Soviet Union span thirty degrees of latitude, fifty degrees of longitude, and five time zones.

The size, physical diversity, and extent of this region can invoke images of unlimited raw materials and vast tracks of virgin land waiting to be developed. With a 1990's population estimated at 210,224,000, comparable to the United States east of the Rocky Mountains, even the market potential for modern consumer products seems immense. However, the factors of distance and accessibility must be considered, for valuable raw materials are located in remote areas and major commercial and industrial activities are located in a few selected sites. Natural and human resources were not used wisely there in the past, and the magnitude of raw materials available and distance from markets encouraged waste.

ATTEMPTS TO ORGANIZE THE REGION. The Soviet Union was the successor to the sprawling Imperial Russian Empire, and guided by Marxist ideology and the Communist Party, its leaders attempted to remold the economy, cultural life, and geography of the union by centralized national planning. Communist planners, recognizing the problems of size and realizing the assets of spatial interaction, remolded most aspects of spatial organization, enhanced the interaction of people and places, and added new elements to the physical and cultural landscape. They constructed new transportation links (roads, canals, and air routes), built thousands of new urban centers, remolded rural life by socializing agriculture through state and cooperative farms, and increased the amount of cultivated land through the Virgin Land Scheme.

Massive internal discontent with communist rule, lack of basic services and necessary amenities, public anger and ethnic group dissension, and a general realization that the political and economic systems could not cope with the complex multifaceted issues of modern economic life led to the disintegration of Communist Party control and the Soviet Union. As other ruling groups had before them, the leaders of the Communist Party failed in their spatial organizations to overcome the problems associated with size, diversity, and space; failed in their attempts to link together all who occupied the space within the boundaries of the huge Soviet Union; and failed in their policies toward nationalities, which fostered disunity and led to the disintegration of the Soviet Union into independent states on December 25, 1991.

LANDFORMS AND PHYSIOGRAPHIC REGIONS. The European nations of the former Soviet Union are underlain by rocks and minerals from almost every geologic period. The various surface configurations—plains, hills, and mountains, rivers, lakes, and seas—are important geographical factors to be considered in any plans to delimit political units and in any scheme for regional and national economic development. There are three basic physiographic regions, each with distinctive physical character and distinctive opportunities for human habitation: the Russian Plain, the Ural Mountains, and the European Arctic Lowlands. All three regions

have been negatively affected by human activities.

RUSSIAN PLAIN. Estonia, Latvia, and Lithuania (the Baltic countries), Belarus, the Ukraine, and Moldova, and Russia west of the Ural Mountains and south of the European Arctic Lowlands are within the vast Russian Plain. This huge area is flat, glacially modified, and has poor internal drainage. Most of the plain is less than 650 feet (200 meters) above sea level. Variations in glacial erosion and deposition give character to this plain. The Valdai Hills, a series of low, rolling glacial depositional features in Russia, are the source of many rivers, including the Volga, Dnieper, and West Dvina. The Pripet Swamp in Belarus and the Ukraine is the largest swamp in Europe.

In the western Ukraine, the Carpathian Mountains, the Podolian Hills, and the

Belarus farm workers. (American Stock Photography)

Dniester Hills are found along the borders of Poland, Slovakia, Hungary, and Romania. Beautiful white limestone mountains, no higher than 5,000 feet (1,500 meters), dominate the Crimean Peninsula and protect the narrow strip of mild Mediterranean-type climate with its Black Sea coast resorts from cold northern air masses.

Rich in five different types of coal, the Donets Basin of the eastern Ukraine is one of the world's leading coal producers. Near the center of this region, the Smolensk–Moscow Hills encompass the large but mineral-poor Moscow basin. The Caspian Sea, noted for its valuable salt deposits and caviar, is below the world sea level. The Russian Plain, a result of continental glaciation, is deficient in mineral energy resources in the north but contains significant deposits of high-quality coal, minerals, and natural gas in the south.

URAL MOUNTAINS. East of the vast Russian Plain lie the historic Ural Mountains. Located within Russia, the Urals are a long, narrow, heavily eroded, low mountain and hill chain best known as the traditional boundary between Europe and Asia. The Urals extend more than 1,500 miles (2,410 km.) from the Arctic Circle to the deserts of Central Asia; only 50 miles (80 km.) wide in the north, they spread out to nearly 140 miles (225 km.) wide in the south. Consisting of a series of north-south ridges with many east-west low mountain passes, the Urals are no barrier to human movement. For centuries, the Urals have been extremely important to the Russian economy. This geographically significant mountain range provides timber, oil, natural gas, iron ore, coal, and a host of valuable minerals and precious metals.

EUROPEAN ARCTIC LOWLANDS. To the north of the Russian Plain and to the west of the Ural Mountains are the flat, marshy European Arctic Lowlands. Located in northwestern Russia, these lowlands are snow and ice-covered in the winter and retain snowmelt water on the surface during the summer. On the large Kola Peninsula of Russia adjoining Finland, repeated glacial action has carved picturesque fjords and left a landscape containing thousands of small lakes, swamps, and streams. Valuable mineral deposits in old basement rock have been exposed and exploited by native inhabitants of the peninsula for centuries. To the east and near the Ural Mountains lies the Pechora Plain. There coal is mined in permanently frozen ground. Far from the core of the Scandinavian Continental Ice Sheet, the glacier was not thick enough or heavy enough to scrape away the coal deposits.

CLIMATES. The landscape of the European nations of the former Soviet Union is stamped with the image of its climate, and it is climate that gives area contrasts in the physical environment. In particular, temperature extremes characterize climates here, and low winter temperatures have a tremendous impact upon basic physical processes and human activities. Extremes in temperature and low annual precipitation are a direct result of the high latitudinal position and the location of this region on the world's largest landmass. Being open to the cold, dry air masses from the Arctic and being a great distances from the warm, moist maritime air masses from the Gulf Stream in the Atlantic Ocean results in extremely cold winters and dry summers.

Direct ameliorating oceanic influence is greatest in the far northwest, and warm Gulf Stream waters give the Murmansk coastal area on the Kola Peninsula some of the mildest winters found in this region. Few areas of the European nations of the former Soviet Union receive more than 20 inches (500 millimeters) of annual precipitation. Most of the precipitation falls in summer, but snow cover gives character to winter. Brief spring seasons intervene between cold winters and hot summers. Winters become increasingly colder eastward; summers generally become increasingly hotter southward. Most major cities are industrial centers and have distinct urban climates with, at times, unusual winter urban fogs.

*Kiev store
Page 1251*

MAJOR ETHNIC GROUPS AND POPULATION. By a process of continuous expansion over four hundred years from the pivotal point at Moscow, the czars and then the commissars governed large numbers of people with diverse racial, cultural, linguistic, and religious backgrounds. The modern national borders of the former republics of the Soviet Union were drawn on the basis of linguistic and ethnic grouping. All seven of the nations in the European portion of the former Soviet Union were named after the ethnic groups making up the majorities of their populations. Some large republics, such as Russia, set aside special administrative regions for ethnic minorities.

SLAVS. The dominant ethnic group in this region is the Slavs. Historically, three main Slavic groups have been distinguished. Different historical experiences, different physical environments in which they lived, and different mixtures through marriage with non-Slavic groups has produced dissimilar cultural and physical attributes. Physical characteristics have played a role in naming the three major Slavic ethnic groups: the Russians (Great Russians), Ukrainians (Little Russians), and Belorussians (White Russians).

The Russians were the great pioneers who moved out of their core area around Moscow and into all the European nations of the former Soviet Union. In the 1989 census, the Russians numbered more than 145 million and were living in every nation of the former Soviet Union. The Ukrainian cultural hearth is the western Ukraine, especially Kiev.

Ukrainians were deeply affected, culturally and racially, by contacts with the Turks, Mongols, Tatars, Lithuanians, and Poles. When the last official census was taken in 1989, there were more than 44 million Ukrainians living in the Ukraine and in every nation of the former Soviet Union. The Belorussians, a Slavic group affected greatly by the Scandinavians, Lithuanians, Poles, and Russians, retained their cultural heritage by taking advantage of the isolation afforded by glacial-induced swamps and thick forests. The 1989 census reported that there were 10 million Belorussians within the Soviet Union.

Moscow's St. Basil's Cathedral. (PhotoDisc)

BALTIC PEOPLES. The Baltic peoples—Estonians, Latvians, and Lithuanians—have diverse ancestry, language, and cultural backgrounds. Estonians are the descendants of pre-Slavic people who lived in an isolated forested area on the shores of the Baltic Sea and the Gulf of Finland. The Estonians, closely related to the Finns, are devout Lutheran Christians. In 1989 approximately 1 million Soviet citizens identified themselves as Estonians.

Latvians reside in fertile lowlands surrounding the Gulf of Riga on the Baltic Sea. Their cultural center is Riga. According to the 1989 Soviet census, 1.5 million people declared themselves Latvians. Lithuanians have lived on the shores of the Baltic Sea south of Latvia, east of Poland, and north of Belarus for more than 1,000 years, and have retained their cultural heritage despite external pressures. Vilnius, their major cultural center and traditional capital, is not located on the Baltic Sea. There were at least 3 million Lithuanians in the Soviet Union when the census was taken in 1989.

MOLDOVANS. Moldovans are a complex ethnic group who speak a Romanian dialect and have strong links to the people of Romania. They live in the extreme southwestern corner of the European portion of the former Soviet Union, in a country formed in 1940 from parts of Bessarabia and Bukovina (taken from Romania). Moldova has few natural resources other than fertile soils and favorable climate; thus, most Moldovans reside in small towns or rural villages. Chisinau (Kishinev) is the center of

Interior of Moscow's GUMM department store, the largest and most famous shopping center in Russia, which began in the late nineteenth century as a series of arcades. (PhotoDisc)

Moldovan cultural activities. More than 3.3 million people identified themselves as Moldovans in the 1989 Soviet census.

ECONOMIC BASE. The nations in the European portion of the former Soviet Union have, for the most part, good-to-excellent soils for agricultural use, excellent pastures, and efficient farmers. The seven countries have different attributes for modern economic development but are basically well endowed with critical mineral resources, particularly coal, iron ore, and oil. Historically, the Ukraine was considered the breadbasket of Europe, and the Donets Basin in the eastern Ukraine was the leading coal-producing center. Iron ore is widely distributed, but large deposits are found in the Ukraine and in the Ural Mountains. Nickel and bauxite are mined in the Kola Peninsula and manganese in the Ukraine. Working as one economic unit, all seven nations have sufficient agricultural and mineral resources to satisfy their needs and for export.

St. Petersburg Page 1250

The pattern of industrial complexes and extractive sites is a result of the emphasis placed upon industrial development in the Soviet Five-Year Plans. Moscow is the most important old center of market-oriented, labor-intensive industries. It accounts for more than 30 percent of the industrial output of the entire seven-country region. The second old center of market-oriented labor-intensive industries is Saint Petersburg, which accounts for at least 10 percent of the industrial output of the seven-country region. The Eastern Ukrainian Industrial Region, centered on the Donets basin, is an old center of heavy industry and contributes at least 25 percent of the region's industrial production. The Ural Industrial Region, also an old center of heavy industry, produces nearly 10 percent of the region's industrial out-

Kremlin Page 1252

put. Every country's capital is an industrial center of some importance. The seven independent nations of the former Soviet Union have the industrial capability of being major manufacturing and food-producing blocs in the world—in many ways, comparable to Western Europe.

William A. Dando

FOR FURTHER STUDY

Baranovsky, Vladimir, ed. *Russia and Europe: the Emerging Security Agenda.* New York: Oxford University Press, 1997.

Brezianu, Andrei. *Historical Dictionary of the Republic of Moldova.* Edited by Jon Woronoff. Landham, Md.: Scarecrow Press, 2000.

Fedor, Helen, ed. *Belarus and Moldova: Country Studies.* Washington, D.C.: Library of Congress, 1995.

Gosnell, Kelvin. *Belarus, Ukraine, and Moldova.* Brookfield, Conn.: Millbrook Press, 1992.

Pauli, Ulf. *The Baltic States in Facts, Figures and Maps.* London: Janus, 1994.

Raymond, Boris, and Paul Duffy. *Historical Dictionary of Russia.* Landham, Md.: Scarecrow Press, 1998.

Ruggiero, Adriane. *The Baltic Countries: Estonia, Latvia, and Lithuania.* Parsippany, N.J.: Dillon Press, 1998.

Smith, Graham, ed. *The Nationalities Question in the Post-Soviet States.* 2d ed. New York: Longman, 1996.

WESTERN EUROPE

Micro States
1. Andorra
2. Liechtenstein
3. Monaco
4. San Marino
5. Vatican City

North
Sea

*Atlantic
Ocean*

English Channel

NETHERLANDS • Hamburg
• Rotterdam
• Leipzig
BELGIUM •Bonn
GERMANY
LUXEMBOURG • Frankfurt
Paris ★ • Nurnberg
• Nantes • Strasbourg • Munich
FRANCE Zurich ② AUSTRIA
SWITZERLAND
• Geneva
*Bay of
Biscay* Lyon• • Milano
•Bordeaux
• Genova ④
Bayonne •
Porto • • Valladolid ① • Marseille ③
PORTUGAL ★ Madrid Corsica ⑤ ITALY
★Lisbon SPAIN • Barcelona • Naples
• Valencia Sardinia
• Cordoba
Balearic
Islands
Mediterranean Sea Palermo •
Sicily

*Chateau de Versailles, the palace of seventeenth century French king Louis XIV,
was the site of the conference that ended World War I.* (PhotoDisc)

Part of the extensive Roman ruins at Conimbriga, a Portuguese town near Coimbra—which takes its own name from Conimbriga. (PhotoDisc)

Canal locks in Amsterdam. One of the Netherlands's two capital cities, Amsterdam is well served by rail and water transportation and is the chief port for the North Sea and North Holland Canals. (PhotoDisc)

BRITISH ISLES

Hill country in southeastern
Scotland, near Edinburgh.
(PhotoDisc)

The most famous, if not the oldest human-made landmark in Great Britain, is the four-thousand-year-old megalithic circle known as Stonehenge, on Salisbury Plain. (PhotoDisc)

Stonehenge cross-pieces. (R. Kent Rasmussen)

Traditional English house with a thatched roof. (PhotoDisc)

Welsh village. (PhotoDisc)

SCANDINAVIA

Balstad, a Norwegian port on the Vestfjord, well above the Arctic Circle. (PhotoDisc)

Norwegian farm valley. (Digital Stock)

MEDITERRANEAN EUROPE

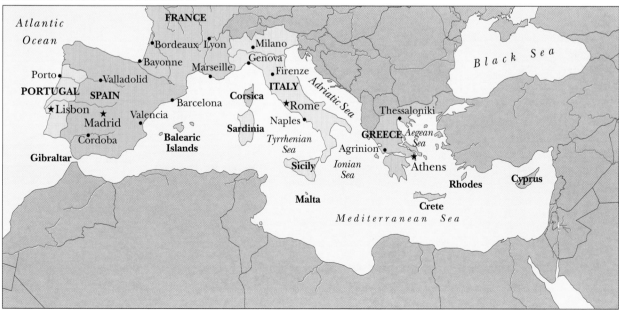

Southern Spain's Andalusia region stretches from the Atlantic to the Mediterranean but has a predominantly Mediterranean climate. It is a primarily agricultural region, producing grapes, olives, tomatoes, wheat, and barley. (PhotoDisc)

Alicante, a port city in Spain, south of Valencia. Like many Mediterranean ports, it has seen a variety of invaders since it was occupied by the Romans in the late third century B.C.E. (PhotoDisc)

Spanish olive groves. Europe grows more than half the world's olives, almost all of them in Italy, Spain, and Greece. (PhotoDisc)

Sheep in Greece. Domesticated animals in the Mediterranean region are similar to those found elsewhere in Europe, but sheep and goats are particularly well adapted to the dry conditions and scanty herbage. (PhotoDisc)

BALKAN NATIONS

Taking advantage of the changing free-market conditions in Russia, residents of St. Petersburg line up to buy milk from a truck. (Charles F. Bahmueller)

An elderly woman studies prices in a Ukrainian grocery store in Kiev. Although the Ukraine is considered the "breadbasket" of the region, many Ukrainians depend on government pensions that are both scanty and slow in being paid. (AP/Wide World Photos)

CENTRAL EUROPE

Former Soviet European Nations

The Kremlin. Taking its name from the Russian word kreml, *for fortress, Moscow's Kremlin is Russia's most famous architecture complex. Its origins go back to the fourteenth century, and it has served as a royal residence, seat of government, and a defensive fort. During the era of communist rule, the Kremlin served as the seat of the Soviet government and the word "Kremlin" itself became synonymous with Soviet rule. After the breakup of the Soviet Union in the early 1990's, the churches of the Kremlin returned to religious use.*
(PhotoDisc)

PHYSICAL GEOGRAPHY OF EUROPE

Barents Sea

Ural Mountains

Ural

Norwegian Sea

Reykjavik ★

Kjölen Mountains

Helsinki ★

Volga

Stockholm ★

P l a i n

Moscow ★

Atlantic Ocean

North Sea

Baltic Sea

Vistula

E u r o p e a n

Caspian Sea

Dublin ★

Jutland

Elbe

Oder

Vistula

Warsaw ★

Volga

Irish Sea

Hartz Mts.

Bohemian Uplands

Dniester

Dnieper

Don

London ★

English Channel

Ardennes

Rhine

Carpathian Mountains

Brittany

Seine

Loire

G r e a t

Black Forest

Danube

Munich ●

Caucasus Mountains

×

Central Massif

Mt. Blanc

ALPS

Danube

Transyl-vanian Alps

Mt. Elbrus

Cantabrian Mts.

Garonne

Rhône

Po

Dinaric Range

Danube

Black Sea

Pyrenees

Douro

Balkans

Tagus ★ Madrid

Adriatic Sea

Apennines ×

Aegean Sea

Guadalquivir

Sierra Nevada

Vesuvius

Athens ★

× Etna

Mediterranean Sea

Ionian Sea

1253

Waters Innvikfjord, Norway. Fjords like this characterize Norway's coastlines, which were shaped, in part, by ancient glaciers. (Digital Stock)

The Wetterhorn, a peak in the Bernese Alps, which contains some of Bavaria's most picturesque Alpine scenery. (PhotoDisc)

PHYSICAL GEOGRAPHY

PHYSIOGRAPHY

*Map
Page 1253*

With an area of 3,837,082 square miles (9,938,000 sq. km.), Europe is the second-smallest of the seven continents, after Australia. Indeed, it is a pygmy in comparison to neighboring Asia, which has an area of more than 17 million square miles (44.6 million sq. km.). Europe's area is close to that of the United States. Geographically, Europe is a peninsula on the landmass of Asia, arbitrarily separated from Asia by the Ural Mountains. Europe has its own series of peninsulas, including Scandinavia, Danish-Jutland, Iberia, Italy, Greece, the Balkans, and Crimea.

PHYSICAL DIMENSIONS OF EUROPE. Europe is surrounded on three sides by water: the Mediterranean Sea on the south; the Atlantic Ocean on the west; the Norwegian and Barents Seas on the north. The Ural Mountains as the eastern boundary separate the more rugged Great European Plain to the west from the flat Siberian plain to the east. To the south, the Ural River is the boundary until it flows into the Caspian Sea.

On the land bridge of the Caucasus between the Caspian and Black Seas, the boundary is the Caucasus Mountains. The line moves through the Black Sea to the Bosphorus and the Dardenelles straits that separate Europe and Asia Minor. Turkey is partially in Europe, but mostly in Asia. The hundreds of islands that surround the continent are also part of Europe. Greenland, the world's largest island and an autonomous part of Denmark is, however, considered part of the North American continent.

As Europe moves toward economic cohesion and globalization, existing boundaries cause problems, and alternative methods of dividing the landmasses of the world are under consideration. With renewed interest on economic strength irrespective of size or possession of natural resources, not only the boundaries of continents but even the boundaries of states and nations are becoming irrelevant.

EUROPE'S FAVORABLE PHYSIOGRAPHY. In relation to its size, no region of the world has so favorable a physiography as Europe, which has been a major factor in Europe's importance in world affairs. Some of its assets are mild climates as a result of Europe's exposure to the North Atlantic Drift, deflecting from the warm Gulf Stream; a long growing season; dependable rainfall; navigable rivers; fertile land; abundant natural resources; an unusually long coast line of 37,880 miles (60,960 km.) with many natural harbors; and no insurmountable natural barriers.

With the exception of the eastern region, no part of Europe is more than a few hours travel time from seas or oceans. Europe also benefits from location. Except for a small part that projects beyond the Arctic Circle, all of Europe lies in a temperate zone with neither arctic frigidity nor tropical heat to sap human strength and energy.

THE LANDFORM REGIONS OF EUROPE. Europe can be divided into four landform regions—three mountain ranges with lowlands between the first and second ranges. These are the northwest highlands, the coastal lowlands or Great European Plain, the central uplands and pla-

*Arctic
Circle town
Page 1246*

CONTINENTAL DRIFT THEORY

Credited to the German geophysicist Alfred Wegener and widely accepted by geographers, the theory of continental drift states that all of the world's continents were part of one great landmass called Pangaea (Greek for "whole earth"). The huge mass broke apart, drifted, and eventually formed the configuration of landmasses that exists today. The drift theory explains the similarity of the Appalachians to the northwest highlands of Europe; more recent computer calculations have established a perfect fit between the western coastline of Europe and Africa with the eastern coastline of Central and North America. Because of lithospheric plate movement, the continental drift continues.

teaus, and the southern mountain region or Alpine system.

A large stable area of resistant rock more than two billion years old underlies parts of present-day Sweden, Finland, Norway, and northwestern Russia. Known as the Fenno-Scandian Shield, it was a resisting element to tectonic pressure, resulting in the breaking of the earth's crust at the shield's boundaries that formed most of Europe's mountains. The greatest thickness (2 miles/3.4 km.) of the terrain-altering European ice cap is on that shield.

THE NORTHWEST HIGHLANDS. The oldest of the mountain regions, the northwest highlands were formed about 420 million years ago. They consist of mountains in Russia, Finland, Sweden, Norway, Scotland, Ireland, and Wales, as well as the Appalachians in the eastern United States, which separated from the European mountains by the divergence of lithospheric plates and the subsequent widening of the Atlantic Ocean. Erosion has worn down the mountains of the northwest highlands, often to mere mounds. Glaciation or ice-sculpting has also changed their contours.

Norwegian fjord Page 1254

The thin soil and hilly terrain make most of the highlands poor areas for farming. As a result, they are thinly populated and the people there seek alternative forms of livelihood, such as shipping and fishing. Because of its proximity to the sea and the moisture-bearing trade winds, the area receives abundant rainfall, which can be used for hydroelectric power. Proximity to other energy sources such as coal and oil has resulted in extensive industrial development in parts of the highlands, especially in the United Kingdom.

LANDFORMS ALTERED BY AN ICE CAP. The ice cap formed 2.5 to 3 million years ago covered much of the northwest highlands and coastal lowlands and greatly altered their landforms. The moving ice, weighing millions of tons, scraped ground cover from thousands of square miles and deposited it as glacial moraine in other areas; and gouged mountains, creating fantastic shapes, inlets, and natural harbors. Ice-sculpting gave Norway a coastline in excess of 11,800 miles (19,000 km.) and caused rivers to be diverted from south-north to east-west flows on the Great European Plain. When the ice finally melted, the excess water caused ocean levels to rise as much as 320 feet (92 meters), created the fjords of Norway, changed shorelines into submerged continental shelves, turned land bridges into waterways, such as the English Channel, and created the shallow Irish, North, and Baltic Seas.

COASTAL LOWLANDS OR GREAT EUROPEAN PLAIN. One of the more interesting features of European topography—and one of the most influential, containing its greatest population concentrations, its richest soils, and its most developed industries—is the coastal lowlands or Great European Plain. Starting at the Pyrenees in southern France, the plain sweeps through France and includes the southeastern part of England as part of the Paris basin.

In Belgium, the plain narrows to little more than 50 miles (80 km.). It continues through the Netherlands, across Germany and Poland, and into Russia—where the plain comprises most of European Russia—terminating at the Urals. At its widest point north of the Black Sea, the Great European Plain is 1,212 miles (1,950 km.) wide. No part of this vast plain rises more than 69 feet (21 meters) above sea level. Because of the ease with which armies could be deployed on it, the plain has been instrumental in shaping Europe's history and is called its "cockpit."

Geographically, the plain was formed when the land mass between the two mountain ranges sank, and was much altered through sedimentation from erosion and glaciation. Parts of the plain were once the bottoms of ancient seas. Calcium carbonate from remains of ancient marine sea life resulted in extensive limestone formations and increased soil fertility, especially in the Paris basin. Continued sinking necessitates the building of sea walls or dikes to keep back the sea in part of northwest Europe.

Glaciation has been a major factor in the curious formation of the northeastern part of the plain. As the ice cap melted and retreated about 10,000 years ago, it left behind glacial moraine, a form of gravel, and a resultant sandy soil. The southern coast of the Baltic Sea from Jutland in Denmark to the Urals in Russia is bordered by a long chain of sandy hills. On the southernmost reaches of the plain, winds deposited fertile soil called loess. Most of Europe's people, many in vast urban complexes, live on the plain, which is crisscrossed by rivers and canals that are easily dug in the channels of ancient rivers.

CENTRAL UPLANDS AND PLATEAUS. More recent than the northwest highlands, the central uplands and plateaus

Norway's long and rugged coastline was sculpted by massive ice movements. (PhotoDisc)

1259

The Matterhorn, seen here in an 1880 engraving, is in Switzerland, near the border with Italy. It is only the third-highest mountain in the Alps at 14,691 feet (4,478 meters) but is famous for its spectacular, sharply rising cliffs that make climbing exceptionally dangerous. (Mark Twain, A Tramp Abroad, 1880)

THE ALPS

The Alps, Western Europe's "belt-buckle," are the continent's dominant mountain range, sprawling over 80,000 square miles (207,440 sq. km.) and covering the greater part of Switzerland and substantial portions of Italy, France, Germany, Austria, Slovenia, and Croatia. The Alpine range and its more important subsidiary ranges run in a rough arc from the Mediterranean coast of French Provence and Nice (Maritime Alps), and the Italian Piedmont (Ligurian Alps) north and eastward into Austria, then southward to the Croatian coast (Dinaric Alps).

The Alps have long been a source of awe and intimidation: In what is still considered one of history's most incredible military exploits, the Carthaginian general Hannibal crossed the range with his army in 218 B.C.E. The Alps are now more noted as a recreational area, specializing in tourism, winter sports, and mountain-climbing excursions. Major resort towns include Chamonix and Grenoble in France; Saint-Moritz, Lucerne, and Zermatt in Switzerland; and Innsbruck and Salzburg in Austria. The Alpine region is particularly noted for the production and export of cheeses, clocks and watches, wood carvings, embroidery and lace, and chocolate.

were formed about 200 million years ago. Later, pressure from the formation of the southern mountain region (Alpine system) to the south recontoured the uplands and raised great plateaus such as the Central Massif in France. Other parts of the uplands include the Brittany Peninsula, the Ardennes, the Black Forest, the

Harz Mountains, and the Bohemian Uplands. Nearly all the coal fields and mineral deposits are located in or near this area, sometimes called "the backbone of Europe." As a result, it is the site of most of continental Europe's heavy industry and its major industrial cities. There is also extensive agriculture in the fertile river valleys such as the Rhine that cut through the central uplands.

SOUTHERN MOUNTAIN OR ALPINE SYSTEM. The most spectacular of Europe's landform regions, this region includes the Cantabrian Mountains, Sierra Nevada, and Pyrenees of Spain; the Alps of Switzerland and Austria; the Apennines and Dolomites of Italy; the Dinaric Range of the Balkans; the Carpathian Mountains of Romania; the Transylvanian Alps of Hungary; and the Caucasus Mountains in the east. The Alpine system also includes the Atlas Mountains of North Africa and, in a continuing movement east, Asia's mighty Himalayas. The highest peak of the system in Europe is Mount Elbrus in the Caucasus Mountains, rising 18,510 feet (5,640 meters) above sea level. The better-known Mont Blanc in the Swiss Alps is 15,770 feet (4,800 meters) high.

A singular feature of the Alpine system is that it is largely formed of what were once marine sediments, which are less dense, of greater bulk, and more flexible than customary earth crust formations—hence the folded recumbent nature of the Alps. Before the mountain-building process of the Alpine system began about fifty million years ago, a much larger sea than the present-day Mediterranean, called Tethys, separated Europe and Africa. Tectonic pressure from the African lithospheric plate forced the seabed upward, forming the mountains.

SEISMIC AND VOLCANIC ACTIVITIES. The Alpine system is the newest of Europe's mountains and is still in the process of being formed, as evidenced by the extensive seismic and volcanic activities that are characteristic of the region. Still not forgotten are the great earthquake and tidal wave that shook Portugal and destroyed Lisbon in 1755. Italy and Greece were devastated in the twentieth century by at least six major quakes. Turkey has perhaps suffered the most, but largely in its Asiatic area. Southern Europe has been the site of two of the greatest volcanic eruptions in history: the blowout of the island of Thera south of present-day Greece about 1550 B.C.E. and the eruption of Mount Vesuvius in 79 C.E. Vesuvius and nearby Mounts Etna and Stromboli, all in southern Italy, are still active and potentially dangerous volcanoes.

*Alps
Page 1254,
1303*

A LAND OF FIRE AND ICE. The part of Europe most affected by earthquakes and volcanoes is Iceland, located in the north Atlantic Ocean about 186 miles (300 km.) east of Greenland and about 620 miles (1,000 km.) west of Norway. Astride the boundaries of two lithospheric plates, Iceland was formed by volcanic action and seven-eighths of the island is made up of uninhabitable lava tablelands, glowing volcanic cinders, hot springs, snow fields, and glaciers. There are more than a hundred active volcanoes, and earthquakes are a regular occurrence. Nevertheless, because of a relatively mild climate and ice-free ports due to the warm North Atlantic Drift, Iceland has an extensive shipping and fishing industry together with a remarkably high standard of living. The resourceful Icelanders even use the water from the hot springs to heat their homes.

*Mt. Etna
Page 1380*

Nis Petersen

FOR FURTHER STUDY

Berentsen, William H., ed. *Contemporary Europe: A Geographic Analysis.* 7th ed. New York: John Wiley & Sons, 1997.

Blij, H. J. de, and Peter O. Muller. "Regions of the European Realm." In *Geography, Realms, Regions and Concepts.* 8th ed. New York: John Wiley & Sons, 1997.

Pocock, J. G. "What Do We Mean by Europe?" *The Wilson Quarterly* 21 (Winter, 1997): 12-29.

Strahler, Alan, and Arthur Strahler. *Introducing Physical Geography.* New York: John Wiley & Sons, 1994.

HYDROLOGY

Watershed map
Page 1304

Trevi fountain
Page 1305

Europe has a complex pattern of rivers. Because Europe is essentially a peninsula surrounded by many irregularly shaped seas, its rivers flow in many different directions and into many different bodies of water. The Volga River flows south to the Baltic Sea, while the Rhine, Elbe, and Vistula Rivers flow toward the north to the North Sea and Baltic Sea. Western Europe's longest river, the Danube, flows eastward to the Black Sea, but many European rivers send their waters westward to the Atlantic Ocean. Many continents have one river system that drains much of their total area, but Europe has many separate river systems, each draining a fairly small part of the continent. Because Europe has few dry areas, there are few areas without rivers.

Compared to rivers on other continents, European rivers are not large. The Volga, Europe's longest river, ranks only nineteenth among world rivers. The Danube and the Volga both send about 280,000 cubic feet of water per second into the sea, but even this great volume of water does not rank them among the top twenty in the world. The amount of water (called discharge) of the Danube or Volga is just over a third the amount of water that flows out of the United States' Mississippi River, and less than 5 percent of that of South America's Amazon River.

The yearly pattern of flow in European rivers reflects the climate. Most large European rivers get much of their water from melting snow. For that reason, they usually contain the greatest amount of water in the spring. For Russian rivers like the Volga, Don, Dnieper, Dniester, and Kama, this melting snow comes from the plains of northern Russia, and the flow of the rivers is closely related to the rate at which snow melts. Western European rivers get their snowmelt from a different source: snow that has accumulated on the mountains of central Europe, especially the Alps. Alpine snowmelt feeds many European rivers, including the Danube, Elbe, Po, Rhine, Rhone, and Vistula. Once the snowmelt ends, the flow of Europe's rivers must be sustained by other sources.

In the parts of Europe where precipitation is regular, river flow is fairly even. Abundant rainfall and steady river flow from season to season characterize northwestern Europe. In Mediterranean Europe, southern Spain, France, Italy, and Greece, rivers receive almost all their rain in winter. Many rivers there are almost empty in July and August. Most Russian rivers also have periods of low water in the summer.

The speed at which water flows through Europe's rivers differs greatly from place to place. This is important because the way a river behaves is partly determined by its slope and by the kind of material over which it flows. The slope of a river is called its gradient. Russian rivers tend to have low gradients and to flow slowly. For example, the Volga River drops only about 840 feet (256 meters) over its entire length of 2,300 miles (3,700 km.). The rivers of Western Europe often have much greater overall gradients. The Rhine River, which is less than one-third as long as the Volga, drops 7,000 feet (2,300 meters). The gradient of any river is rarely even. European

EUROPE'S INLAND WATERWAYS

Far from constituting insurmountable barriers, Europe's rivers and straits have long been gateways for commercial and exchange routes, migrations, and invasions. European rivers such as the Rhine, the Danube, and the Volga were privileged communication routes. Around 5000 B.C.E., Neolithic Near East settlers traveled up the Danube to reach Europe. Crusaders traveled down the Danube toward Jerusalem, as the Goths, Huns, and Hungarians had previously traveled in the opposite direction. The Celts and the Germanics traveled on the Rhine and the Danube, and the Huns penetrated Europe on the Volga and the Don.

The extensive and accessible European river system contributed to the revival of trade during the Middle Ages, when the Rhine became a main commercial axis. The straits of Gibraltar, the Bosporus, and Pas-de-Calais also constituted important passageways. Arab peoples passed through the Gibraltar Strait, expanding their territories over the entire Iberian Peninsula. On the other side of the Mediterranean, the Turkish Empire, and the earlier Byzantine Empire, developed on both sides of the Bosporus Strait. The Strait of Dover, or Pas-de-Calais, despite being 20 miles (32 km.) wide at its narrowest point, did not cut off the British Isles from Europe. In the twentieth century Great Britain and France solidified their ties with the construction of a tunnel across the strait.

rivers usually drop much more swiftly near their start than near their mouth.

GREAT RIVERS OF EUROPE. The Volga is by far the longest river in Europe and one of the hardest-working rivers in the world. It begins in the Vladi Hills northwest of Moscow. On its long journey to the landlocked Caspian Sea, more than two hundred tributaries join it. The Volga drains 533,000 square miles (1,380,000 sq. km.) of central Russia. From spring through fall, almost the entire length of the Volga is navigable. A series of large dams on the Volga begin at the city of Rybinsk. From here to Volgagrad, the river is a series of wide lakes separated by large dams.

South of Volgagrad, the character of the river changes. There, evaporation from its surface increases and the flow of new water into the river lessens. There is less water in the Volga when it reaches the Caspian Sea than there was 250 miles (400 km.) upstream. Before reaching the sea, the Volga breaks up into many branches. Each of these branches takes a different course over a wide swampy delta that occupies 7,330 square miles (19,000 sq. km.) of land.

The Danube is the largest river in Western Europe. It twice crosses mountains of the Alpine system, once near Vienna and once at a narrow gorge known as the Iron Gate. The Danube touches ten independent countries, more than any other single river in the world: Germany, Austria, Slovakia, Hungary, Croatia, Yugoslavia, Bulgaria, Romania, Moldova, and the Ukraine. More capital cities are located on the Danube than on any other river in the world, including Vienna, Austria; Bratislava, Slovakia; Budapest, Hungry; and Belgrade, Yugoslavia. An international treaty guarantees the Danube is open to ships from all countries.

The Danube begins in the Black Forest of Germany only 15 miles (24 km.) from the Rhine River. Many geologists believe that what is now the southern part of the Rhine River was once part of the Danube. In Hungary, the river flows through the center of Budapest. On the border between Yugoslavia, the Danube enters another gorge known as the Kazan Defile. The narrowest part of this gorge is called the Iron Gate. Until a dam and canal were built, the raging waters of the Danube where it passes Iron Gate were almost impossible to navigate. Beyond the Iron Gate, the Danube becomes a wider but gentler river. It passes through the rich farmland of Bulgaria and Romania and forms much of the boundary between these two countries. At last, the Danube makes a great loop to the north and west and enters the Black Sea.

The Rhine is Europe's busiest river. It begins with glacier-fed streams high in the Swiss Alps. The upper Rhine is a swift-flowing mountain river with far too many waterfalls and cataracts to be useful for navigation. Only when it reaches Basle, in Switzerland, where the river makes a turn to flow northward, does it become useful for transportation. North of Basle, the Rhine forms the boundary between France and Germany. The part of the Rhine River between Basle and Bingen is known as the Rhine Graben. When the Rhine reaches the German town of Bingen, it takes on a different character. It is forced to pass through volcanic and metamorphic rocks that are difficult to erode. This area, known as the Rhine Gorge, is one of the most scenic parts of Europe.

The Rhine narrows from more than 2,600 feet (762 meters) north of the gorge to 400 feet (121 meters). In the Rhine Gorge, black cliffs, made of hard slate rock, rise steeply from the water and leave little room for roads or railroads along the banks. The water there is deep, swift-flowing, and dangerous. Dozens of castles stand on the cliffs above the river. For many years, the Rhine Gorge has been a major attraction for tourists. White-painted tour boats share the gorge with

hard-working barges. The Rhine Gorge ends near the German city of Bonn, which was the capital of West Germany from the end of World War II until shortly after the reunification of Germany in 1989.

Downstream from Bonn, the Rhine becomes a wider, more gently flowing river. The land along its banks is flatter and more densely populated. Until the 1980's, the waters of the river reached the North Sea by flowing through many channels (called distributaries) that made a huge flat delta. Each distributary found its own path to the sea. The two largest of these distributaries, the Lek and the Val, were sealed off by a massive engineering project in 1986. The water of the Rhine now reaches the sea through an entirely artificial channel, and its flow is carefully regulated by a series of sluices and gates. Another artificial channel has been built to divert Rhine water to the Dutch town of Rotterdam, which handles more ships than any other port in Europe. None of these changes have been able to prevent the flooding that plagues the Rhine delta.

RIVERS AND TRANSPORTATION. Rivers have been extremely important in the development of Europe. At the end of the twentieth century, Europe relied more on river transportation than any other continent. Canals connecting almost all of the large rivers of Europe have been constructed. Some of these canals go back to the nineteenth century, but many are recent. In 1997 the Rhine-Main-Danube, which linked western Europe's two largest rivers, was opened.

There are problems with the use of European rivers for transportation. Many Russian rivers, and their connecting canals, are frozen during the winter. Russian economic problems also have brought about a sharp decline in river traffic there. In Western Europe, where an efficient system of highways and railroads now pro-

Barges
Page 1373

Amsterdam
canals
Page 1241

Southwest France's Canal du Midi was built during the seventeenth century to link towns to the Mediterranean. Construction of a tunnel for part of the canal stimulated an advance in the use of gunpowder for blasting. (PhotoDisc)

Thames flood gates Page 1318

vides competition for river traffic, the volume of river traffic has begun to decline also. Still, rivers remain the cheapest way to move many bulk products through Europe, including coal, iron ore, gravel, chemicals, building material, timber, and agricultural machinery.

The importance of European rivers for transportation has influenced the location of cities. Many European capitals are located on major rivers. The same is true of port cities. During rises in sea level the valleys of many European rivers were flooded. These flooded river valleys, called estuaries, look like long narrow bays. Estuaries enabled ships to dock a considerable distance from the open ocean and unload their cargoes further in-

land. Some of Europe's most important seaports are located on these estuaries. London is on the estuary of the Thames River, about 64 miles (100 km.) from the sea. Hamburg, Germany's largest port, is 69 miles (109 km.) from the sea. Bremen is 43 miles (73 km.) from the sea.

HUMANS CHANGE RIVER SYSTEMS. Every major river system in Europe has been altered by human activities such as building dams, diverting water into irrigation channels, and straightening riverbeds. The biggest change in Europe has been the elimination of wetlands. Before humans interfered, most European rivers were surrounded with thousands of square miles of wetlands. By draining these wetlands, reducing natural flooding, and filling in land along the banks of the rivers, humans have eliminated most of Europe's wetland environment. This has helped people by improving navigation on rivers, permitting the construction of roads and buildings along riverbanks, and increasing the amount of farming. However, these activities have greatly altered the ecology the continent.

Many species of animals and plants that once flourished in Europe have almost disappeared because the swampy and marshy environments that once supported them are gone. Species of animals and plants that once used these rivers as routes of travel find their journeys interrupted by dams. The elimination of waterfalls and rapids improved navigation but destroyed the habitat of fish that need rapidly flowing water.

Pollution also has been a major problem for European rivers. Some pollution comes from dumping waste into rivers. For example, by the 1980's, most of the large rivers in Poland no longer had any animal or plant life. In recent years, major efforts have been made to clean up those rivers.

Many European countries have passed laws that require ecology to be considered before river systems are altered. The clean-up effort has had its best results in Western Europe. The European Union has become a major force in the work to clean up the continent's rivers. For example, after Germany was reunified and the former East Germany became part of the European Union, more than sixty purification stations were built on the Elbe River. These stations cut phosphorus and organic contaminants to less than half their previous level.

LAKES. The hydrology of Europe includes many large lakes. Most are found in northern Europe, especially in Scandinavia and northwest Russia. Many of the northern lakes were created or greatly modified by the glaciers that once covered much of northern Europe. Among these glacial lakes are the largest lake in Europe, Lake Ladoga, with a surface area of 7,100 square miles (18,390 sq. km.), and Europe's second-largest lake, Lake Onega, with a surface area of 3,850 square miles (9,970 sq. km.). Both are located in Russia.

EUROPE'S TEN LONGEST RIVERS

River	Length		Begins in	Empties into
	Miles	Kilometers		
Volga	2,293	3,692	Russia	Caspian Sea
Danube	1,776	2,859	Germany	Black Sea
Ural	1,575	2,536	Russia	Caspian Sea
Dnieper	1,420	2,286	Russia	Black Sea
Kama	1,261	2,030	Russia	Volga River
Don	1,224	1,971	Russia	Black Sea
Dniester	877	1,412	Ukraine	Black Sea
Rhine	820	1,320	Switzerland	North Sea
Elbe	724	1,166	Czech Republic	North Sea
Loire	634	1,021	France	Bay of Biscay

Lake Constance. (PhotoDisc)

Sweden also has many glacial lakes, and about 20 percent of the surface of Finland is covered with freshwater lakes.

Lakes in the Alpine area of Europe occupy only a tiny fraction of the area of northern lakes. Some Alpine lakes were formed where rivers flowing out of the Alps encountered layers of rock that resisted erosion. Lake Constance, part of the Rhine River, and Lake Geneva, part of the Rhone River, are examples of this kind of lake. Other Alpine lakes were formed when glaciers scooped out deep valleys. Such lakes may be seen on both sides of the Alps.

William D. Walters, Jr.

FOR FURTHER STUDY

Bentley, James. *The Rhine.* Topsfield, Mass.: Salem House, 1989.

Bryson, Bill. "Main-Danube Canal: Linking Europe's Waterways." *National Geographic* (August, 1992): 2-31.

Bullock, Alan, ed. *Great Rivers of Europe.* London: Weidenfeld and Bullock, 1966.

Clark, Miles. "A Russian Voyage from the White Sea to the Black Sea." *National Geographic* (June, 1994): 114-138.

Kaplan, Marion, and Stephanie Maze. "Iberia's Vintage River." *National Geographic* (October, 1984): 460-489.

CLIMATOLOGY

Map
Page 1307

Europe's overall climate can be described as mild—much more so than would be expected given the continent's high latitude. Latitudinally, most of Europe exists near or poleward of the U.S.-Canadian border, but most of Canada experiences a rather harsh, cold climate, while most of Europe is considerably more temperate. Southern Italy, for example, lies at a latitude that approximates New York City. When one thinks of southern Italy, images of warm, sunny days typically come to mind—hardly the image one associates with New York City.

TEMPERATE CLIMATES. The two primary reasons that the European continent is so temperate for its latitude are the warm North Atlantic Drift and its mountain ranges. The North Atlantic Drift is a warm ocean current that flows across the North Atlantic basin to the Arctic Sea north of Scandinavia. The current is an extension of the warm Gulf Stream that occupies the western portion of the North Atlantic basin off the eastern seaboard of the United States. As the Gulf Stream travels north along the U.S. east coast, it slowly curves away from the North American continent toward the mid-ocean basin.

Along North America, the cold Labrador Current replaces the departing Gulf Stream as far south as Maryland. In the mid-ocean region, the Gulf Stream is renamed the North Atlantic Drift. Waters of the North Atlantic Drift are quite warm because most of the water originates in the North Equatorial Current of the Atlantic Ocean. Most of the remainder comes from waters of the warm Caribbean Sea and the Gulf of Mexico. The small remaining portion is made up of North Atlantic waters that traverse the lower latitudes, warming considerably in these high temperature zones.

The North Atlantic Drift is the northern extension of the circulation gyre that occupies the North Atlantic basin. The term "gyre" refers to the coupling of atmospheric circulation with oceanic circulation. The North Atlantic gyre owes its existence to the huge atmospheric subtropical high (STH) pressure cell that occupies the central North Atlantic basin year-round. The STH waxes and wanes seasonally, reaching a maximum intensity during the summer months and a minimum during the late winter. The position of the STH also fluctuates seasonally. It reaches its maximum poleward position during the summer months and its maximum equatorial position during the winter months.

Because the ever-present STH is a zone of high pressure, it spins clockwise, or anticyclonically. This spin imparts considerable frictional force on the waters of the North Atlantic. Surface currents, therefore, mimic the atmospheric flow. Waters that are fairly warm for their latitude flow poleward along the western edge of the basin, near North America, while cooler waters flow equatorward along the eastern edge of the basin, near Africa. Because Europe lies poleward of the mean central gyre position, waters off its coast are much warmer than expected for their latitude. This is the Gulf Stream extension, the North Atlantic Drift, which completes the northern gyre circle.

THE OCEAN'S INFLUENCE ON RUSSIAN CLIMATE

The warm waters of the North Atlantic Drift keep the Russian port of Murmansk open through the entire winter, even though the city lies at a latitude of approximately 68 degrees north, well poleward of the Arctic Circle. Murmansk and Saint Petersburg are Russia's only two European ports open year-round.

The North Atlantic Drift splits into two distinct currents near the southern coast of England. Part of the drift flows south, along the coasts of France, Spain, and Portugal. This water is eventually incorporated into the cooler Canary current that flows south along the west coast of Northern Africa. The remaining portion of the North Atlantic Drift flows north along the west coast of England and Norway, eventually flowing eastward north of the Scandinavian countries and into the Arctic Ocean. The waters are so warm that the area remains ice-free even during the coldest winters.

EFFECTS OF MOUNTAIN RANGES. The second major reason for Europe's mild climate relates to its mountain ranges. The major mountain system of Europe, the Alps, extends along an east-to-west transect. This is radically different from the north-south mountain axes of North America, which allow warm equatorial air and cold polar air to traverse virtually the entire continent.

In Europe, warm air originating over the warm Mediterranean basin is confined to the southern regions of the continent. Colder air, originating in higher-latitude, polar locations, is confined to the northern regions of the continent. Thus, on average, much of Europe—especially its southern region—is warmer than other locations of similar latitude. The mountains also have a profound effect on the daily weather, especially storms. Storms in Europe are rarely severe, because the mixing of radically unlike air masses is almost nonexistent as a result of the mountain barrier. In North America, severe weather is common, especially during spring when the mountain configuration allows unlike air masses to converge. Therefore, the frequency and magnitude of severe weather events has been dramatically less in Europe than in North America.

DRY CLIMATES. Europe has no true deserts—its driest areas are the steppes. Steppe climates are transition zones between drier desert climates and wetter climates. Steppe climates typically have enough precipitation for tall steppe grasses to grow, but usually are too dry for forests. In Europe, steppe areas occur mainly in the Iberian Peninsula and near the Black and Caspian Seas.

Steppe also occupies eastern Turkey, expanding southward into the Mideastern countries. All steppe climates of Europe can be classified as midlatitude steppe. This is because they have overall lower temperatures and smaller temperature ranges (both seasonally and diurnally) than true deserts. Normal temperature ranges approach 50 degrees Fahrenheit (10 degrees Celsius) between high and low sun periods. Precipitation ranges between 10 and 30 inches (25 to 76 centimeters) depending on local and regional factors.

Iberian Peninsula steppe regions exist predominantly from rain shadow induced by the surrounding mountains. The mountains help wring out available moisture only on the windward sides, usually those sides facing the sea. The protected interior regions have less precipitation, leading to steppe climates. Steppe regions of the interior, near the Black and Caspian Seas, exist primarily from continentality. Those regions are located far from major water sources such as the North Atlantic Ocean, the Mediterranean Sea, and the Indian Ocean.

The rain shadow effects of mountains also prevent high levels of precipitation. These eastern steppe areas are true transition zones to the harsher, drier, Gobi Desert, which occupies central Asia, and the true desert of the Middle Eeast.

MEDITERRANEAN CLIMATE. Possibly the most identifiable climate of Europe is the Mediterranean climate, found in southern Spain, southern France, Italy, and Greece. This climate, which typically occurs along the western edges of continents, is named for the southern edge of Europe, the Mediterranean basin. Mediterranean climates are characterized by a distinct and pronounced summer dry period and a rather wet winter. The summer dry occurs as precipitation processes are thwarted by a distinct cell of high pressure that builds over the Mediterranean Sea. The high develops in response to thermal differences between the hot land regions and the cooler Mediterranean waters.

The jet stream, which typically induces much of the precipitation falling on Europe and other midlatitude locations, is pushed north of the Alps. Precipitation falling as a result of migratory frontal cyclones embedded within the jet stream is confined to regions north of the Mediterranean basin. This, combined with the Mediterranean high, ensures dry summers. Occasional rainfall may occur as a result of surface heating-induced convective thunderstorms.

During winter, cooler temperatures developing near the North Pole expand to lower latitudes. The jet stream denotes the upper atmospheric border between this cold air and warmer air originating from lower latitudes. The jet expands southward, ultimately positioning south of the Alps, over the Mediterranean basin. Cyclonic frontal storm systems provide the area with abundant rainfall through the winter season. Annual rainfall amounts typically are between 10 and 20 inches (25 to 51 centimeters).

Because of the huge sea influence, temperatures in the Mediterranean region are mild, especially given the latitude of the region. The Mediterranean Sea is quite warm, which causes air temperatures in the region to be greatly moderated. Monthly average temperatures for winter are approximately 50 degrees Fahrenheit (10 degrees Celsius), while summer averages approach 80 degrees Fahrenheit (27 degrees Celsius).

Seville
Page 1305

MARINE WEST COAST. The marine west coast climate occupies the bulk of Western Europe. This high-latitude climate is usually confined to the edges of a continent. In Europe, however, the climate type is quite extensive because of the prevalence of the extremely warm North Atlantic Drift and the east-west alignment of the Alps Mountain range, which allows maritime air to penetrate deep into the continental interior. The marine west coast climate region extends from northern Spain through France, England, Norway, and across the northern tier of Europe to Russia.

The marine west coast climate is typified by the moderating influence of the warm ocean current, which keeps the region warmer than it would be otherwise, given its high latitude. The entire region lies within the global westerlies, the wind system that occupies regions between 30 and 60 degrees north latitude. Winds and storms, therefore, traverse this region from west to east, carrying the ocean-moderated winds far inland.

EUROPE'S HIGHEST TEMPERATURE

The highest temperature ever recorded in Europe was 122 degrees Fahrenheit (50 degrees Celsius), recorded at Seville, Spain, on August 4, 1881.

Precipitation is rather evenly distributed throughout the year as storms embedded within the polar jet stream traverse the region nearly year-round. Precipitation typically ranges between 30 and 50 inches (75 to 125 centimeters) for most locations, but much higher totals can be common in highlands. Snow is uncommon in many locations but common in others, especially in the hills and mountains. While the chance of precipitation is quite high during much of the year, actual precipitation intensity is low. This stems from the nature of the precipitation, which commonly is generated by low-lying stratus clouds. These clouds often produce drizzle and rarely produce heavy precipitation events. Because of the high frequency of frontal cyclone passage and the associated persistent cloudy conditions, the climate is often thought of as being rather dreary.

Temperatures are quite moderate considering the latitude of the region as the moderating effects of the sea are transported inland. Temperature ranges are also kept rather low by the persistence of cloud cover virtually year-round. Average monthly temperatures are normally no lower than 36 degrees Fahrenheit (2 degrees Celsius) during the coldest month and no higher than 70 degrees Fahrenheit (21 degrees Celsius) for the warmest month for most locations. Extreme temperatures, although they do occur, are rather rare.

Baltic Sea beach Page 1306

HUMID SUBTROPICAL. The humid subtropical climate region occupies an area of south central Europe that includes portions of Italy, Austria, and Hungary. The region is bordered by the marine west coast climate to the north and the Mediterranean climate to the south. This region has mild winters and long, hot summers. Abundant precipitation is evenly distributed through the year. Warm-season precipitation is usually convective in nature while cool-season precipitation is triggered by frontal cyclones. Precipitation amounts range from 39 to 60 inches (100 to 150 centimeters) per year. Temperatures can be quite high during the summer, reaching 95 degrees Fahrenheit (35 degrees Celsius) or higher in some locations. Average summer temperatures are typically between 79 to 82 degrees Fahrenheit (26 to 28 degrees Celsius). The coldest month, January, has average temperatures around 50 degrees Fahrenheit (10 degrees Celsius) for most locations.

HUMID CONTINENTAL. Humid continental climates exist inland from marine west coast climates throughout Europe. Therefore, the climate type is associated with eastern Europe from Poland and east through Russia. Most of Sweden, southern Finland, and eastern portions of Norway also have this climate classification. The climate is typified by cold, long, harsh winters, and rather short but sultry summers. Much of the pronounced climate variation is related either to continentality (in the case of Russia) or to extreme variations in the length of day that accompanies the high latitudes (as in Scandinavia). Much of Scandinavia is located so close to the Arctic Circle that some areas receive only a few hours of daylight in winter. During the summer, temperatures may be hot along the continental interior but milder near the Baltic Sea. Monthly temperature averages vary from about 82 degrees Fahrenheit (28 degrees Celsius) during summer to the freezing mark during winter.

Precipitation is generally even from month to month across the region, as frontal cyclones traverse the region on a fairly consistent basis. Annual precipitation totals are usually between 20 and 40 inches (50 to 100 centimeters) for most locations. Quite a bit of this precipitation comes in the form of snowfall during the winter months.

SUBARCTIC. North of the humid continental climate region lies the subarctic climate. This region is confined to northern portions of Scandinavia, largely Sweden and Finland, and northern Russia. It is characterized by extensive boreal (coniferous) forests that are well suited to the harsh climate. Winters are frigid and long, with average monthly temperatures below freezing for up to seven months. The average temperature of the coldest month may approach –36 degrees Fahrenheit (–38 degrees Celsius) for some locations. Some of the coldest temperatures on record outside of the ice cap climates of Antarctica and Greenland have been recorded in subarctic climates. Average summer temperatures show a dramatic reversal, with monthly averages near 68 degrees Fahrenheit (20 degrees Celsius). The variation in temperature between summer and winter may be as high as 122 degrees Fahrenheit (50 degrees Celsius).

Precipitation is sparse, because the frequent cold air has little moisture-carrying capacity. Summer precipitation maximums are pronounced in most locations, while winter remains dry and cold. Warm-season precipitation is primarily convective and sporadic. However, there is enough soil moisture to support the boreal forests because the overall cold temperatures limit evaporation rates. Moisture, therefore, remains frozen in the ground (permafrost) for extensive periods. When temperatures rise enough for evaporation to deplete this moisture, the soil moisture is replaced through precipitation. Annual precipitation amounts are usually between 5 and 20 inches (12 to 50 centimeters). Although precipitation amounts are rather meager, fairly impressive snow amounts are common in some areas because sporadic, light snowfalls remain from year to year with little melting.

TUNDRA. The boreal forest of northern Europe culminates at the border between the subarctic and tundra climates. The tundra is a colder, drier version of the subarctic climate type. Temperatures are too cold, and precipitation too meager, to support tree growth. The tundra is characterized by stunted, low-growing lichens, mosses, and shrubs. The average temperature of the warmest month does not exceed 50 degrees Fahrenheit (10 degrees Celsius), and may be as low as the freezing mark at the northern boundary of the climate region. This region occupies the extreme northern sections of the continent, namely the northern half of Iceland, Scandinavia, and Russia.

Winters are long, dark, and freezing, while summers tend to be cool and brief. Average winter temperatures may be as low as –31 degrees Fahrenheit (–35 degrees Celsius) with little, if any, sunlight present. Because of the extreme differences in the length of day between winter and summer, there are large variations (40 to 60 degrees Fahrenheit/5 to 20 degrees Celsius) in annual average temperature ranges.

Precipitation is sparse as a result of the extreme cold. Annual precipitation amounts are below 10 inches (25 centimeters) with most locations receiving less than 5 inches (13 centimeters). Although some precipitation typically falls in every month, a distinct warm season maximum is discernable. Snows remain at the surface for long periods, and in some areas, from year to year.

HIGHLAND. Highland climates exist where mountains are prevalent. The extreme variations of temperature and precipitation that occur in mountainous regions supersede other climate features. In Europe, highland climates prevail through the central Alps region centered on Switzerland and in the Caucasus Mountain region between the Black and Caspian Seas. The extreme differences in elevation, slope, and orientation give highland climates remarkable spatial variations in weather elements. Vertical zonation, the progression of climatic zones with increasing elevation, also prevails. For example, the Swiss Alps are surrounded by a marine west coast climate. In the lowlands, this climate prevails, but with increasing elevation, characteristics of a humid continental, then subarctic, then tundra, and finally ice cap (if the mountain is snow-capped) climate regime are apparent. Such small spatial scale variations are impossible to correctly characterize; therefore, these regions receive the all-inclusive highland climate designation.

Anthony J. Vega

FOR FURTHER STUDY

Battan, Louis, J. *Weather in Your Life.* New York: W. H. Freeman, 1983.

Critchfield, Howard J. *General Climatology.* 4th ed. Englewood Cliffs, N.J.: Prentice Hall, 1983.

Lutgens, Frederick K., and Edward J. Tarbuck. *The Atmosphere.* 7th ed. Englewood Cliffs, N.J.: Prentice Hall, 1998.

Lyons, Walter A. *The Handy Weather Answer Book.* Detroit, Mich.: Visible Ink, 1997.

Suplee, Curt. "Untangling the Science of Climate." *National Geographic* (May, 1998): 44-70.

Tufty, Barbara, *1001 Questions Answered About Hurricanes, Tornadoes, and Other Natural Air Disasters.* New York: Dover, 1987.

INFORMATION ON THE WORLD WIDE WEB

European climate information can be found at Database Europe, which hosts detailed information on a variety of topics. (www.asg.physik.uni-erlangen.de/europa/indexe.htm)

Additional information can be found through the Permafrost and Climate Web site. (www.cf.ac.uk/uwcc/earth/pace/)

BIOGEOGRAPHY
AND
NATURAL
RESOURCES

NATURAL RESOURCES

Resource map Page 1308

European resources have supported an expanding population for centuries and through the commercial and industrial revolutions that emerged from European societies. Many European resources, such as forests and some mineral reserves, have been depleted during the past millennium as a result of the advance of human settlement. The remaining resources of the continent are essential components in sustaining the quality of European life.

The diversity, extent, and quality of European resources varies among the specific regions of the continent. Stretching from the Atlantic Ocean on the west to the Ural Mountains in the east and from the Arctic Ocean in the north to the Mediterranean Sea in the south, Europe's natural resources are distributed unevenly and have contributed to internal political instability, wide disparities in rates of economic development, and centuries of imperial and colonial expansion throughout the world. European resources include significant water, mineral, forest, and energy-developing assets.

To examine the resources of Europe, the continent can be divided into four regions: Western Europe, Mediterranean Europe, Central Europe, and Eastern Europe. Western Europe stretches from Ireland in the west to Switzerland in the east and from Scandinavia in the north to France in the south.

WESTERN EUROPE. The natural resources of Western Europe were the basis of the commercial and industrial revolutions; access to these resources was supported by moderate weather and an extensive river system that was enhanced through the development of a complex network of canals. The early emergence of nation-states, capitalism, and democracy in Western Europe accelerated the effective application of resources and contributed to an uneven distribution of wealth between the West and the other regions. As a result of the exploitation of the North Sea oil fields and the integration of its national economies, first through the Common Market and later through the European Union, Western Europe has sustained its dominant position.

In the Treaty of Rome in 1957, six Western European nations (France, West Germany, Italy, the Netherlands, Belgium, and Luxembourg) formed the European Economic Community (EEC), also known as the Common Market. During the next three decades, that organization developed into a political and economic organization, the European Union.

During the late twentieth century, the Central and Mediterranean regions closed the gap; but Eastern Europe, although rich in resources, did not have the economic and political base that was needed for the effective use of its resources. Thus, Eastern Europe is poorer than the other regions, and many of its people continue to have a lower standard of living than do those elsewhere on the continent. While Eastern European states have developed nuclear energy resources, the absence of sound development policies and practices and the general inefficiencies associated with their economies have rendered these efforts both unreliable and unsafe.

MEDITERRANEAN EUROPE. This region covers the northern coasts of the Mediterranean Sea from Spain, through Italy and the Balkans, to Greece and Turkey. This region was the home of the classical cultures of Greece and Rome; it is noted for soil that is difficult to cultivate, negligible mineral resources needed for industrial and postindustrial economies, and river systems that historically have been difficult to control. Many of the original and limited mineral resources of this region have been depleted by human consumption during the past twenty-five centuries.

CENTRAL EUROPE. Central Europe includes Germany, Poland, Austria, Hungary, the northern Balkans, and Romania. Rich in arable land, this region also has significant mineral resources that support heavy industry and electrical power to sustain a modern living standard. One major problem in Central Europe is the environmental damage that is the legacy in the former Eastern Bloc nations; reckless use of fossil fuels without effective environmental standards have made many cities in these countries ecologically unsafe.

Trevi fountain Page 1305

EASTERN EUROPE. Eastern Europe consists of Russia, Belarus (fomerly Byelorussia), and the Ukraine—all components of the former Soviet Union. Based on mineral and energy resources, these states are self-sufficient and continue to export these commodities to the rest of Europe and throughout the world. Nevertheless, their economies and societies do not reflect the value of these natural treasures; mismanagement of the region's resources has been a continuing theme during the post-Soviet period.

WATER. Of all of Europe's resources, water is most evident when looking at a map of the continent. Three of its four major boundaries are among the world's largest bodies of water—the Atlantic and Arctic Oceans and the Mediterranean Sea. Not only did these masses of water promote commerce and exploration, but they also have been a major source of food for the coastal peoples of Western, Northern, and Southern Europe.

Fishing grounds, such as the Dogger Bank in the North Sea, have supplied a reliable source of protein for centuries.

RENEWABLE ENERGY: EUROPE'S GIFT FROM THE SEA

The prevailing southwest winds that nudge the warm Atlantic waters of the Gulf Stream eastward give Europe its temperate climate and have for centuries turned Europe's windmills for pumping water and grinding grain. These same winds also perform an even more valuable service: the production of renewable electric energy. The nations of the European Union lead the world in the production of electric energy from wind, producing 6,572 megawatts in 1998, compared to 2,141 megawatts produced in the United States. Germany, Europe's largest consumer of electricity, has been a leader, along with the Scandinavian states, in the development of wind-powered electricity. Ten percent of Denmark's electricity was produced by wind in 1999, and the figure is expected to rise to 50 percent by 2030.

Two features of Europe's physiography make the development of wind energy possible: the flat terrain of the Great European Plain and the shallowness of the surrounding seas, allowing for offshore construction of the increasingly efficient wind turbines. The wind resources over the shallow European seas theoretically could provide all of Europe's electricity supplies several times over. Wind-powered electricity's benefits, in the form of reduction in pollutants alone, are incalculable.

Other major bodies of water include the Irish Sea between Ireland and England, the Baltic Sea and Gulf of Finland in Scandinavia, the Bay of Biscay west of France, the Adriatic and Tyrrhenian Seas of Italy, the Ionian and Aegean Seas of Greece, the Black and Caspian Seas in extreme southeastern Europe, and the White and Barents Seas north of Russia.

Despite developments that jeopardize their environments, these water resources continue to serve as venues for fishermen and commerce. Because of the nature of European geography, these major water resources have been used heavily for transport; the distribution of the fishing yields from the seas produced distinct coastal communities that have thrived for almost a millennium.

While the oceans and seas are significant European resources and contributed greatly to European exploration of the rest of the world, Europe's river and stream systems were the focus for early settlement and the emergence of urban centers during the early modern era. The availability of access to sufficient supplies of freshwater was the essential resource necessary to support a growing population that had settled on a continuing basis. The agricultural, commercial, and industrial revolutions were made possible as the result of access to abundant supplies of freshwater.

In the British Isles, the Shannon, Thames, and Avon Rivers are significant in understanding both the history of Great Britain and Ireland and their economic development. The construction of hundreds of canals (most notably the Manchester Ship Canal) has connected industrial sites to rivers and other large bodies of water. Through this network of canals, goods can be transported throughout the British Isles.

On the mainland of the continent, the major rivers are the Ebro, Duero, and Tagus in Spain and Portugal; the Seine, Loire, Rhone, Moselle, and Garonne in France; the Rhine in the Netherlands and Germany; the Main, Weser, Elbe, Danube, and Oder in Germany; the Drave, Danube, and Save in the Balkans; the Oder and Vistula in Poland; the Dnieper and Dniester of the Ukraine; the Dvina of Latvia and Russia; and the Volga, Don, and Ural in Russia.

Bay of Biscay Page 1377

During the nineteenth and twentieth centuries, most of these rivers were interconnected through the construction of canals. In most instances, these rivers are not only sources of water for drinking and crop irrigation and a conduit for trade, but also provide hydroelectric power. With the advent of electricity at the end of the nineteenth century, the demand for inexpensive power to light homes and streets and provide energy to industry resulted in the harnessing of water power to produce electricity. Until the 1970's, hydroelectric power and generators fueled by coal and oil supplied Europe's electric needs; during the late twentieth century, nuclear power plants replaced many of the older hydroelectric plants as the major source of electric power.

MINERALS. Many of the mineral resources of Europe have been depleted because of their use since ancient times and the impact of the Industrial Revolution. During the Greco-Roman and medieval periods, the limited reserves of gold, silver, bronze, tin, and other such metals were exhausted.

As the modern age developed and the population grew, iron and coal resources were used to support the Industrial Revolution and urbanization. While these resources are still available, Europeans, with the exception of Russia, Ukraine, and Byelorussia, have become dependent on imported minerals to support their standard of living. Europeans need coal, ura-

EUROPE'S NORTH SEA OIL FIELDS

The discovery and exploitation of the North Sea oil fields have tempered but not eliminated European dependency on imported petroleum. European political and diplomatic actions during the Gulf War of 1991 reflected the importance of sustaining access to Mideast oil. The primary beneficiaries of the North Sea oil fields have been Norway and Great Britain.

nium, oil, and natural gas to support the heating and electric needs of industry and society; they also require significant quantities of high-grade iron ores to produce the steel necessary for economic renewal and growth.

Coal
Page 1318

European coal resources are dispersed throughout the continent, with the most significant and accessible seams being located in Northern Europe. The major coal deposits are in Great Britain's Midlands; the Lorraine region of France; eastern Belgium; the eastern Netherlands; the Saar Valley, Westphalia, and North Rhine districts of Germany; Upper Silesia in Poland; Silesia in the Czech Republic; and the Ural Mountains of Russia. In each of these areas, coal production has been actively pursued for more than a century, but the deposits are still plentiful and accessible. Exploration for new coal fields has led to the development of new fields in Germany and Great Britain. Smaller but significant coal resources have been exploited in Norway and Hungary.

Nuclear
power plant
Page 1309

The value of coal resources depends on several factors. One is how accessible it is. Known coal deposits that are not readily or reasonably accessible are not cost-effective and remain untapped until their need justifies the expense; thus, many of the small deposits located across Northern Europe have not been mined. Second is the type of coal that is available—anthracite (hard) or bituminous or coking (soft). The type of coal determines and limits its applications and therefore its need. Another factor that must be considered is the environmental impact of using this fossil fuel.

During the 1970's, Europeans started becoming more aware of the need to eliminate sources of pollution that have corrupted the quality of the air and water and that may contribute to human health problems. Environmental priorities have been reflected in the deliberations before the European Union, and policies have been adopted that are designed to eliminate sources of air and water pollution throughout the member states. Nevertheless, the use of coal as a major energy source continues. The European demand for energy is expanding. In 1997 Russia, Great Britain, and Norway were listed among the world's ten major producers of energy; in the same year, Russia, Germany, Great Britain, France, and Italy were ranked among the world's ten leading consumers of energy.

European societies have become dependent upon nuclear energy. Of the top ten nations in the world reliant on nuclear energy in 1998, only South Korea was not European. Lithuania, France, Belgium, Sweden, Ukraine, the Slovak Republic, Bulgaria, Switzerland, and Slovenia are highly dependent on nuclear energy, with percentages of their power coming from nuclear plants ranging from 77 percent in Lithuania to almost 40 percent in Slovenia.

Deposits of uranium, required for production of nuclear energy, appear throughout Europe, with the most useful resources located in central France, Spain, Hungary, Estonia, and the Ukraine; additional uranium must be imported. The problem of the disposal of nuclear waste is another environmental concern with which Europeans and their governments are grappling.

While the discovery of new oil and natural gas reserves in the North Sea during the last half of the twentieth century have, at least temporarily, resolved the petroleum crisis for Great Britain and Norway, Europe, with the major exception of Russia, is largely dependent upon the importation of most of its oil needs. The old oil fields in Romania, once so important in European economic and military history, no longer meet the oil needs of that country.

In 1998 Western European oil reserves were 18.3 billion barrels and those in Eastern Europe were 59 billion barrels; natural gas reserves in the same year were 173.1 trillion cubic feet for Western Europe and 2,000.4 trillion cubic feet for Russia and Eastern Europe. The continent's largest oil reserve is the Volga-Ural field in Russia. During the 1990's, new oil fields in the Black Sea and its surrounding coastal areas were developed by Romania, Turkey, and Russia.

With the exception of rich deposits in eastern France and Sweden, Europe's principal iron resources are located in Russia and the Ukraine. The Ukraine has the world's largest known manganese resources, at Nikopol; Russia also has extensive holdings of this mineral and significant reserves of nickel, chromium, and vanadium. Vanadium, titanium, and cobalt deposits are located in Finland.

LAND AND FORESTS. The European landmass consists of plains, mountains, forests, and a number of significant river systems. The major agricultural zones in Europe are the great Central Plain that starts in France and expands in Germany and into Eastern Europe; almost all of the Ukraine is a highly arable region. In other areas, Europeans have maximized food production by effective scientific management of the available land. Nevertheless, Europeans have continued to import an increasing amount of the food that they consume.

The major mountain ranges in Europe are the Alps in France, Italy, Switzerland, and Austria; the Carpathians in the Slovak Republic and Romania; the Pyrenees in France and Spain; the Apennines in Italy; and the Caucasus in Georgia and Russia.

The density and diversity of European forests are largely dependent upon the climate. In the Arctic, the high elevations of the Alps, and the tundra of northern Russia and Scandinavia, cold temperatures prevent the development of forests. The more temperate sections of Northern Europe are dominated by coniferous trees—trees with needles rather than leaves, such as firs, pines, and spruces. In the central temperate sections of Europe, birch and oak have survived the onslaught of the expanding population and the impact of the Industrial Revolution and wars. In the warm Mediterranean region, forests have almost disappeared because of the impact of human development. The few sections of olive, cork oak, holm oak, and Lebanon cedar trees that survive are endangered by the instability of the terrain and the mounting brush that is frequently ignited by lightning or humans.

Most, if not all, of the original forests of Europe have been replaced by the existing forests, which are limited by the encroaching needs of society. As forests disappeared, they were replaced in the more arid zones with grasslands or steppes or prairie lands; the steppes developed as regions between the forest lines and dry, desert-like areas in the south. In spite of these ecological conditions, moderate forests still exist in Britain, France, Germany, and throughout Eastern Europe. Reforestation efforts to restore Western Europe's forests have been moderately successful.

OTHER RESOURCES. Perhaps the most important physical resource enjoyed by Europeans is the moderate weather that has supported a long growing season. The absence of extreme shifts in European temperatures has resulted in greater mobility and longevity, and provided for economic growth that has enhanced the living standards for its people. From the European perspective, the primary resource concerns to be addressed in the future are a mounting dependency on imported oil and most minerals, the continuing concentration of the population in a few major metropolitan areas with the accompanying need for clean air and water, and the need to import substantial amounts of foodstuffs from throughout the world.

Another major resource factor relates to the European dependency on nuclear energy and the accompanying problems associated with the stability of nuclear plants and the disposal of radioactive hazardous waste. Most of the issues are readily manifested in internal political and foreign policy debates. The European Union and the nation-states that are not members must undertake initiatives that address common resource concerns. The future direction of Russia raises both hope and anxiety. Resource-rich Russia can move toward a partnership with the new Europe or it can sustain a national resource policy that may lead to political instability and conflict.

William T. Walker

FOR FURTHER STUDY

Buchanan, K. *The Geography of Europe.* London: Spokesman Books, 1972.

Dawson, Andrew H. *A Geography of European Integration.* New York: Halstead Press, 1993.

Gottmann, Jean. *Geography of Europe.* 4th ed. New York: Holt, Rinehart and Winston, 1969.

Hoffman, George Walter, ed. *A Geography of Europe: Problems and Prospects.* 4th ed. New York: Ronald Press, 1977.

Kaa, Dirk van de, ed. *European Populations: Unity in Diversity.* Boston: Kluwer, 1999.

Knox, P. L. *The Geography of Western Europe: A Socio-Economic Survey.* Beckenham, England: Croom Helm, 1984.

Nelsen, Brent F. and Alexander Stubb, eds. *The European Union: Readings on the Theory and Practice of European Integration.* 2d ed. Boulder, Colo.: Lynne Rienner, 1998.

Thomas, Kenneth P. and Mary Ann Tétreault, eds. *Racing to Regionalize: Democracy, Capitalism, and Regional Political Economy.* Boulder, Colo.: Lynne Rienner, 1999.

FLORA

The flora—flowering plants—of Europe are divided into three principal groups—trees, shrubs, and herbs—all of which reproduce through their flowering parts. Trees have a central, woody stem; shrubs have multiple woody stems; and herbs do not have woody stems. Many of Europe's flowering plants are similar to those in North America, for example, belonging to the same genus, or second-to-last biological category, but of different species, the last biological category. Some of the most common North American flowering plants have cousins in Europe, but their location varies according to their latitude—how far they are from the equator—and altitude—how far they are above sea level.

LOCATION. Other factors besides latitude and altitude determine where flowering species will be found. The most important is climate: The continent of Europe ranges from the coastal areas on the northern shore of the Mediterranean Sea and Black Sea to the Arctic Ocean north of the Scandinavian peninsula. Although most of Europe is in the temperate climate zone, the areas that border the Mediterranean Sea are nearly all frost-free, while the parts of Europe that form the Scandinavian peninsula and northern Russia have frost-free periods each year of as little as two months. As a result, there is a south-to-north gradation of the flowering plants.

Another important factor in determining where flowering plants will be found is the soil. The soil in the south of Europe tends to be sandy; the low annual rainfall at the Mediterranean shoreline means that what little rain there is flows rapidly through the soil, leaving relatively little for plants. In the north, much of the soil is permanently frozen, so only plants that can grow in a short period of time in the summer and survive many months of frozen life will be found there. In between these areas, European soils vary between those that make ideal growing conditions for flowering plants, the black earth soils of central Europe, and those that are thin layers over underlying rock or that trap water in the soil layers just below the surface, creating marshy conditions.

An east-to-west factor also influences which flowering plants are found where in Europe. The Atlantic coastline is warmed all year round by the Gulf Stream, so that normal temperatures in the parts of the continent touched by this current (including much of the western Baltic Sea) have warmer temperatures in winter than their latitudes would indicate. Southern Norway, for instance, is on the same latitude as Greenland, most of which is covered with ice and snow throughout the year; but many plants, including agricultural crops, grow in southern Norway because of the Gulf Stream. Because rainfall is high, these parts of Europe tend to be wetter and cooler in summer than in other parts of the world at the same latitude.

Although Europe is a favorable location for many flowering plants, the fact that it has been occupied by humans for such a long period of time means that there are almost no parts of Europe where the vegetation has been unaffected by humans. There are virtually no "virgin forests" in Europe.

EUROPE'S VANISHING PLANT SPECIES

German authorities estimate that, because the European landscape has been exploited by humans for so many centuries, fourteen plant species totally disappeared between 1870 and 1950, and 130 disappeared from 1950 to 1980. Fifty more species are threatened or endangered. Intensive agricultural development of the land is largely responsible, stimulated by an agricultural price support system that encourages growth of agriculture.

FORESTS. Most of Europe's trees are similar to those in North America, but they are essentially cousins, not members of the same immediate families. The numerous varieties of oaks in Europe are different species from American oaks. There are also maples, ashes, elms, birches, beeches, chestnuts, walnuts, apples, and hornbeams in Europe, but they are not the same species as the members of these families native to North America. The same is true of the conifers or evergreens: The pines, spruces, firs, and larches native to Europe are not the same as those native to North America.

Some of the native tree species of Europe have been brought to America and have become a natural part of the American forest. The sycamore, for example, is the same species in North America as in Europe. The sycamore is a long-lived tree; some sycamores that were planted in North America during the colonial era are still alive. The mountain ash, with its bright orange berries, is another tree from Europe (where it is known as the rowan) that has emigrated to America. The horse-chestnut is yet another tree native to Europe that has long been settled in North America.

Among the evergreens, the Norway spruce has been widely planted and now seeds itself in North America. The Scots pine has been widely planted in North America; many Christmas trees sold every year in the United States are Scots pine. The European larch has become popular with the forest industry, because it is suited to reforestation after clear-cutting. Some North American species have made the opposite journey: Much of Scotland has been reforested with the Sitka spruce, a native of the Pacific Northwest. Another native American evergreen that has made the trip to Europe is the white pine, known in Europe as the Weymouth pine, after the Englishman who first discovered it. Plantations of white pine have been set up all over Europe, because Europe did not have a soft pine, and the wood of the white pine is easily worked.

One important European tree that has had a large impact on America is the apple. Only the crabapple is native to North America; other apple varieties are imports. The apple tree that produces the familiar fruit appears to have originated in southern Russia, but soon made its way throughout Europe. Many apple varieties were cultivated by the Romans. The English and other European settlers of North America, finding only crabapples when they arrived, imported familiar apple varieties from Europe, and orchards were among the first things the English settlers of New England planted in Massachusetts Bay.

SHRUBS. Many European shrubs have become immigrants too. The box and holly are much prized for foundation planting, and the privet makes a neat hedge. The buckthorn bush has also made the journey, although it is less popular with nurserymen. The juniper in Europe is the same as the juniper in North America, but the raspberry is not. Currants and gooseberries are European shrubs that have been widely transplanted to America, although one of the European currant varieties harbors a disease that affects the North American white pine. By contrast, the cranberry is a North American shrub that has lately been transplanted to Europe, and North American blueberries are quite different from the related species in Europe.

The raspberry bush found everywhere in eastern North America is a European native, but it has been planted throughout America. Because birds are frequent consumers of its fruit, it has spread well beyond the beds where it was originally planted. The heather that covers many of the hills of northern Europe is native to Europe, and has become popular with florists as a filler for bouquets. One of the most common landscape shrubs in America, the lilac, is of European origin, but it was among the earliest to make the trip to America. Today the foundations of old colonial homesteads can often be located because, although the house is gone, the lilacs that once surrounded it survive.

HERBS. Herbs or wildflowers have spread across the continents much as shrubs have. Many of the most common North American wildflowers, such as the dandelion, are, in fact, immigrants. So is the wild strawberry, whose tiny fruits are merely a suggestion of their domesticated cousins. Among the less-favored immigrant plants is the plantain that infests lawns.

Many wildflowers are both European and American in origin, although in most cases the species differ: that is, they are cousins rather than siblings. Among them are the violets, some of the cinquefoils, many buttercup varieties, and the marsh marigold. While the common ox-eye daisy is an import, the daisy fleabane and the black-eyed susan are American. The clovers that are so familiar to Americans are all imports—the white clover, the red clover, and the alsike clover are all natives of Europe.

Plants that are thought of as grasses also are really flowering plants. Kentucky bluegrass is really the European smooth meadow grass. Annual rye grass, often used to green up new lawns quickly, is a European import, as is red fescue, common in hayfields. Timothy hay, cultivated all over America as feed hay, is also an import from Europe.

The marshes and swamps of Europe are populated mostly by indigenous plants. Large numbers of sedges that are native to Europe are grouped together in the *Carex* genus; these can be found in Europe's wetlands. Wetlands may have more "virgin" plant communities than anywhere else in Europe, because they were unsuitable for cultivation. Europeans have drained many of the continent's wetlands to convert the land to farmland; the most notable case is the Netherlands, where land has been reclaimed from the sea so that crops can be grown on it. Among the shrubs, Europe's wetlands, like those in North America, harbor alders, but Europe's are different species from those found in America. The same can be said for the willows, which grow well where ample moisture is available.

COMMERCIAL PLANTS. Ever since the first agricultural revolution, ten thousand years ago, humans have adapted plants to their needs. This is especially true for the grains, most of which originated in the Middle East. Wheat, oats, barley, rye, and others that could become food for hu-

Tulips. (Digital Stock)

mans were altered from their original form by careful plant breeding. This is also true for the flowers that are the staple of the florists' trade—roses, chrysanthemums, begonias, and carnations are all adaptations of wild plants.

Tulips Page 1309

One of the most widely known flowers that originated in Europe is the tulip, which the Dutch have cultivated for centuries and have made into a staple export. While there is a wild hyacinth that is native to America, the grape hyacinth that is seen in gardens is an immigrant in America, as is the full-size hyacinth. The crocus flowers that herald spring in gardens all across America are natives of the Mediterranean region.

Olive groves Page 1249

OLIVE TREES. One native flowering plant of Europe deserves special mention: the olive tree. It originated along the shores of the Mediterranean Sea, but has been cultivated and modified to increase the size of its fruit since ancient times. It remains an important agricultural resource for the nations fronting on the Mediterranean, especially Greece, Italy, France, and Spain, in all of which it is cultivated. The Spanish conquerors of Central America carried it to the new world, and it has been successfully introduced into California.

Uncultivated olive trees form part of the vegetation of the maquis, an area in France and Spain where the native olive grows with the carob, a small, native tree like the olive, and the holm oak. Most of these trees are so stunted by the impoverished soil, heavily eroded over the centuries, that they are little more than bushes. There are also a variety of shrubs characteristic of the maquis, such as a clematis vine, the Mediterranean buckthorn, and the common myrtle. A local variety of grass covers the ground between the trees and shrubs. Similar communities can also be found in Greece, where they provide grazing for goats.

VINES. The grapevine has been of commercial importance for centuries. Both Greeks and Romans raised grapes and made wine from them. The wine grape appears to have originated in the Mediterranean region, but since it has been cultivated for so many centuries, many variations on the original native vine have developed. Grapevines of European varieties have been transplanted to North America, and the process has also worked in reverse. In the late nineteenth century, when a devastating disease known as *phylloxera* ravaged French vineyards, Ameri-

can grapevine rootstock was imported into France, and the French vines grafted onto it, since the American rootstock had shown itself less subject to the disease.

Also in the category of vine is the ivy. There are ivies native to almost every continent, but European ivy, sometimes called English ivy, has spread far beyond its native ground. It is popular as a wall covering and is frequently seen in gardens.

In considering European flora, it must be remembered that in Europe, the kinds of plants that grow in a particular location vary according to the climatic conditions that apply there. The climate and soil of the land bordering the Mediterranean Sea differs greatly from that north of the Alps. The division is perhaps more marked in Europe than on other continents, because the Alps run west to east, the highest

Italian vineyard Page 1314

French vineyard. (PhotoDisc)

INVASIVE EUROPEAN PLANTS THREATEN NATIVE AMERICAN PLANTS

American botanists have discovered that the purple loosestrife, a European plant, is successfully invading some American wetlands, particularly in Maine. It has spread prolifically and threatens to eliminate native American plants in those areas. More problematic are Asian plant species such as the bittersweet vine, which chokes trees, but European plants are also a threat. A well-known example is Dutch elm disease, which actually originated in Belgium and has killed vast numbers of elms that once lined North American streets.

peaks being without vegetation, whereas the mountains in North America run north to south. Thus in Europe, the mountains separate land that is also separated by latitude, whereas in America the mountains only separate elements at the same latitude. Since climate is strongly a function of latitude, there is, in effect, a double line separating the vegetation of the part of Europe along the Mediterranean from the part that is north of the Alps, instead of the gradual gradation that is more characteristic of America.

Nancy M. Gordon

FOR FURTHER STUDY

Bryson, Bill. "England's Lake District." *National Geographic* (August, 1994): 2-34.

Peterson, Roger Tory, and Margaret McKenny. *A Field Guide to Wildflowers of Northeastern and North-Central America.* Boston: Houghton-Mifflin, 1968.

Polunin, Oleg, and Martin Walters. *A Guide to the Vegetation of Europe.* Oxford, England: Oxford University Press, 1985.

Shreeve, James. "Secrets of the Gene." *National Geographic* (October, 1999): 42-75.

Shupe, John F., et al., eds. *The National Geographic Atlas of the World.* Washington, D.C.: National Geographic Society, 1992.

Swerdlow, Joel L. "Biodiversity: Taking Stock of Life." *National Geographic* (February, 1999): 2-5.

FAUNA

The number of wildlife species in decline across Europe increased during the second half of the 1990's. Eleven of Europe's twelve most urgent environmental problems, including waste, climate change, and stratospheric ozone depletion, have remained static or worsened over the latter half of the 1990's. The threat to Europe's wildlife continues to be severe, with more than a third of bird species in decline, most severely in northwestern and central Europe. Up to half the known vertebrate species were under threat in many countries.

In the countries of the European Union (EU), intensive and subsidized agriculture has devastated the wildlife. Italy is a good example. The extent of animal life in Italy has been reduced greatly by the long presence of human beings. The primary locales in Italy where wildlife survive are the Italian Alps, the Abruzzi (east central Italy on the Adriatic Sea), and Sardinia. Only in those areas can one find the Alpine ibex, brown bear, wolves, foxes, fallow deer, mouflon (wild sheep), and wild boar.

Portugal and Spain are somewhat different from the rest of Europe in that their wildlife is a mixture of European and North African species. In Portugal, about two-thirds of the wildlife overall is Mediterranean, but the farther south one is in Portugal, the more North African the fauna becomes. Birdlife is rich in both countries of Iberia because the peninsula lies on the winter migration route of western and central European species. Nevertheless, major species in Portugal and Spain are endangered.

Despite its reputation for pollution, the eastern portion of Europe is the stronghold of Europe's wildlife. Agriculture in Eastern Europe is starting to intensify, however. One notable exception to the situation of Europe's fauna is Latvia. Although a small country, Latvia contains a number of species and ecosystems rare in other European nations. As many as four thousand Eurasian otters can still be found in Latvian rivers.

Less fortunate European countries struggle to re-establish their beavers, but Latvia has a population of forty-five to fifty thousand beavers, which were reintroduced in 1952 from Russia. There are two hundred to four hundred wolves, as well as three hundred to four hundred lynx. Latvia has more than two hundred breeding species of birds, some of which are rare elsewhere. These include the white-backed woodpecker, lesser-spotted eagle, and black stork. Estonia, which borders on Latvia, is similar in some respects. The moose is the largest animal, along with roe deer and red deer. In the forests of northeast Estonia, bears and lynx are found. Along the riverbanks, mink and nutria are common.

THE EFFECTS OF HUMANS. Wild animals have been in retreat since Upper Paleolithic times (30,000 B.C.E. to 3500 B.C.E.), when small human groups held their own against such big game as aurochs, a type of bison, and mammoths, now extinct. In more recent centuries, settlers won the land for crops and domesticated animals. As the population increased in industrializing Europe, humans inevitably destroyed, or changed drastically, the wild

Map
Page 1311

Loch Ness
Page 1310

EFFORTS TO SAVE EUROPE'S LARGE CARNIVORES

Habitat destruction and the loss of prey species have contributed to the decline of large carnivores in Europe. In the year 2000, large carnivores occupied fragmented landscapes dominated by humans. The Iberian lynx population is confined to about ten isolated pockets of Spain and Portugal and numbers less than eight hundred. Elsewhere, relic brown bear populations are dangerously small and highly fragmented in southern, central, and western Europe. Like wolves, brown bears face a hostile reception whenever they move into new areas. Wolverines have been reduced to a few hundred in remote areas of Scandinavia. The Eurasian lynx has disappeared from much of its original habitat; where populations are starting to recover, conflict with humans remains a major stumbling block.

The World Wildlife Fund's (WWF) Campaign for Europe's Carnivores aims to challenge ancient prejudices and to help fund projects supporting peaceful coexistence between people and predators. Wolves are beginning to return to old haunts in France, Switzerland, and even Germany. This fact, along with continuing human conflicts with the wolverine, lynx, and brown bear in other areas, emphasizes the need to secure public support for carnivores. WWF's strong European network is working across international boundaries to help secure pan-European cooperation for carnivore populations and to gain public acceptance of their important place in Europe's natural heritage.

vegetation cover and the animal life. With difficulty, and largely due to human tolerance, animals have nevertheless survived.

In January, 2000, a dike holding millions of gallons of cyanide-laced wastewater gave way at a gold-extraction operation in northwestern Romania. The collapse of the dike sent a deadly waterborne plume across the Hungarian border and down the nation's second-largest river. Two hundred tons of dead fish floated to the surface of the blighted waters or washed up on the Tisza River's banks. The toxic brew also killed legions of microbes and threatened endangered otters and eagles that ate the tainted fish.

WILDLIFE PRESERVES. Even when there are parks and reserves, human activities endanger the fauna and environment. Doñana National Park, an area of wetlands and sand dunes on the Guadalquivir River delta in southern Spain, is one of the most important wildlife sanctuaries in Western Europe. More than 250 bird species, over half of Europe's total, are found there. It is also home to the rare Iberian lynx. The park covers 190,830 acres (77,260 hectares) and is a World Heritage Site. In the 1990's, the park was threatened by falling water levels caused by thirty dams along the Guadalquivir River.

In 1998 the park was further threatened by a flood of toxic waste from a breached dam that was holding back a reservoir used for dumping mining waste. The waste was successfully diverted, but not before wetlands surrounding the park were contaminated by heavy metals. Those heavy metals may yet poison many of the birds that fly there to feed. The aquifer that supplies the park was contaminated and thousands of fish and amphibians died. These had to be removed to prevent carrion-eating birds from being poisoned.

MAMMALS. Larger mammals are mostly gone from Western Europe, with the possible exceptions of Spain and Portugal. In the tundra of European Russia and of Lapland in Finland, Norway, and Sweden, caribou or reindeer thrive. In the short summer of the tundra, arctic fox, bear, ermine, and the wolverine may appear. In the deep forests of Poland, Belarus, and European Russia, one still finds the moose, reindeer, roebuck, and brown bear. The brown bear no longer inhabits Scandinavian forests, but the moose is common in Norway, Sweden, and Finland.

Finland is the home of the only species of freshwater seal in the world—an animal depicted on one of the country's coins. The lynx is mostly gone, but wolves, fox, marten, badgers, polecats, and white weasels survive. The sable, which is much hunted for its valuable fur, only just survives in the northeastern forests of European Russia. In Romania, there can still be found bears, wolves, wild goats, and even the European bison.

In much of the rest of Europe, wild fauna are limited to foxes, squirrels, marmots, and other rodents. In higher elevations in France, Italy, and Austria, one can still find the chamois and ibex. Italy's renowned Gran Paradiso National Park in the Valle d'Aosta saved the alpine ibex from extinction. Alpine marmots and chamois can be seen in the Bavarian Alps near Berchtesgaden, Germany. In the steppes of the Ukraine and European Russia, large wildlife is gone except in the semidesert areas north and northwest of the Caspian Sea. There one can still find two types of antelope, the saiga and the jaran, along with rodent sand marmots, desert jerboas, and the sand badger.

REPTILES, AMPHIBIANS, AND FISH. Europe's reptiles are most common in Mediterranean and semidesert areas. In the coastal Mediterranean, vipers and similar snakes, lizards, and turtles are found frequently. In the semidesert areas north and northwest of the Caspian, cobras and steppe boas are found, along with lizards and tortoises.

In Italian waters, freshwater fish are the brown trout, sturgeon, and the eel. Off the coast of Italy, one finds the white shark, bluefin tuna, and swordfish. There is an abundance of red coral and commercial sponge on the rocks of the warm southern seas. Spanish waters contain a diversity of fish and shellfish, especially in the southeast where Atlantic and Mediterranean waters mix. Species include red mullet, mackerel, tuna, octopus, swordfish, pilchard, and anchovy. Bottom-dwelling species include hake and whiting. The striped dolphin and the long-finned whale are found off southeastern Spain, and the bottle-nosed dolphin off the delta of the Ebro River. In Scandinavian waters, salmon trout, and the much-esteemed *siika* (whitefish) are relatively abundant in the northern rivers. Baltic herring and cod are the most common sea fish.

BIRDS. In the short summer of the tundra, seabirds and immigrant birds such as swans, ducks, and snipes can be found. In the great forests of Eastern Europe, black grouse, snipe, hazel hen, white partridge, owls, and blackbirds are common. The steppes have a more abundant selection of fowl. There are eagles, falcons, hawks, and kites and water and marsh birds such as the crane, bittern, and heron.

INSECTS. Different kinds of locusts and beetles are common in the steppes of the Ukraine and European Russia. In the summer months of 2000, much of the Eurasian steppes was hit by a plague of locusts, devastating Russia's vital grain crops. In Mediterranean and semidesert areas, scorpions, the karakurt spiders, and the palangid are insects dangerous to humans.

CONSERVATION EFFORTS. In a remote part of northwestern Greece, the lakes of

Mikri Prespa and Megali Prespa combine to form rich wetlands. The area has more than fifteen hundred plant species, forty mammals, including the brown bear, otter, and wolf, eleven species of amphibians, twenty-two species of reptiles, and seventeen fish species. Since 1974 Prespa has been a national park, but there was no management plan. In 1991 the World Wildlife Fund (WWF) helped to establish the Society for the Protection of Prespa (SPP) to intervene at a local level and develop the necessary strategies to maintain the area.

Scientists trying to save the Iberian lynx, the most endangered cat in the world, from extinction are using the latest DNA technology to track the cat by its droppings. The scientists want to put several healthy cats in a captive-breeding center in the Doñana National Park. Once the population is located, DNA testing will reveal whether inbreeding is further endangering the dwindling species by producing unhealthy offspring. The idea is to capture several cats from different regions and bring them to the breeding grounds. In 2000 there was no stock to breed. There are no more than six hundred lynx in Spain and fifty in Portugal. If the rate of decline continues at the current trend, the animal could be extinct by 2010.

The Mediterranean monk seal is one of the ten most endangered species in the world. At the beginning of the twentieth century, it was prevalent throughout the Mediterranean. It is now a rare sight, although still spotted, particularly in the eastern Mediterranean and out in the Atlantic off the Madeira Islands of Portugal. The monk seal is a shy animal with low reproduction rates. It is thus highly sensitive to changes in its habitat and external disturbances. Increasing pollution from industrial waste, plastics, insecticides, and heavy metals have also affected its habitat, food, and most probably its mating ability. More important, since the seals are perceived by commercial fishermen to be in competition for limited fish stocks, they have been deliberately killed.

The WWF began a project in 1993 in the eastern Mediterranean to monitor the presence of the seal and to determine its interaction with the local population. The WWF has mounted information campaigns and government lobbying in Greece, Turkey, and Cyprus in order to

---

WILDLIFE DROWNING UNDER THE HIGH SEAS

Some of Great Britain's best-known nature reserves are expected to be covered by the sea before the middle of the twenty-first century. The British government forecast that the sea level around southeast England would rise by 2 feet (60 centimeters) by mid-century. A wildlife-rich chain of low-lying grazing marshes, reedbeds, and lagoons behind the shingle beaches of Suffolk and Norfolk in southeast England are at risk. In February, 1996, a combination of storms and exceptionally high tides flooded the freshwater Cley and Salthouse Marshes in Norfolk with saltwater to a depth of 6 feet (2 meters) along a 2-mile (3-kilometer) stretch of coast. The marshes there are one of the few British haunts of the bittern, a large heron-like bird that is one of the most critically endangered species in Britain. No bitterns bred there in 1996 because the salt stunted the reeds that give the bitterns cover and killed the freshwater fish they eat.

pass protective measures to achieve a balance between increasing human use of decreasing marine resources and the basic survival needs of the monk seal.

Dana P. McDermott

FOR FURTHER STUDY

Arnold, Edwin Nicholas, and John S. Burton. *Reptiles and Amphibians of Britain and Europe.* New York: Viking Penguin, 1999.

Arnold, H. R. *Atlas of Mammals in Britain.* London: Stationery Office Books, 1993.

Griffiths, Richard A. *The Newts and Salamanders of Europe.* Fort Worth, Tex.: Harcourt Brace, 1996.

Hayward, Peter J., and John S. Ryland, eds. *Handbook of the Marine Fauna of North-West Europe.* New York: Oxford University Press, 1995.

MacDonald, David, and Priscilla Barrett. *Mammals of Britain and Europe.* New York: HarperCollins, 1998.

Morrison, Paul. *Mammals, Reptiles, and Amphibians of Britain and Europe.* London: Pan Books, 1994.

INFORMATION ON THE WORLD WIDE WEB

A good source of on-line information about European fauna is the European Center for Nature Conservation (www.ecnc.nl). Another source is the World Wildlife Fund (www.wwf.org), at which viewers can access information about endangered species in individual countries.

HUMAN GEOGRAPHY

PEOPLE

Population Density map Page 1312

Humans first appeared in Europe in prehistoric times. As human societies evolved through the millennia, they struggled against a cold, arid European environment. The melting of the glaciers, which modified Europe's configuration, deeply influenced human migratory patterns and spatial distribution. Consequently, over the millennia, and with the impacts of such historical events as migrations, agriculture, population growth, and invasions, the peoples' lifestyle progressively shifted from hunting and gathering to farming, and their primitive cave habitats evolved into highly developed communities. These factors, plus the subsequent development of urban civilizations and feudal states and the intermingling of various populations, formed essential elements in the peopling of Europe.

FIRST INHABITANTS. The earliest European inhabitants, members of the species *Homo erectus*, began trickling into Mediterranean Europe approximately 1.5 million years ago. The first tribes came from Africa, where evidence of their existence has been traced back to 5 or 6 million years ago. Starting about 200,000 B.C.E., other hominids, *Homo sapiens neanderthalensis*, an evolution specific to Europe, began peopling a large part of Europe. Neanderthals practiced funerary rites, and were physically strong. They disappeared approximately forty thousand years ago.

Europe's prehistoric climate had a great effect on the development of early European populations and explains Europe's setback compared to human activities occurring simultaneously in the Middle East. Because glaciers formed a natural barrier to their movement, the two species of primitive Europeans initially settled in the meridional regions of Europe, where they were confined for many millennia. Europe at that time had a small and scattered population that numbered perhaps a few hundred thousand and a maximum of one to two million people.

Until about 12,000 B.C.E., and despite periodic warming, glaciers intermittently covered Northern Europe and part of Central Europe, and humans had to adapt their habitats and hunting grounds to climatic variations. To survive, they depended at first on picking and gathering whatever plants and wild fruits were available, as well as capturing sickly animals; later, they gradually developed hunting techniques. Glaciary cycles, which consisted of cold glaciary periods alternating with warm interglaciary ones, inflicted terrible hardships on inhabitants, with gigantic meltings and torrential rains often leaving the population preoccupied with the search for food and shelter. Cold, arid periods led to the fragmentation and isolation of the population, while warm periods led to its dispersal. As the glaciers melted toward the north, the animals followed and so did the humans, thus beginning their progressive expansion northward.

By about 45,000 B.C.E., a new species appeared that gradually began peopling the entire European continent: *Homo sapiens sapiens*, also known as the people of Cro-Magnon. These modern-type humans achieved spectacular progress compared to their predecessors and introduced a

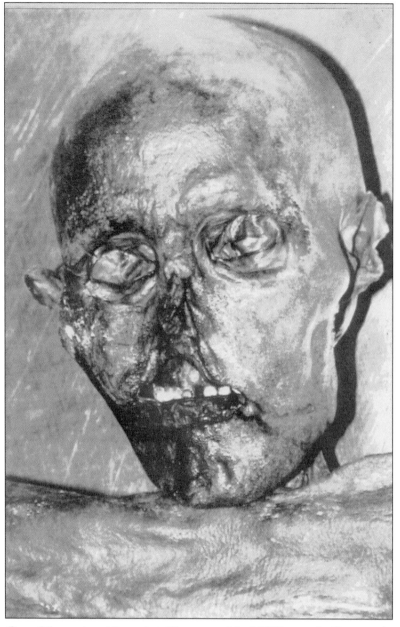

One of the most exciting scientific events of the 1990's was the discovery in the Alps of an unusually well-preserved mummy believed to be more five thousand years old. The discovery held out the promise of new break-throughs in the study of the Bronze Age. (AP/Wide World Photos)

provided a safer lifestyle, and led to more mutual aid among tribes. In addition to living near coastal regions, the populations also settled close to lakes and rivers, where hunting, gathering, and fishing were also made easier. Cro-Magnon communities continued growing, thus setting the stage for a more modern Europe, where drastic changes were yet to come.

SPREAD OF FARMING COMMUNITIES. Around 10,000 B.C.E., glaciers were melting, forests were replacing the steppe, and deer and bovines were multiplying. An event of great importance in Europe's history was also taking place, bringing drastic changes perhaps unequaled in importance until the Industrial Revolution of the nineteenth century. The first agrarian and stock-raising civilizations, which were developing in the Middle East at that time, started their western expansion. Between 6000 and 3000 B.C.E., they colonized Europe from east to west, reaching Scandinavia and the British Isles in the fourth millennium B.C.E. The Mediterranean basin provided an easy access route to Middle East settlers, who reached Europe by traveling along the Mediterranean coast and up the course of the Danube River.

wealth of significant cultural innovations, the most important being the invention of art. They also revolutionized hunting-tool technology and developed a great hunting civilization, with hunts becoming more systematic, strategic, and organized. New tools resulted in safer, more distant hunts,

This Neolithic front either pushed back or absorbed hunting and gathering populations, gradually changing their precarious but free lifestyle into a stable but sedentary one, and progressively transforming predators into stock breeders and food gatherers into food producers. The extensive spread of the farming economy was made possible primarily by climate change and the melting of the glaciers in Northern Europe, but also by the population increase of hunting and gathering tribes, the diminishment of Europe's big game supply, and the transformation of local habits.

THE FIRST HIERARCHICAL SOCIETIES. New food production methods resulted in an enormous population growth. Life expectancy, which was twenty to thirty years for the hunting population, increased considerably. The milder climate, improved tools, and forest clearing allowed populations to abandon their caves and settle in the plains, where farmers began building real houses, which were to become Europe's first villages. The widespread multiplication of such villages is the most obvious sign of population growth.

The extensive peopling of the European continent by farmers, however, and the establishment of a production economy based on agriculture and stock-raising, modified internal relations within peasant societies. Furthermore, farming tasks such as tending herds, stocking food, and harvesting crops, and specialized tasks such as pottery-making, mastering fire, and cutting and polishing stone, required collective organization and gradually created a difference between the rich and the poor. With social differentiation and no more lands to conquer, peasant communities began restructuring, thus resulting in the first hierarchical societies.

Around 4000 B.C.E., tensions began to rise and violence multiplied within these primitive chieftaincies, which evolved into warring forms distinguished mainly by fortified defense sites, different-sized habitats, princely tombs, and the development of metallurgy. Although these societies, some of which were already acquiring urban characteristics, remained in existence in Northern Europe until the Middle

---

THE MEGALITHIC CIVILIZATION

From approximately the fifth millennium B.C.E. until the end of the third millennium B.C.E., a mysterious civilization, or cult, developed in Western Europe and multiplied along the Atlantic Coast—from Portugal to Brittany (northwestern France), from the British Isles to Denmark, and throughout the territories of France, Switzerland, and the Iberian Peninsula. Menhirs, or single-standing stones, dolmens (upright stones supporting a horizontal stone slab), alignments, and cromlechs (circular monuments) were dragged over long distances and erected. They served as tombs or religious temples and testify to the spread of the first civilization common to all Western Europe.

The construction of such gigantic monuments required a religious motivation, technical knowledge, social organization, and physical effort, since approximately one thousand men were needed to advance a fifty-ton slab about two-thirds of a mile (one kilometer) in one day. France has five thousand dolmen chambers, the British Isles have two thousand, and Denmark has more than three thousand megalithic tombs. Among the most impressive settings are the circular stone groupings found at Stonehenge in southern England, where complex structures reveal a solar cult or astronomic observation site, and the parallel-row alignments in Carnac, Brittany, where nearly three thousand menhirs were aligned over a distance of about 4 miles (6.44 km.).

Ages, they were gradually absorbed by the forthcoming urban Mediterranean civilizations.

BIRTH OF CITIES. Around 2000 B.C.E., as a result of commercial networks and contacts with Middle East urban civilizations, the first European urban societies—the Cretans, Greeks, Etruscans, Carthaginians, and Romans—began developing on Mediterranean shores. The revolutionary technique of metallurgy and the invention of bronze not only played an important role in the establishment of trade networks but also contributed to the rise of new civilizations. During the European Bronze Age, for example, the island of Crete was, from 2000 to 1450 B.C.E., the meeting point of intensive economic and cultural activity between Europe and the Middle East, and became the first real state to form in Europe.

Roman ruins
Page 1240

Despite lasting many centuries, however, the first European states were a limited phenomenon, even subject to returns backward, such as the collapse of the Minoan, Mycenian, and Etruscan civilizations. This was followed by an unprosperous period characterized mainly by a cultural, economic, and political decline that lasted until the rebirth of Greek culture and the domination of the Roman Empire, both of which profoundly shaped the development of European civilization.

GREEK, CELTIC, AND ROMAN EXPANSION. Starting in the eighth century B.C.E. and continuing for the next four hundred years, the Greeks, as a result of a tremendous population increase and internal social, economic, and political tensions, multiplied their urban cities around the Mediterranean basin and the Black Sea. The population of classical Greece is estimated to have been approximately two million inhabitants and it became an economic and political power, but Greece did not contribute much to the peopling of

Athens, Greece
Page 1310

Europe. Its influence on Europe was mainly cultural, with its democratic government, written laws and philosophy, monetary and social class system, and regional product specialization. Politically and economically weakened by Persian and internal wars, the Greek civilization, like the aristocratic Celtic civilization that had developed to the north, was gradually conquered by the Roman Empire.

The neighboring Celts, the first people whom historians classify as "Europeans," had begun their expansion around the fifth century B.C.E. in Central Europe, Northern Italy, Greece, and Spain. For many centuries, the Celts transmitted their linguistic and artistic heritage, but, like the Greeks, their civilization was conquered by the Roman Empire.

The Roman Empire, from the third century B.C.E. and until the fourth century C.E., progressively absorbed all urban outbreaks and used the force of arms to impose an urban lifestyle on a large part of Europe and the Mediterranean basin. During its glory, the empire covered approximately 1.3 million square miles (3.5 million sq. km.) and counted an estimated 70 million inhabitants. In contrast to the Greeks, who were fascinated with philosophy, the Romans were preoccupied with organizing and building the structures of the state. For several centuries, the Roman Empire marked Western Europe with its political, administrative, and economic unity, as well as the diffusion of Christianity.

Beyond this apparent unity, however, and undoubtedly because of its extension all the way to Africa and Asia, the Roman Empire did not possess a specific identity. In addition to linguistic and religious differences, internal problems such as social, fiscal, and economic difficulties contributed to its disappearance. Furthermore, despite its gigantic size, the Roman Em-

HUMAN HISTORY IN EUROPE

1.5 million years B.C.E.:	Appearance of *Homo erectus*, of African origin, in Europe.
200,000 B.C.E.:	Appearance of Neanderthal humans, a local evolution specific to Europe.
45,000 B.C.E.:	Gradual appearance of *Homo sapiens sapiens*, coming from oriental Africa and the Near East.
30,000 B.C.E.:	Beginning of cave art drawings.
12,000 B.C.E.:	Melting of glaciers in Northern Europe.
6000-3000 B.C.E.:	Gradual colonization by Near East farmers; megalithic cults.
3500 B.C.E.:	First hierarchical and warring civilizations; first violent population movements.
2000-1500 B.C.E.:	First urban civilizations in Crete, then in the Mycenaean world.
8th century B.C.E.:	Gradual development of cities in Greece and Italy.
4th-2d century B.C.E.:	Celtic migrations toward eastern and southern Europe; first urban Celtic States.
3d century B.C.E.-4th century C.E.:	Roman expansion.
4th century C.E.:	Beginning of great invasions and migrations.
15th century C.E.:	Beginning of European colonial expansion.
18th-20th century C.E.:	Widespread drift away from rural areas—first within each state, then from the poorest European states, and finally from underdeveloped countries outside Europe.

pire covered only part of Europe. Beyond the fortified zones limiting its territories lived the rebellious and menacing Germanic people whom Rome called the barbarians.

INVASIONS AND MIGRATIONS. Beginning in the third century C.E., warring societies such as the Sarmates, the Huns, and the Germanics stormed into romanized Europe through great waves of invasions and migrations. The struggle, which lasted more than three centuries, resulted in medieval feudal states that lasted until the thirteenth century, and the divided Roman Empire subsided under the increasingly reduced form of the Byzantine Empire and then the Ottoman Empire. Even though medieval states were the start of modern Europe, during the first two millennia of the Christian era, the continent remained exposed to numerous migratory movements as a result of wars of conquests, European colonization of other continents, and migrations from underdeveloped non-European states to rich European states.

The peopling of Europe was the result of numerous movements and mixtures that began in prehistoric times and continued through subsequent centuries. After having reached a considerable cultural diversity, European states moved toward a new form of unity with the birth of Christianity and continued their unification in the twenty-first century with the establishment of a common market and currency.

Joyce Sakkal-Gastinel

FOR FURTHER STUDY

Alexander, Caroline. "Echoes of the Heroic Age: Ancient Greece, Part 1." *National Geographic* (December, 1999): 54-79.

Edwards, Mike. "Searching for the Scythians." *National Geographic* (September, 1996): 54-79.

Gore, Rick. "The First Europeans." *National Geographic* (July, 1997): 96-112.

_____. "Neanderthals." *National Geographic* (January, 1996): 2-35.

Ilbery, Brian W. *Western Europe: A Systematic Human Geography.* 2d ed. New York: Oxford University Press, 1986.

Reed, T. R. "The Power and the Glory of the Roman Empire." *National Geographic* (July, 1997): 2-41.

Switzerland's Matterhorn is not the highest peak in Western Europe, but it is probably the most picturesque. Its sides rise too steeply to retain snow, even in the heaviest snowfalls, ensuring that it maintains a year-round variegated ap-pearance. (PhotoDisc)

The Trevi Fountain is one of Rome's most famous tourist attractions because of the popular belief that any visitor who throws a coin into the fountain is certain to return to Rome. However, the fountain is also an important symbol of Italy's water resources, as it was built in the mid-eighteenth century to mark the spot where an ancient Roman aqueduct delivered water to the city. (PhotoDisc)

Seville, in southern Spain, experienced the highest temperature ever recorded in Europe: 122 degrees Fahrenheit (50 degrees Celsius) in 1881. (PhotoDisc)

German beach. In the colder climates of northern Europe, people seek whatever sunshine they can find. (PhotoDisc)

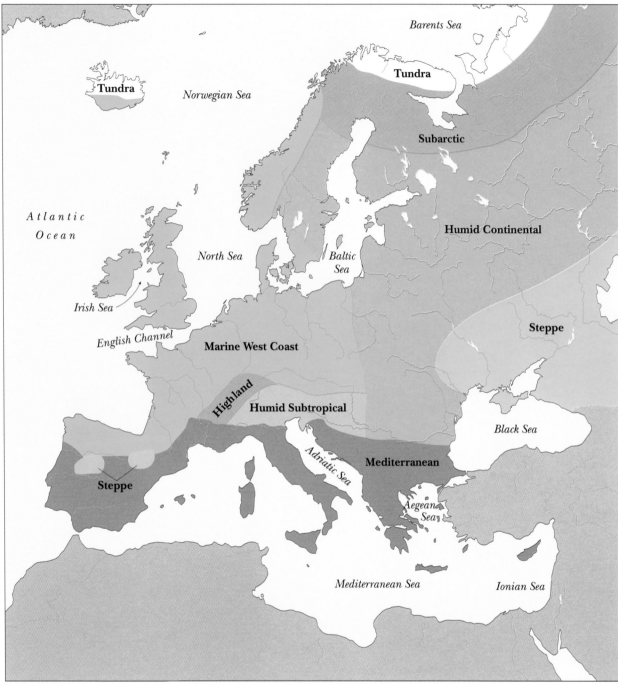

Nuclear power plant in Germany. Until the late twentieth century, hydroelectric power and generators fueled by coal and oil supplied Europe's electric needs. As old hydroelectric plants were retired, they were replaced by nuclear plants. (American Stock Photography)

One of the most widely known flowers that originated in Europe is the tulip, which the Dutch have cultivated for centuries and made into a staple export. (Digital Stock)

A long, narrow, lake in northern Scotland, Loch Ness has long been said to be the home of a great aquatic creature, which many people believe to be a survivor from a prehistoric era. However, no tangible evidence for the "Loch Ness Monster's" existence has yet been found. (PhotoDisc)

Standing on the Acropolis above modern Athens, the Parthenon was built in the fifth century B.C.E. as a temple to the goddess Athena. It now stands as a visual reminder of Greece's preeminent role in early Western civilization. (PhotoDisc)

HABITATS OF SELECTED VERTEBRATES OF EUROPE

Caribou

Gray Seal

Wolverine

TUNDRA

Lemming

Brown Bear

Sable

Moose

BOREAL FOREST

Reindeer

Freshwater
Seal

Otter

Roe Deer

Red Squirrel

Pine Marten

Jerboa

Eurasian Otter

Fox

Red Deer

Baltic
Herring

Antelope

Beaver

Hedgehog

Lynx

Nightingale

GRASSLANDS

DECIDUOUS FOREST

Pheasant

Partridge

Gazelle

Fallow Deer

Wolf

Badger

Marmot

Wild Boar

Wild Boar

European
Bison

Rabbit

HIGHLANDS

Chamois

Stag

Red Squirrel

Ibex

Falcon

MEDITERRANEAN

Iberian
Lynx

Dolphin

Mackerel

Monk
Seal

Sea Turtle

Octopus

POPULATION DENSITIES OF EUROPEAN COUNTRIES

(BASED ON MID-1999 ESTIMATES)

St. Peter's Cathedral in Vatican City, a microstate surrounded by Italy's capital, Rome. (PhotoDisc)

Venice, the most famous tourist attraction in Italy after Vatican City, originated on islands in a lagoon off the coast of northern Italy. Water-buses provide the city's main urban transportation. (PhotoDisc)

Dutch streetcar. The development of electric streetcar transportation in the early twentieth century enabled European cities to expand physically. (PhotoDisc)

Vineyard in central Italy's Chianti region, which is famous for its red table wines. (Digital Stock)

Major Urban Centers in Europe

SELECTED AGRICULTURAL PRODUCTS OF EUROPE

Wares in an Italian cheese shop. Europe produces more than half the world's cheese. (PhotoDisc)

Long-haired highland cattle are a breed closely identified with Scotland. (PhotoDisc)

Coal waiting to be loaded at a shipyard. Long the primary source of energy in Europe, coal is gradually being displaced by other forms of energy. (PhotoDisc)

One of the most ambitious flood-control projects undertaken anywhere in the world was the construction of barrier doors on Great Britain's Thames River, which would flood London if the waters of the North Sea were to rise. (PhotoDisc)

POPULATION DISTRIBUTION

Europe's population is divided into three major linguistic and religious patterns, which generally follow a west-east and, to a lesser degree, a north-south axis model. In western and southwestern Europe, the populations speak Romance languages such as French, Italian, and Spanish, all representing a Roman (Latin) legacy. In England, Scandinavia, and Central Europe, Germanic languages are dominant; in Eastern Europe and Russia, Slavic languages are spoken. There are minor language groups, such as Hungarian (Magyar) and Basque, that are not related to any of the three dominant language groups in Europe.

Europeans also are divided into three major religious groups. Western, southern, and many central Europeans are predominantly Roman Catholic, while the populations of Britain, Scandinavia, north and east Germany, and some of the Baltic countries adopted Protestantism after the sixteenth century. Russians and many Balkan people are generally Greek Orthodox Christians. As with the language groups, there are small exceptions to the major religious patterns because Judaism and, increasingly, Islam is practiced in Europe. In some regions of Europe, particularly in former communist countries, many people have abandoned organized religion altogether.

DISTRIBUTION AND DENSITY. Demographers suggest that at the beginning of the common era (1 C.E.) Europe had a population of 33 million people, representing 16 percent of the world's total population. By 1650 Europe's population had reached the 100 million mark, but this still represented only 18 percent of the world's total. With the declining infant mortality in the nineteenth century, the European population expanded to 400 million by 1900, or 25 percent of the world's population. At the end of the twentieth century, the 700 million Europeans west of the Ural Mountains represented only 13 percent of the world's population.

Between 1 C.E. and 1992, as a percentage of Europe's total population, the populations of southern and western Europe decreased, while those of Britain and east-central, southeastern, and northern Europe increased. Ten European nations had 75 percent of Europe's population. Russia had the largest population in Europe, while Germany had the second-largest. These two countries and Great Britain, France, Italy, and the Ukraine each had more than 50 million inhabitants. Excluding such tiny states as Liechtenstein, Andorra, Malta, Luxembourg, and Iceland, the rest of the European countries had populations between 1.46 million (Estonia) and 39.7 million (Spain).

The density of Europe's population varies greatly from a few people for each square mile to a high of 43,000 persons per square mile (16,550 persons per sq. km.) in the principality of Monaco. Various factors such as soil quality, climate, and coal and iron resources influence population density. The core density area stretches north-south from England to Italy and west-east from eastern France to the Donets region of the Ukraine.

Vatican City Page 1313

In much of the core area, more than 500 people occupy each square mile. Excluding such microstates as Liechtenstein and Monaco, the five most densely populated countries in Europe are the Netherlands, with 1,155 persons per square mile (446 persons per square kilometer); Belgium, with 855 persons per square mile (330/sq. km.); Great Britain, with 612 persons per square mile (236/sq. km.); Germany, with 570 persons per square mile (220/sq. km.); and Italy, with 500 persons per square mile (193/sq. km.).

Liechtenstein Page 1431

In the periphery, the ratio is 130 persons per square mile (50/sq. km.). For example, in Sweden few people live in the subarctic regions of the north. The five countries with the lowest density are Iceland, with 6.5 persons per square mile (2.5 persons/sq. km.); Norway, with 34 persons per square mile (13/sq. km.); Finland, 39 persons per square mile (15/sq. km.); Sweden, 52 persons per square mile (20/sq. km.); and Estonia, 90 persons per square mile (35/sq. km.). All these countries are in northern Europe.

CULTURE AND POPULATION DENSITY. A variety of customs and practices affect population density and distribution. In southern Europe, inheritance laws based on Roman law decreed that property had to be divided among all survivors. As a result, farms became smaller and smaller and population density increased dramatically. This Roman law legacy also caused massive rural overpopulation in the Rhine region, particularly in the German states of Hessen and Baden. In the 1840's, many people left these regions and emigrated to the United States and Australia.

Another example of the cultural impact on population growth can be seen in Belgium. Between 1900 and 1996, the country's population increased by 30 percent. However, the population in the Flemish provinces increased three times as fast as the population in the French-speaking Walloon provinces.

Wars caused by cultural clashes also impact population density and distribution. During the seventeenth century, the German religious wars reduced Central Europe's population by at least 30 percent. On the Mediterranean island of Cyprus, a clash over religion and language resulted in a major division of the population. The island won its independence from Britain in 1960, but conflicts between the Greeks (Orthodox Christians), who made up 80 percent of the population, and the Muslim Turks eventually resulted in a Turkish invasion of the northern parts of the republic in 1974. Two hundred thousand Greeks fled to the southern regions of Cyprus, while fifty thousand Turks escaped to the northern parts of the island.

ENVIRONMENT AND POPULATION. Traditionally, European population was densest in the fertile agricultural lowlands of the Great European Plain. In the nineteenth century, however, massive population concentrations occurred in the cities that grew around major coal and iron deposits. The mountain regions and colder climate areas are much more sparsely populated. In the Alpine regions of Austria, Switzerland, and Italy, people have usually selected the sunny southern slopes of the mountains for their homes. In fact, twice as many people live on the southern slopes and they often think themselves superior to those living on the dark side of the mountains, who are sometimes referred to as "shady characters."

In Scandinavia and in mountainous Mediterranean areas, people settled on or near the coastline. In these areas and in the Baltic region, 77 percent of the population is within twenty-five miles of the coastal areas. In the rest of Europe (excluding Russia), only 30 percent live near the coast. The majority of the French, German, and Irish populations, who have access to good coastlines, concentrated in areas away from the seashores. In some Mediterranean areas, however, malaria reduced the population. In Campagna, the plain between Rome and the coast, malaria was endemic in the seventeenth and eighteen centuries. Only twentieth century reclamation of the wetlands increased the population of this area.

MIGRATION. People move because of either the "push factor" or the "pull factor." The first is caused by a region's overpopulation, famine, or instability. The "pull factor" is created by the attraction of an area or country because of its opportunities or religious and political freedoms. In the nineteenth century, the key population shift was from rural to urban areas. Between 1861 and 1901, the rural migration to Paris was so large that 96 percent of France's population growth during this period occurred in Paris. Many other European capitals also attracted numerous people. For example, 30 percent of the population of Ireland is concentrated in the greater Dublin region, and 40 percent of Austria's population is concentrated in Vienna and Lower Austria.

This rural-urban migration continued in the twentieth century, particularly in Eastern Europe after 1945. As a result, in many regions of Europe, the rural labor force represents only 3 percent of the nation's total workforce. The decline in the number of farmers has been most pronounced in the periphery areas of the North Sea region, but the same is true in Baltic regions like Finland, where farm populations declined by one-half between 1960 and 1990.

The second type of migration affecting population patterns is the periphery-to-core migration. For example, many Irish migrated to Great Britain (as well as emigrating to the United States), and, beginning in the 1950's, Europeans from the underdeveloped southern regions like Spain, Greece, Portugal, and Croatia migrated north to the core of Europe to obtain jobs. By 1995 seven million foreign workers and their families lived in Germany alone. In Luxembourg, 26 percent of the population is foreign.

EUROPE'S NOMADIC HERDING POPULATION

National boundaries forced roaming herding populations on the periphery of Europe to settle primarily in one country. The Saami people of Sapmi (Lapland), a group linguistically related to the Finns, used to herd domesticated reindeer on the vast arctic tundra of the Scandinavian countries. The Saami followed the animals across the boundaries of modern Norway, Sweden, Finland, and Russia to obtain food, clothing, housing, and tools from reindeer herds. When countries began to close their borders to migration in 1852, the Saami were forced to accept citizenship in one country. In addition, part of the reindeer range was fenced on the Norwegian-Finnish border. Finnish dairy farmers expanded to the north, intruding into traditional Saami lands. By the 1990's most Saami no longer followed reindeer herds; those who did used snowmobiles and lived in permanent housing.

MODERN MIGRATIONS. The 1980's saw a population shift to areas of prosperity or better climate, such as southern England, the southern coasts of France and Spain, and southern Germany. The two German states of Bavaria and Baden-Württemberg accounted for 60 percent of Germany's population growth in the 1970's and 1980's. In the 1980's, Spain attracted 200,000 foreigners who retired there.

The rural area south of London became one of the fastest-growing population and economic centers in Great Britain. This pattern continued a periphery-to-center population movement, from northern to southern Britain, that went on during the last half of the twentieth century. London and southeastern England benefitted most from this population trend, while the towns in the West Midlands (Birmingham, Coventry, and the coal area known as Black Country) lost one-third of their manufacturing jobs between 1974 and 1982 alone.

After 1989 the largest migration was from Eastern Europe and Russia to Western Europe, particularly to Germany. Between 1990 and 1995, l.5 million people sought asylum in Germany alone. In addition, l.65 million ethnic Germans, primarily from the former Soviet Union, were resettled in Germany. With the disintegration of the Soviet Union after 1991, three major population movements affected the European parts of Russia. First, ethnic Germans resettled to Germany or Kaliningrad, a German region (Königsberg) annexed by the Soviet Union after 1945. In addition, between 1989 and 1994, more than half a million Russian Jews left the country for Israel, the United States, and Germany. Finally, during these same years, 2.4 million Russians returned to Russia from Central Asia, Belarus, the Baltic countries, and the Ukraine. They were joined in Russia by returning military men from former East Germany.

EMIGRATION. During the nineteenth century, Europe's population increased dramatically. In addition, sixty million Europeans emigrated to such regions as Australia and the Americas. Between 1600 and 1880, most people who arrived in North America came from northwestern Europe, particularly from the British Isles and Germany. The potato famine in the 1840's reduced Ireland's population, both by starvation and illness and by massive emigration to the United States. In 1990 the Irish population was still 62 percent smaller than it had been in 1841 (8.1 million). Sweden and Norway lost the largest percentage of their total population to emigration in the nineteenth century. Between 1880 and 1914, most Europeans who left for the Americas came from southern and eastern Europe, including two million Jews from Russia. The U.S. immigration laws after World War I dramatically limited further immigrations from eastern and southern Europe.

IMMIGRATION. Because of labor shortages after 1950, immigration into Europe from abroad greatly overshadowed emigration from Europe. Only Iceland, which did not allow non-Europeans into the country, did not experience this massive influx of foreigners. Initially, southern and southeastern Europeans from Spain, Italy, and Greece came to the core areas of France, Germany, and the Benelux countries to find jobs. Beginning in the 1960's, immigrants from Africa, Turkey, Vietnam, and the West and East Indies flocked to Europe.

Germany became the place of choice for three-fourth of all Turks who left their homeland in search of work. Berlin's Turkish community is the largest Turkish urban community in Europe outside of Istanbul. In addition, 95,000 Vietnamese and 15,000 Africans from Mozambique were recruited by the former communist government of East Germany. The foreign population, concentrated primarily in urban areas, constitutes between 14 and 25 percent of the population in the German cities of Berlin, Munich, and Frankfurt.

The Third World population migration particularly affected the former colonial powers, Great Britain, France, the Netherlands, and Portugal. In Britain, for example, South Asians (from India, Pakistan, and Bangladesh) are the largest ethnic group, comprising 49 percent of all immigrants in 1991. They settled primarily in major industrial centers like London, Birmingham, and Coventry. Chinese from Hong Kong moved to both rural and urban centers in Britain.

Immigrants from the Afro-Caribbean countries make up 77 percent of Britain's black population. For example, the Caribbean island of Montserrat sent one-third of its population to Britain between 1955 and 1961. During this same period, Jamaica sent 10 percent of its population to Britain. Blacks and South Asians have suffered from urban residential segregation, even though the government has passed several antidiscrimination laws. Two-thirds of all ethnic minorities in Britain live in Birmingham, Bradford, Leicester, and central London. Tensions caused by racism and impoverished urban conditions produced urban riots in 1958 in London's Notting Hill area and in 1980-1981 in several other British towns.

"ETHNIC CLEANSING." One of the most brutal population phenomena of the twentieth century was "ethnic cleansing." Between 1920 and 1950, thirty-three million Europeans were expelled from their homelands. The process started outside of Europe's borders in 1915, when Ottoman Turkish rulers decided to eliminate their Armenian minority. Hundreds of thousands were killed or forcibly marched from eastern Anatolia to Mesopotamia. In Europe proper, the first massive transfer of populations occurred after World War I. In the early 1920's, one million Greeks left Turkey and hundreds of thousands of Turks and other Muslims were forced out of Greece.

During World War II, Germany's Nazi government uprooted 600,000 ethnic Germans from Eastern Europe and brought them "home" to Germany. In a nightmarish period remembered as the Holocaust, the German government killed millions of European Jews, particularly Polish and Russian, and destroyed a rich Yiddish culture in Eastern Europe. After the war, millions of Germans were expelled from areas occupied by Poland and Czechoslovakia. Two million Poles were forced out of Russian-occupied former Polish areas and settled in newly acquired German lands.

Some population transfers continued in Eastern Europe after 1945. For example, Bulgaria expelled Turks in the 1950's and in 1989, and Greeks and Turks on the island of Cyprus were resettled after the Turkish occupation of the northern part of Cyprus in 1974.

After the disintegration of Yugoslavia between 1990 and 1992, massive ethnic cleansing occurred in the Balkans. Serbs, Croats, and Bosnians battled each other and terrorized civilians. Before a truce was signed in 1996 to end the conflict in Bosnia-Herzegovina, 700,000 people fled the disputed regions of former Yugoslavia, and half of these came to Germany.

Further ethnic cleansing occurred in Kosovo, a province of the remnant of Yugoslavia (Serbia and Montenegro), which had a majority ethnic Albanian population. After troops of the North Atlantic Treaty Organization (NATO) launched air attacks on Serbia and Serbian military positions in Kosovo, the Serbians killed thousands and expelled hundreds of thousands of Kosovo's ethnic Albanians. Only a NATO victory allowed Kosovo's refugees to return home.

DEMOGRAPHIC TRANSITION. The demographic transition started in Europe in the nineteenth century. In that century, European death rates, particularly infant deaths, declined drastically. Although the birth rate also fell, the population of Europe increased because the death rate declined faster. The second stage of the demographic transition also started in Europe. In this stage, the birth rate declined because of a continuous fertility dip. When the birth rate falls below the death rate, the population declines. Beginning in 1965, the fertility rate in Germany, Austria, and Hungary declined to those low levels. By 1990 the birth rate was low in most European countries. Only massive immigration helped stabilize the population of many European countries.

Eastern Europe reached those low birth levels after 1989. Until the collapse of communism, policies favoring births in East Germany gave that country a larger growth rate than West Germany. Likewise, Nicolae Ceausescu in Romania outlawed abortion and contraception, increasing population growth dramatically. After the fall of the region's communist regimes around 1989, Eastern Europe and Russia experienced dramatic declines in the birth rate. The Russian birth rate fell from 17.2 per 1,000 in 1987 to 10.8 per 1,000 in 1992. Death rates exceeded births by 200,000 in 1992 and by 800,000 in 1993. In the European area of the former Soviet Union, only Moldava and Belarus do not have negative population growth rates.

Europe has the lowest birth rate in the world. To maintain a stable population,

the average woman must bear 2.1 children; however, the average in Europe in 1985 was only 1.69 births, and only 1.28 in West Germany. The European population growth rate is 0.2 percent, compared to 3 percent in Africa and 2.1 percent in Turkey. Hungary has the lowest population growth (−2.4 percent), while Albania has the fastest-growing population in Europe (2.4 percent). Ireland has a high birth rate, but its population is declining because of massive migration and emigration. In the Netherlands and Portugal, one-third of a small population increase is due to immigration.

On average, the population of Europe is also the world's oldest population. Eighteen countries with the highest percentage of people age sixty-five and older are in Europe. In part, this is a reflection of the increase in life expectancy. In France, Sweden, and the Netherlands, women have an average life expectancy of eighty-one years, while men average seventy-five years. Because of lifestyles and economic hardships, in Russia in 1993 the average life expectancy for women was only seventy-four and for men, fifty-nine. The older population also affects population patterns. Older people in Western Europe often move to the warmer southern regions of their countries. This is the pattern in England, France, and Norway. In Eastern Europe, however, the elderly move to urban centers to be closer to their children.

Johnpeter Horst Grill

FOR FURTHER STUDY

Boulat, Alexandra. "Albanians: A People Undone." *National Geographic* (February, 2000): 52-71.

_____. "Eyewitness Kosovo." *National Geographic* (February, 2000): 72-83.

Eberstadt, Nicholas. "Demographic Shocks in Eastern Germany, 1989-

1993." *Europe-Asia Studies* 46 (1994): 519-533.

Edwards, Mike. "A Broken Empire: Russia, Kazakhstan, Ukraine." *National Geographic* (March, 1993): 4-53.

Hall, Ray, and Philip Ogden. *Update: Europe's Population in the 1970's and 1980's.* Cambridge, England: Cambridge University Press, 1985.

Noin, Daniel, and Robert Woods, eds. *The Changing Population of Europe.* Oxford, England: Basil Blackwell, 1993.

Range, Peter Ross. "Europe Faces an Immigrant Tide." *National Geographic* (May, 1993): 94-126.

Szulc, Tad. "The Great Soviet Exodus." *National Geographic* (February, 1992): 40-65.

INFORMATION ON THE WORLD WIDE WEB

Population.com, a Web site sponsored by the World News Network, collects current articles, resources, and directories relevant to European population and population statistics. (www.population.com)

Culture Regions

Europe has three primary culture regions—Northern European, Southern European, and Eastern European—that have great significance as meaningful ways of understanding the cultural similarities and differences among the peoples of Europe. The Northern and Southern European culture regions have so much in common that they might be combined into a single, enormous Western European culture region. However, there are still significant differences between Northern European culture and Southern European culture. Keeping these two culture regions separate, along with Eastern European culture, provides a three-part framework for comparing and contrasting the diversity of cultures that exist in modern Europe.

SOUTHERN EUROPE. Geographers sometimes refer to language as "the mother of culture." Knowledge of the language of a people often is the key to understanding the history, literature, and even the religion of that people. The Southern European culture region may be defined on the first level by a common heritage of Romance languages. These are the most direct descendants of the Latin language that developed originally in the region surrounding Rome at approximately 500-600 B.C.E. The countries that share this linguistic heritage begin with Italy and the various Italian dialects, from Sicily in the south to the Alps Mountains in the north and westward to the large Italian island of Sardinia in the Mediterranean Sea. North of Sardinia in the Mediterranean lies the island of Corsica; although part of France, its language is a dialect of Italian.

French is the dominant Romance language throughout nearly all of France; however, there are some linguistic minorities. In the south of France where the border between France and Spain meets the Mediterranean Sea, there is a French population of Catalan (Romance) speakers who are a French extension of the Catalan population of northern Spain.

Where the French-Spanish border meets the Atlantic Ocean, the large, minority linguistic group of Basques inhabit both sides of the border. The Basque language is not a Romance language; in fact, no other language in the world has been found to be closely related to Basque. Farther north in France, the large peninsula of Brittany juts westward into the Atlantic Ocean. The people of Brittany are called Bretons and the language they speak is Breton. Breton is not a Romance language, but a Celtic language related to Welsh and Irish and Scottish Gaelic. For centuries, the French government tried to stamp out Breton and force the Bretons to use only French. In recent years, the French government has started to tolerate the use of Breton. In eastern France in the Alsace-Lorraine area along the border with Germany, a large percentage of the population speaks German as well as French.

Spain and Portugal are also countries in the Southern European culture region that are overwhelmingly dominated by the Romance linguistic heritage. The language of the majority of people of Spain is Castillian Spanish, which dominates most of central and southern Spain, including the capital, Madrid. In northeastern Spain along the French border, Catalan is the dominant Romance language. It is also the language of Spain's second-biggest city, Barcelona, and of the Spanish Mediterranean islands of Majorca and Minorca. Along the northwestern border with France, the non-Romance Basque people dominate the region, including the cities of Pamplona and Bilbao, Spain.

In the extreme northwest corner of Spain above Portugal is the region of Spain known as Galicia. The language spoken there is Galician, which is a form of Portuguese. Throughout Spain, almost all the minority language groups have fought, sometimes violently, for autonomy in cultural affairs. Changes made in the Spanish Constitution indicate that the government may try to give more autonomy to these groups. In Portugal, nearly everyone speaks the national Romance language—Portuguese.

In addition to these four countries, parts of two other countries could be said to be part of the Southern European culture region. In Belgium, the people in the southern 40 percent of the country, called Walloons, are French speakers. In Switzerland, the western part of the country, including Geneva, is dominated by French-speakers and the part of Switzerland near the Italian border is predominantly populated by Italian-speakers. Therefore, these three small Romance language areas should be included as part of the larger Southern European culture region.

ROMAN CATHOLICISM. The second important cultural trait that distinguishes this culture region is religion. The Roman Catholic faith is the overwhelmingly dominant religion in nearly all of this region. This is partly a result of the lengthy period of Roman rule and the persistence of the legacy of Rome throughout Southern Europe. It is also the result of the forceful ac-

tion of the Catholic Church to eliminate other faiths in this region by the Inquisition, from the thirteenth to the nineteenth centuries. The Inquisition reached its worst levels in Spain, where many non-Catholics were burned at the stake or forced into exile from the fifteenth to the nineteenth centuries.

In sixteenth century France, Protestants known as Huguenots made up about 25 percent of the population. As a result of the subsequent religious conflicts in France, many Huguenots migrated to America, Germany, the Netherlands, and especially to French-speaking Switzerland, where the Protestant reformer John Calvin preached and virtually ruled over the city of Geneva. As a result of Calvin's activities, French-speaking Switzerland is the only part of the Southern European culture region that is predominantly Protestant today. In France itself, Protestants are only about 5 percent of the population. However, as a result of heavy migration to France from former French colonies in Africa, Muslims were more than 10 percent of the population of France in the 1990's. This has become a controversial issue in France. There is also a Jewish minority in France, which is approximately 1 percent of the population.

Beyond language and religion, the major countries of the Southern European culture region have had similar historical experiences with regard to the development of political institutions, especially democratic, parliamentary government. In general, the countries of Southern Europe did not establish themselves as stable, permanent democracies until the period from 1870 to 1980. This was later than the countries of Northern Europe, but generally earlier than the countries of Eastern Europe. The transition to democracy in Southern Europe was slowed by the reluctance of ruling monarchies to yield power

*Barcelona
Page 1375*

to democratically elected parliaments. In this confrontation, the Roman Catholic Church generally supported the supremacy of traditional monarchies over the rise of elected parliaments.

Although in 1789 the French Revolution overthrew the monarchy, this did not immediately lead to a stable, lasting democracy. In the nineteenth century, France experienced a reestablishment of the monarchy. Stable, democratic rule did not emerge until the regime of Napoleon III ended and was replaced by France's Third Republic in 1871.

In Italy, the rise of fascism under Benito Mussolini held back the establishment of democracy until the end of World War II in 1945. Spain and Portugal were ruled by fascist dictators, Francisco Franco and Antonio Salazar, from the 1930's to the 1970's. After the deaths of these dictators, both Spain and Portugal became democracies in the 1970's.

NORTHERN EUROPE. The Northern European culture region may be defined first as those countries of native Germanic language or those areas where Germanic culture has become established through colonization. The heartland of this region is those areas where German, in its various dialects, is the dominant language. This includes Germany, Austria, the northeastern two-thirds of Switzerland (including the capital, Bern, and the largest city, Zurich), and the small countries of Luxembourg and Liechtenstein.

The Germanic linguistic subfamily also includes the North Germanic group or Scandinavian languages: Danish, Norwegian, Swedish, Icelandic, and Faeroese, the latter being spoken in the Faeroe Islands, a possession of Denmark located between Scotland and Iceland. In addition, there are the languages of the West Germanic group: Dutch, spoken in the Netherlands; Flemish, spoken in the northern

half of Belgium; English; and Frisian, which is spoken in the Frisian Islands off the coast of the Netherlands and Germany and is the closest surviving relative of modern English.

In addition to the Germanic peoples, the Northern European culture region is home to various non-Germanic peoples who have been highly influenced culturally by their Germanic-language neighbors. An example of this is the influence of the English language in Scotland, Wales, and Ireland. The native languages of those three countries are Celtic, not Germanic. However, as the English conquered and colonized these lands, the English language ultimately became dominant in those three countries. Some of the greatest writers from each of these three countries have written in English and made great contributions to English literature, including James Joyce, Robert Burns, and Alun Owen.

In the Baltic region of Northern Europe, Germanic peoples dramatically changed the culture of non-Germanic peoples such as the Lapps (the Saami people of Lapland), the Finns, and the Estonians. These people are all linguistically part of the Uralic language family, which is concentrated on both sides of the Ural Mountains on the border of Europe and Asia. The Lapps reside in large numbers in northern Norway, Sweden, and Finland.

Finland and Estonia were both independent in the year 2000, but each had been part of the Swedish Empire in earlier centuries. That experience left a profound legacy, especially in Finland. Under Swedish rule, Swedish was the official and literary language of Finland for centuries. It was not until the nineteenth century that the Finnish language achieved official status and reawakened as a literary language. At the end of the twentieth century, both Finnish and Swedish were official in

Finland, and 6 percent of the population spoke Swedish as their first language.

South of Estonia is the country of Latvia. The Latvian language is part of a small linguistic subfamily known as Baltic. However, the Latvians were ruled for centuries, alternating between Swedish and German rulers; thus, they also were drawn into the Northern European culture region.

The second important distinguishing characteristic of the Northern European culture region is the Protestant religions. By the end of the Reformation, most of Northern Europe had broken with the Roman Catholic Church and had adopted some form of Protestantism. Most of the independent principalities of northern Germany adopted the Lutheran faith, which in Germany has always been called the Evangelical Church. From Germany, Lutheranism spread north to become the religion of more than 90 percent of the population of Denmark, Sweden, Norway, Iceland, and Finland. From Sweden, Finland, and Germany, Lutheranism spread to Estonia and Latvia, where it became the religion of the majority of the population.

From Geneva, Switzerland, Calvinism spread throughout western and northern Switzerland, where it is known as the Reformed Church. It spread to the Netherlands, where it is called the Dutch Reformed Church. Calvinism became dominant in Scotland as the Presbyterian Church, which Scottish settlers took to Northern Ireland. Calvinism also became an important minority religion in England, where it was known as Puritanism.

During the Reformation, the great majority of the people of England and Wales

Statue of Martin Luther in Worms, where he began the Protestant revolution in the early sixteenth century. The modern Lutheran Church takes its name from him. (PhotoDisc)

adopted the new Church of England (also known as the Anglican faith) as their religion. In the eighteenth century, most of the people of Wales switched to the Methodist faith, which had broken away from the Church of England at that time.

Some parts of Northern Europe remained overwhelmingly Roman Catholic: Austria, Ireland, southern Germany (especially Bavaria), Flanders (the Flemish-speaking northern half of Belgium), parts of the southeastern Netherlands, and the small countries of Luxembourg and Liechtenstein.

The third distinguishing characteristic of Northern Europe was the establishment of stable, democratic government at an early date, in most cases before 1870. One important event in this regard was the Glorious Revolution in England in 1688. As part of this agreement, King William III and Queen Mary II jointly agreed to recognize the supremacy of Parliament over the monarchy. This came to be known as constitutional monarchy.

By the early nineteenth century, the royal families of Denmark, Sweden, and the Netherlands also accepted parliamentary supremacy and became constitutional monarchies. Iceland was an independent republic from 930 to 1262. Then it became linked with Norway, and subsequently was a territory of Denmark from 1380 until 1941. Ever since 930, Iceland had its own elected assembly, called the Althing. When Denmark was occupied by Germany during World War II, Iceland declared itself an independent republic and the Althing became the Parliament of Iceland. Thus, Iceland can claim to have the oldest elected parliament still operating in the world today.

Although Norway was ruled by Sweden from 1814 to 1905, the Swedes allowed Norway to have its own independent, elected Parliament. The two countries peacefully separated in 1905, at which time Norway established its own constitutional monarchy. Finland was ruled by Sweden for more than six hundred years before Sweden had to cede it to Russia in 1809. Finland was then ruled by Russia until it declared independence in 1917. Finland was able to maintain most of its democratic traditions, even during the period of Russian rule. It is not an exaggeration to say that stable democracy emerged earlier

and more permanently in Northern Europe than in most of the rest of Europe.

In Germany, some of the independent German states had developed as constitutional monarchies by the middle of the nineteenth century. However, when the German Empire was created in 1871, these democratic traditions were overwhelmed. United Germany tried to establish democratic rule under the Weimar Republic in the 1920's, but this democracy was destroyed by the Nazis. Germany would not finally achieve a stable, lasting democracy until the creation of the Federal Republic of Germany (West Germany) in 1949, which was expanded to include East Germany in 1990.

EASTERN EUROPE. The last of the primary culture regions of Europe is the Eastern European culture region. The core group of this region is the Slavic language subfamily in Europe. Of the approximately 720 million people of Europe, roughly 270 million speak Slavic languages. Russian, by itself, has the most native speakers of any language in Europe, approximately 140 million. German, the second-most widely spoken language, has only approximately 95 million native speakers. Beyond the Slavic peoples, the Eastern European culture region also includes three non-Slavic groups: the Greeks, the Romanians, and the Lithuanians. As the Eastern European culture region is the most populous of Europe's three primary regions, it is also the most heterogeneous region, with significant cultural divisions even within the Slavic peoples.

The most fundamental division among the Slavs is the difference between Western and Eastern Slavs. As used here, the term Western Slavs refers to those Slavic peoples who use the Latin alphabet and practice Roman Catholicism. This category includes the Poles, the Czechs, Slovaks, Slovenes, and Croatians—a total of nearly sixty million people. However, the Slovenes and Croatians have been so affected by contact with Western Europe that they are not considered part of the Eastern European culture region.

The vast majority of the people of the Eastern European culture region are the 210 million people who may be considered Eastern Slavs, Slavic peoples who use the Cyrillic alphabet, which was derived from the Greek alphabet. In addition, the Eastern Slavs predominantly follow branches of the Eastern Orthodox Church derived originally from the Greek Orthodox church. These Eastern Slavic churches include the Bulgarian Orthodox Church, the Macedonian Orthodox Church, the Serbian Orthodox Church in Yugoslavia, the Ukrainian Orthodox Church and, largest of all, the Russian Orthodox Church.

The religious division between Eastern and Western Europe ultimately came to a head in 1054 in the Schism of East and West. At that time, the pope excommunicated the patriarchs (religious leaders) of the Eastern Orthodox churches. In retaliation, the patriarchs collectively excommunicated the pope. This cemented the lasting division between the Latin-based Roman Catholic Church and the Eastern Orthodox churches originally based upon Greek cultural roots. Although Greeks are not Slavs, the profound influence of Greek culture in the formation of the East Slavic nations justifies the inclusion of Greece in the Eastern European culture region.

The division of the Slavic peoples between those linked most closely to Rome and those oriented primarily to Greek culture is a replication of the circumstances in the Roman Empire nearly 1,700 years ago. In the Roman Empire, Greek culture dominated the eastern half of the Mediterranean world, while Latin culture dom-

Cathedral of a Bulgarian Orthodox Church. (PhotoDisc)

inated the western part of the Mediterranean world from Italy westward to modern-day Spain and Portugal. The Greek-Roman cultural division eventually led to a partition of the empire into the Western Roman Empire, centered upon Rome, and the Eastern Roman Empire, with its new capital at Greek-speaking Constantinople. The Western Roman Empire collapsed under the successive barbarian conquests of Rome beginning in 410. The Eastern Roman Empire evolved into the Greek-culture Byzantine Empire, which survived until the Turkish capture of Constantinople (now Istanbul) in 1453.

In addition to the Slavs and Greeks, the Eastern European culture region includes the Romanians and Lithuanians. From a linguistic perspective, the Romanian language is a Romance language descended from Latin. This is a legacy of the Roman Empire, which ruled the province of Dacia, generally corresponding to present-day Romania. Although they held on to their Romance language, over the centuries, the Romanians became more influenced by their East Slavic neighbors—especially in religion. Eventually, the Romanians adopted Eastern Orthodoxy and established their own Romanian Orthodox Church.

Farther north, the Lithuanian people also experienced a cultural transformation. Lithuania is a small country wedged in between Poland and Russia. The Lithuanian language is a member of the small Baltic linguistic subfamily. Over the centuries, the Lithuanians adopted the Latin alphabet and the Roman Catholic religion. Thus, although they are not technically Slavs, over the centuries the Lithuanians developed increasing cultural ties with their West Slavic neighbors, especially the Poles. In fact, Lithuania twice merged with Poland to form a common, unified state.

With regard to political evolution, the Eastern European culture region lagged far behind both Northern and Southern Europe in the development of stable, lasting democracy in modern times. In 1850 there was only one independent nation-state in the Eastern European culture region: Greece, which had freed itself from Turkish rule with the help of the major powers of Europe. All the rest of the Eastern European culture region was ruled by the Russian Empire, the Austro-Hungarian Empire, and the Ottoman Turkish Empire. In the late nineteenth and early twentieth centuries, these empires disintegrated and were replaced by numerous nation-states. Some of these nation-states had brief periods of democracy before ultimately succumbing to fascist, communist, or military dictatorships. Even Greece, the homeland of democracy, did not achieve stable, lasting democracy until the overthrow of a military dictatorship in 1974.

Most of the rest of the East European culture region established democratic rule between 1989 and 1991, as the Soviet Union disintegrated and communist regimes were ousted throughout Eastern Europe. Some countries in the region, including Yugoslavia and Belarus, had not instituted true democratic rule by the end of the twentieth century. Nevertheless, the political changes that have occurred in this region as a whole bewteen 1989 and 2000 have been the most positive move toward democracy since the end of World War I.

Other Regions. Europe contains various areas that do not readily fit the model of Europe divided into the Southern, Northern, and Eastern European culture regions. One of these is the European part of modern Turkey, which has approximately 12 million people including those in Istanbul. Although these Turks live in

Europe, they cannot be said to be part of traditional European culture. They are 98 percent Muslim in religion and speak a non-European language. From a linguistic and religious perspective, the closest cultural relatives of the Turks are in Central Asia in newly independent countries such as Kazakhstan, Uzbekistan, and Turkmenistan.

In the Balkan region of Europe, it is difficult to classify the people of Albania and their close relatives, the Kosovars of Yugoslavia. Both the Albanians and Kosovars are overwhelmingly Muslim. They all speak Albanian, which is a European language but not closely related to any other European language. The newly independent republic of Bosnia-Herzegovina is also difficult to classify. The population of the country has been estimated to be 40 percent Serbian, 38 percent Muslim, and 22 percent Croatian. These three groups have a long history of animosity toward each other. Ironically, they all use the same language, Serbo-Croatian; however, the Serbs write it with the Cyrillic alphabet while the Muslims and Croatians use the Latin alphabet.

Farther north in the Balkans are two other countries that split off from Yugoslavia in the 1990's: Croatia and Slovenia. Both of these peoples speak Slavic languages that they write with the Latin alphabet and are overwhelmingly Roman Catholic. Thus, it may seem that they should be classified as part of the Eastern European culture region, along with other West Slavic peoples. However, the unique history of these two peoples makes it difficult to classify them as part of Eastern Europe. Both peoples were subjected to centuries of rule by Venice, which was followed by centuries of rule by the Austrian Empire; thus, they are far more westernized than any other Slavic peoples.

The last country that does not fit easily into the three primary culture regions of Europe is Hungary. The most important characteristic of the Hungarian culture is the language, known as Magyar. Magyar, like Estonian and Finnish, is a Uralic language that originated in the vicinity of the Ural Mountains, the boundary between Europe and Asia. However, Magyar is such a distant cousin of Finnish and Estonian that Hungarian-speakers cannot understand those languages. This is because the Finns and Estonians migrated into Northern Europe at least 3,000 years ago, making them among the earliest peoples of Europe.

The Hungarians, on the other hand, are among the most recent arrivals in Europe. They began migrating into central Europe in the ninth century and established the Kingdom of Hungary in 1000. The Hungarians became somewhat westernized through centuries of political association with Austria. Nevertheless, because of its unique language and its location along the cultural boundary between Eastern and Western Europe, it is difficult to classify Hungary definitively.

SUMMARY. There is a well-known adage among scholars of Europe: "Europe marches in threes." This saying is based on the observation that Europe can readily be divided into three major parts based upon various characteristics: linguistic subfamilies, branches of Christianity, climate types, agricultural patterns, and even racial subtypes. One way to achieve greater understanding of Europe is by studying it from the perspective of three primary culture regions. No system of regional divisions can be perfectly applied to Europe; however, the examination of primary culture regions should provide a framework for greater insight and understanding of this complex part of the world.

Kenneth A. Johnson

FOR FURTHER STUDY

Gore, Rick. "The First Europeans." *National Geographic* (July, 1997): 96-112.

Ilbery, Brian W. *Western Europe: A Systematic Human Geography.* 2d ed. New York: Oxford University Press, 1986.

Jordan, Terry G. *The European Culture Area: A Systematic Geography.* 3d ed. New York: HarperCollins, 1996.

King, Russel, et al. *The Mediterranean: Environment and Society.* New York: John Wiley & Sons, 1997.

Matvejevic, Predag. *The Mediterranean: A Cultural Landscape.* Translated by Michael H. Heim. Berkeley: University of California Press, 1999.

Panayi, Panikos. *An Ethnic History of Europe Since 1945: Nation-States and Minorities.* Harlow, England: Longmans, 2000.

URBANIZATION

*Map
Page 1315*

In contrast to the United States, where a city is defined as a place with a population greater than twenty-five hundred people, in the countries of Europe, there are many different classifications for cities. In Sweden and Norway, even a small community with two hundred people is classified as a city, while in Spain or Greece, a city must have at least twenty thousand inhabitants. In Hungary, some large villages with twenty thousand people are called giant villages. Notwithstanding the size of an urban community, European cities have played an important role as political, religious, economic, and educational centers in both European and world history.

By 1914 Europe was the most urbanized continent, and its culture was essentially an urban culture. For example, London, the capital of the United Kingdom, was the financial capital of the world; and Vienna, the capital of Austria-Hungary, was the center of innovative modern cultural trends ranging from music to psychoanalysis. The World's Fair in 1900 in the French capital, Paris, attracted fifty-one million visitors.

Northern and Western Europe were the first world regions with a majority urban population. Even as late as 1960, Europe still claimed 20 percent (more than three hundred) of the cities in the world with populations greater than 100,000 people. Asia had only 215 cities in that category, followed by the Americas with 155 such cities. Although by the late twentieth century many cities around the world were larger than those in Europe, its cities continue to be vital political, economic, and cultural centers. Moreover, European cities host the headquarters of many regional and international organizations, ranging from the International Court of Justice in The Hague to the United Nations' International Maritime Organization in London.

ORIGINS AND HISTORY. Urban centers in Europe appeared first in the Mediterranean region. By 2000 B.C.E., cities were thriving on the island of Crete, and soon after that, city-states appeared on the mainland of Greece, which flourished until 1200 B.C.E. A new urban revival occurred by 600 B.C.E., when hundreds of Greek urban colonies were established around the Mediterranean area. Greek cities often were built on high ground and surrounded by walls. Greek city-states included the agricultural population of the region. These cities usually had small populations of 5,000 people, although larger communities averaged between ten thousand and 15,000 inhabitants. Athens's population may have reached 150,000. Many Western cultural and political ideas, ranging from drama to the concept of democracy, emerged in Athens, the intellectual center of the classical Greek world.

*Athens
Pages
1310, 1375*

By the second century B.C.E., Greek cities were dominated by a new power in the Mediterranean—the Roman Republic, which became an empire. Unlike the independent Greek city-states, Roman cities were part of an empire. The most urbanized parts of the Roman Empire were Italy, Greece, and Andalucia in southern Spain. Like Greek cities, most Roman urban places were small, with populations between two thousand and five thousand people. Larger cities had between fifteen thousand and thirty thousand people. Rome itself may have had close to one million inhabitants at the height of its power around 100 C.E.

Rome conquered much of the Mediterranean world and expanded into northern Europe, including England, where it established cities. Almost all major mod-

ern cities in that part of Europe, such as London, Vienna, and Budapest, have Roman roots. England's London was called Londinium by the Romans. Many of the cities established in northern Europe grew out of Roman military camps. The names of many English towns, such as Lancaster, can trace their origins to the names of Roman military camps, since the Latin word for army camp is *castra*.

After the collapse of the Roman Empire in the West in the fifth century C.E., urban life continued in the eastern parts of the empire centered on Constantinople. In the West, however, Germanic invasion, political instability, and economic decline reduced the former Roman cities to miniatures of their former size. The Catholic Church, whose organization centered on the Roman cities, was important in maintaining some continuity of urban life during the period between 500 and 1000 C.E.

Beginning in the eleventh century, the expansion of trade and increasing agricultural productivity contributed to the revival of urban life. Medieval towns, which were encircled by protective walls, were unique because they were legally separated from rural and noble society. Charters obtained from the princes and kings granted the towns self-government and the right to engage in commerce. The phrase "Town air makes free" reflects the uniqueness of the medieval town. By 1300 approximately three thousand communities in Europe were recognized as towns. Over 90 percent of these cities had fewer than two thousand citizens. A few towns in Italy and Flanders could claim a population in excess

One of the most famous religious buildings in the world is Istanbul's great domed Church of Hagia Sophia, originally built in the sixth century as a basilica. After the Turks conquered Constantinople in the fifteenth century, the church became a Muslim mosque. In 1934 Turkey's secular government made it a state museum. (PhotoDisc)

of fifty thousand. Only the largest cities in Western Europe, such as Paris and Naples, had more than one hundred thousand inhabitants in 1400.

By the sixteenth century, sixteen cities in northern Italy, Spain, and west-central Europe had grown to more than fifty thousand people. As late as 1600, however, only about 5 percent of Europe's population lived in towns. European expansion after 1500 furthered the growth of towns in Western Europe and expanded the size of capitals like London, Paris, and Madrid, but this did not radically change the distribution of towns. In Eastern Europe, the Russian ruler Peter the Great built a new capital, St. Petersburg, in the early eighteenth century. Nevertheless, rapid urbanization in Europe, which changed the landscape of the continent, did not occur until the impact of the Industrial Revolution was felt after 1800.

THE INDUSTRIAL CITY. Massive urban expansion occurred in Europe during the nineteenth century. By 1850 half of England's population was urban; half a century later, three-fourths of its population lived in cities. In 1900 Germany became the second European nation to have half its citizens inhabiting towns. By 1930 many other countries in northwestern Europe had become predominantly urban. Between 1800 and 1900, the number of European cities with populations over 100,000 increased from twenty-two to one hundred. London was the first European city to reach a population of one million by 1800. By 1900 six European cities—London, Paris, Berlin, Vienna, St. Petersburg, and Moscow—had more than one million inhabitants. These urban centers grew primarily because of the massive rural-to-urban migration of Europeans between ten and forty years of age.

Nineteenth century urbanization contributed to Europe's great economic expansion. Cities became key sources for culture and values. The term "urbane" means polite and mannerly, while "provincial" implies unsophisticated and narrow-minded. Nevertheless, the positive aspects of cities came only after years of suffering by many of the rural migrants who flocked to them. Many problems stemmed from the rapid, often unplanned, urban growth. Sanitation facilities were completely overwhelmed. There were simply not enough apartments and rooms for the many newcomers. In Liverpool, England, one-third of the inhabitants lived in cold cellars.

During the first half of the nineteenth century, the water supply in Paris was safe only at fountains, and in London water was distributed by a private company for only a few hours a day. Paris had enough water for two baths a year per individual. In Manchester, England, only one-third of the houses had toilets in the 1830's. Often, one privy in the courtyard served dozens of residents. One London engineer found cellars of houses filled with three feet of human soil. In 1858 the sewage odor in London was so repulsive that the British House of Commons suspended sessions. By the beginning of the twentieth century, many of these problems were solved because of public health laws and modern sanitation and water systems. In addition, electric streetcar transportation enabled cities to expand physically.

MODERN CITIES. European cities suffered from both neglect and actual physical destruction during World Wars I and II (1914-1918 and 1939-1945). During World War II, 33 percent of the housing in Germany was completely destroyed and another 44 percent was damaged. After 1945, all the European countries devoted between 3 and 5 percent of their gross national product to rebuilding what had been damaged. In many towns, particu-

St. Petersburg Page 1250

larly in Germany, efforts were made to reconstruct old historic buildings. By 1950 Western Europe had more houses than it had before the war.

Industrial expansion during the 1950's and 1960's meant continued urbanization, primarily through rural-to-urban migration. In 1996 Europe was still the most urbanized continent in the world, with 73 percent of its population living in cities. The urban population ranged from a high of 97 percent in Belgium to a low of 21 percent in the small principality of Liechtenstein. Only four small countries west of the Ural Mountains (Liechtenstein, Albania, the Republic of Bosnia-Herzegovina, and Portugal) have fewer than 50 percent of their populations living in cities. Sixty-eight cities in Europe claim populations greater than one million people, but only seventeen of the ninety-two largest urban centers in the world are in Europe. The largest urban area in Europe, London, is only the sixteenth-largest city in the world.

Europe saw a period of counterurbanization between the late 1960's and the 1970's. Britain experienced this trend first in the 1960's, followed by West Germany, France, and Denmark. Between 1975 and 1982, France's rural population grew more than its urban population, particularly in the Atlantic and Mediterranean coastal areas. During the 1960's, thirteen of twenty cities in West Germany with populations greater than 250,000 experienced a decline in population, because many people moved to the suburbs. In Germany, for example, commuter villages such as Perlach eventually became suburbs of Munich. Seven miles north of central Paris, large apartment complexes provided housing for Parisian workers who left the city center. In contrast to the West, suburbanization was not prominent in Soviet and East European cities until after 1989.

Moscow's Kremlin Page 1252

By the 1980's, counterurbanization slowed and Europe again experienced the growth of large urban centers that engulfed the suburbs. Supercities (megalopolises or conurbations), similar to the urban sprawl between Boston and Washington, D.C., exist in several European countries. The largest conurbation, with almost nine million people, is in the Parisian area. One-fifth of the population of France lives within one hour by car from Paris. The same percentage of the population of Britain can reach London by car in one hour. Six million inhabitants live in the megalopolis Ranstad, Holland, and the Rhein-Ruhr area contains three metropolitan areas with more than 1 million inhabitants each and three more with populations greater than 500,000.

Similar megalopolises exist in the Donbas region of eastern Ukraine and in Greater Moscow. By the 1980's, the Soviet Union had 297 cities with populations over 100,000, and 75 percent of Soviet citizens lived in cities of more than 2,000. In 1935 communist leaders planned to limit the capital, Moscow, to five million inhabitants. By 1965 Moscow had more than seven million people, and by 1990, the Moscow conurbation had grown to nine million residents. Only with the impending breakup of the Soviet Union did a Russian region like the Karelian Republic experience a massive decline in its urban population. Because of a declining birthrate, Europe's urban population growth in the 1990's was only 2.6 percent, compared to 12 percent in sub-Saharan Africa.

GOVERNMENT POLICIES. European governments played a crucial role in urban developments after 1945. Beginning with the French in the 1950's and then the British (and the United States), a "growth-pole strategy" was adopted. The governments wanted to stimulate economic growth in peripheral areas that had lagged in economic development. Planners also hoped to direct urban and economic growth away from the most developed cities and regions. In France, attempts were made to shift growth away from Paris to such cities as Lyons, Marseille, Strasbourg, and Bordeaux. Although Paris continued to grow, the policy did create a more balanced French urban system.

Not all such French government programs proved to be a success. The famous architect Edouard J. Le Corbusier prepared plans for a "linear city" in Marseilles in 1946. The complex had 337 units, ranging from studios to family duplexes, to ensure a mixed social residential profile. A large shopping mall was created on the sixth and seventh floors, and a track, theater, and swimming pool were added to the roof. However, the French public did not like the new construction. Tenants wanted to shop in traditional ground-level stores. The residents in Marseilles called the project "the nut house," and after 1955, the French government allowed for more private developments to meet the public's demands.

In Great Britain, a New Town program was introduced by legislation in 1946 to shift people from overcrowded cities. In 1950 fourteen New Towns were established, all built according to strict land-use zones. Eight of the towns were built in southeastern England, twenty to forty miles from the center of London, and the rest were established in the northeast, the Midlands, and the Scottish highlands. Half a century after the creation of the New Towns, two million people in Britain lived in thirty of the settlements. Unlike on the Continent, British New Towns offered single-family houses, not just apartments. By the 1990's, New Towns were no longer fashionable, and the government's Development Corporation was abolished. Similar attempts at building New Towns were

introduced in France in the 1940's and in the Netherlands and Sweden in the 1970's. In Scandinavia and the Netherlands, 80 percent of the housing in the New Towns consists of apartments.

The most extreme government control of urban planning occurred in Eastern Europe and the Soviet Union. Communist planners wanted to destroy the "contradiction" between urban and rural lifestyles. Government officials adopted comprehensive growth-pole strategies that put new plants and industrial towns in peripheral areas, both to decentralize production and to increase industrialization. The Romanian ruler Nicolae Ceausescu adopted the most extreme form of settlement planning. His program, called "systematization," called for the transformation of villages into towns. Between three and four hundred villages were transformed, destroying traditional rural culture in the process.

URBAN PATTERNS AND LOCATIONS. Towns were established in physical locations that satisfied either defense or economic requirements. Paris originated on an island in the river Seine and the capital of Sweden, Stockholm, began on a number of small islands in an areas where Lake Mälaren meets the Baltic Sea. Venice, the most famous tourist attraction in Italy after Vatican City, originated on islands in a lagoon off the coast of northern Italy. Water-buses provide Venice's main urban transportation. Other towns, like Belgrade in Serbia, are located on high ground for protection. Many towns are on river or coastal trade routes. The Romans used a bridge in London to cross the Thames River. London was not only at a key crossing of the Thames, but also functioned as a major port city. Some cities, such as Salzburg ("Salt castle") in Austria or Bath in England, were located near natural resources.

Welsh village Page 1245

Vatican City Page 1313

Venice Pages 1313, 1370

Venice's famous Bridge of Sighs, which was built around 1600, crosses the Palace Canal. The bridge gets its name from the suffering that prisoners experienced when they had to walk across the bridge to be interrogated by inquisitors in the palace of the ruling Doge. Directly above the inquisitors' offices was a torture chamber. (Photo-Disc)

*Paris
Page 1367*

No city has the relative importance in Europe that New York City enjoys in the United States, but London, Paris, and Moscow enjoy pan-European roles. These urban centers each have metropolitan populations close to ten million people. Several European cities also have significant international functions. London has the reputation of being a world city like Tokyo and New York. Vatican City, within Rome, is the center of the Roman Catholic world, while Strasbourg and Brussels host the headquarters of the Council of Europe and the European Union. Paris and Milan dominate the world of opera and fashion. The new central bank of the European Union is located in Frankfurt am Main, Germany.

Most capitals are also centers of culture and business. The only exception is Bern, the capital of Switzerland. Most capital cities are at the center of national rail and road transportation networks. In Britain, Austria, and Hungary, the capital dominates national life. Hungarians say they are living in "the country" when they want to say that they are living in Budapest. When the capital or largest city is that dominant, it is called a primate distribution. Italy, Belgium, Norway, and Germany are examples of countries with a more balanced urban system, where no single town or capital dominates the country.

TYPES OF CITIES AND MORPHOLOGY. European cities are more compact than those in the United States, because they have less landmass. As in the United States, a large percentage of British urban residents live in single-family houses. On the Continent, apartment living is more prevalent because land is too expensive and because governments have built large public housing apartment complexes. Because Europeans tend to move less frequently than Americans do, there is more permanence in the urban neighborhoods. In general, wealthier citizens in Europe tend to live closer to the city center than they do in the United States. In Vienna and Budapest, however, the wealthy prefer western suburbs because they want to live upwind from the prevailing westerly winds of Continental Europe.

Unlike in U.S. cities, there are no skyscrapers in the skylines of most European city centers. Instead, one sees Gothic church spires or landmarks like the Eiffel Tower in Paris. Most European cities have building restrictions that prohibit tall buildings in the center of cities. This is why tall buildings were constructed outside Paris in the La Defense area, which has skyscrapers for corporate business headquarters. In the former communist countries of Eastern Europe, tall buildings were built primarily for public use.

In most Western and Central European cities, the preindustrial central urban areas, where many of the museums, cathedrals, and marketplaces are located, are too small for two-way car traffic. A study of 141 German cities revealed that 77 percent of all urban streets in these cities were too narrow for two-way traffic. Beginning in the 1970's, many European cities banned car traffic from the central areas. In 1992 Amsterdam closed off the old sections of the city to cars. Many cities are bringing back the streetcar (tram) systems that were eliminated in the 1960's and 1970's. In Mediterranean cities, however, there is less urban planning. These cities have a high residential density, and many have not restricted car traffic in inner-city areas. By contrast, the inner-city areas of Scandinavian cities (Stockholm, Oslo, Helsinki, and Copenhagen) have lost populations to the suburbs. One-fourth of all

Dutch streetcar Page 1314

Skyline of modern Paris. (PhotoDisc)

THE NEW GERMAN CAPITAL: BERLIN

Berlin, a city of 3.5 million people on the river Spree, was the capital of Germany until the conclusion of World War II in 1945, when it was divided between the Soviets and the Western powers. In 1948-1949 a Soviet blockade failed to subdue the West Berliners. Between 1961 and 1989 the communists divided the city with the Berlin Wall, which was dismantled after German reunification in 1990. Berlin is now the capital of a healthy, democratic Germany. Like Bremen and Hamburg, it is also one of sixteen German states.

After 1989, Berlin leaders faced monumental problems in unifying the Western part of the city with the former communist Eastern section. East and West Berliners had to overcome a mental wall in addition to the physical one that had separated them for decades. The former border crossing between the two sections of Berlin, known as "Checkpoint Charlie," became the massive American Business Center. Over $135 billion was spent on rebuilding and unifying Berlin.

Swedes and Danes live in cities concentrated around the shores of the Oresund, the strait separating the countries of Denmark and Sweden.

MODERN URBAN PROBLEMS. European cities, particularly British and East European cities, have faced structural problems because of shifting industrial patterns, especially in steel-manufacturing cities. In addition, many European cities have become multicultural societies, because millions of immigrants and "guest workers" came from North Africa, Turkey, and the rural periphery of the European Union. Finally, the end of communist rule in Eastern Europe has revealed decades of government-tolerated pollution and decay of the urban environment.

The influx of immigrants after the 1950's, particularly from Muslim countries or rural regions, caused considerable tensions in European cities. In 1980, 20 percent of the population of the German city of Frankfurt am Main was made up of foreigners. The Turkish population in Berlin is the largest Turkish urban population outside of Turkey. West Indians and East Indians flocked to British cities, and Algerians and North Africans to French cities. Many of the poorer immigrants set-

tled in urban areas that already suffered decay. In 1980 the British cities of London, Liverpool, Birmingham, Manchester, and Bristol experienced urban riots. Ethnic and racial conflicts spread to French, German, and even Swedish cities.

Economic changes and the decline of traditional industrial occupations fueled urban problems. Much of the urban housing constructed in the 1940's and 1950's was of poor quality and needed repair by the 1980's. Many cities initiated inner-city redevelopment programs in the 1970's. In Britain, for example, the government started an Enterprise Zone in 1980 to encourage urban renewal through tax breaks and deregulation. In order to privatize urban areas, one million public housing units were sold. In Belfast, Northern Ireland, unfit housing was reduced from 25 percent to 8 percent between 1978 and 1992.

The renovation of the London Docklands represents one attempt at urban renewal. The London Docklands cover an area 3 miles (5 km.) from the financial center of London. In 1981 the docks of the Port of London Authority were closed and shipping shifted downstream on the Thames River to Tilbury. Fifty-five miles of waterfront were abandoned, leaving residents of public housing without jobs. Then Canadian investors and some London newspaper headquarters moved to the area and established offices. Unfortunately for public housing residents, most office jobs went to well-trained commuters from other areas of London.

The collapse of communism in Eastern Europe caused massive problems for many East European cities. Government-planned industrial cities like Eisenhütten-stadt in eastern Germany and Leninvaros in Hungary may not be able to compete in a free market system. Much of the housing in Eastern Europe was made of poorly constructed prefabricated blocks. Moscow's total urban density is as high as that in London's central city area. In 1991 the new Russian government initiated the privatization of Russian urban apartments. By 1993 one-quarter of Moscow's housing and five thousand businesses were in private hands. The greatest urban renewal occurred in former East German cities, primarily because the wealthier West German government and industries poured billions of dollars into the effort. Prague, the capital of the Czech Republic, illustrates a successful transition from a socialist command system to a Western free-market system.

Johnpeter Horst Grill

FOR FURTHER STUDY
Bryson, Bill. "Oxford." *National Geographic* (November, 1995): 114-137.

Conniff, Richard. "Monaco." *National Geographic* (May, 1996): 80-95.

Hohenberg, Paul M., and Lynn Hollen Lees. *The Making of Urban Europe, 1000-1994.* Cambridge, Mass.: Harvard University Press, 1995.

Ludwig, Gerd. "Reinventing Berlin." *National Geographic* (December, 1996): 96-117.

McCarry, John. "Milan—Where Italy Gets Down to Business." *National Geographic* (December, 1992): 90-119.

Raymer, Steve. "St. Petersburg, Capital of the Tsars." *National Geographic* (December, 1993): 96-121.

Remnick, David. "Moscow: The New Revolution." *National Geographic* (April, 1997): 78-103.

Vries, Jan de. *European Urbanization 1500-1800.* Cambridge, Mass.: Harvard University Press, 1984.

Zwingle, Erla. "Venice." *National Geographic* (February, 1995): 73-99.

INFORMATION ON THE WORLD WIDE WEB

The Federal Statistical Office of Germany provides current data in English on the urban population of Europe. (www.statistik-bund.de/)

Cities.com is an Internet database of information on over 4,000 cities, including those in Europe. (www.cities.com)

*Prague
Page 1439*

POLITICAL GEOGRAPHY

The political geography of Europe divides along two imaginary lines, or axes: One line runs from east to west, the other from north to south. The east-west axis is mainly political and divides free from authoritarian or quasi-authoritarian countries. The north-south axis divides southern countries that historically have been poor from more prosperous northern countries. Since authoritarian countries are generally poorer than free countries, both historically and in modern times, northwest Europe has been freer and more prosperous than other regions.

The east-west axis has been and remains more influential than the division between north and south. The division between east and west played a profound role in twentieth century Europe, especially in the second half of the century. From soon after the end of World War II in 1945, communism, as embodied by the Soviet Union, dominated the east, installing regimes not just friendly to its interests, but obedient to its will. In 1946 Winston Churchill gave a famous speech in Fulton, Missouri, declaring that "an Iron Curtain has descended across Europe." The line that this Iron Curtain traced precisely defined the east-west axis of European political geography as it then existed.

GOVERNMENT IN THE WEST. In the West, forms of liberal democracy, which differed fundamentally from communism, were practiced by Germany (divided into eastern and western sectors), Austria, Switzerland, France, the Low Countries (Belgium, the Netherlands, and Luxembourg), Scandinavia, and the British Isles.

Liberal democracy, in which the power of government is limited and the liberty of the individual is valued and protected, was supported in this region by the resources of the United States, Western Europe's postwar partner and ally.

Through the Marshall Plan, the United States began transferring billions of dollars to Western Europe in 1948 to shore up the region's war-weakened economies against communism. The following year the U.S. partnership was institutionalized in a formal political and military alliance, the North Atlantic Treaty Organization (NATO). The Soviets responded by creating the Warsaw Pact, comprising itself and its Eastern European puppet states. At the end of 1991, the Soviet Union (USSR) collapsed, disintegrating into fifteen separate states, the largest of which was Russia. The Warsaw Pact was disbanded, but NATO has survived into the twenty-first century. The Western alliance continued to play a prominent role in European politics, and therefore in the continent's political geography.

Emphasis on the political and cultural basis of the east-west and north-south axes does not imply that features of physical geography play no significant role in Europe's political geography. Switzerland's long-standing policy of neutrality in international affairs is based principally on its geographical position surrounded by a high wall of protective mountains, the Alps. Poland's vulnerability to aggression from east and west is based on its closeness to Russia, its border with Germany, and its lack of natural barriers to invasion. This vulnerability has enabled Poland's neighbors through history to have appropriated large portions of its territory, even to a point that the state of Poland ceased to exist for a time. Similarly, the Baltic Republics have been denied their freedom through military occupation by the Russian colossus to the east. For decades after the outbreak of the Cold War in 1946, Finland, which bordered the then Soviet Union, found it prudent to mute its comments on its eastern neighbor.

ORIGINS OF THE EAST-WEST AXIS. The political geography of Europe in the twenty-first century has deep roots in the distant past. The most important origins of the east-west axis are found in the division of the Roman Empire into eastern and western branches. This effectively took place in 330 C.E., when the emperor Constantine moved the capital to Byzantium. At that time, Christianity was an officially tolerated religion. The Eastern Empire, whose capital was renamed Constantinople (later Istanbul), lasted until the fourteenth century, when it fell to the Muslim Ottoman Empire. The Western Roman Empire had a far different history, succumbing to barbarian invaders in 476.

One result of the fall of the Western empire was that when secular institutions were reestablished, they seldom cooperated closely with the West's nearly universal religious institution, the Christian Church. Religious and secular authorities were considered part of a single society called the Christian Republic, but they clashed with each other in an ongoing struggle for power. This division came about through the influence of Christianity, which, in the West, caused divided loyalties between ecclesiastical and political authorities.

Struggles between political and religious powers broadened as the Middle Ages waned, and cities, increasingly proud of their emerging independence, gained the economic strength to resist the demands of rulers. In the Orthodox civilization to the East, church and state collaborated so closely that their relationship, while not completely unitary, is known as "Caesaropapism."

ELEMENTS OF WESTERN SOCIAL PLURALISM. In the West, a further element of social pluralism developed by the seventeenth and eighteenth centuries, when some political writers conceived society as distinct from the political order. The fact that early modern Western Europe developed competing centers of power distin-

---

WESTERN EUROPEAN CONFLICTS THROUGHOUT HISTORY

Known for violent and long-continued conflicts over territorial control, Western Europe—particularly the areas that are now eastern France, western Germany and the Benelux countries—has often been labeled the "cockpit." In the nineteenth and twentieth centuries, the following major conflicts were waged throughout the region, accounting for the deaths of millions.

1792-1802:	Wars of the French Revolution
1803-1815:	Napoleonic Wars
1820-1823:	1820 Revolts
1830-1831:	1830 Revolts
1848-1849:	1848 Revolts
1859:	Franco-Austrian War
1864:	Schleswig-Holstein War
1866:	Seven Weeks War, or Austro-Prussian War
1870-1871:	Franco-Prussian War
1914-1918:	World War I
1939-1945:	World War II

guished it further from the East and allowed the eventual development of what is known as "civil society," which is the realm of autonomous, independently organized social groups of all varieties.

After the religious violence of the Reformation, pluralism in Protestant Western Europe included a realm of independently organized social organizations, beginning with a variety of Christian sects. By the eighteenth century, countries such as England and the Netherlands were taking strides to assure liberal freedoms of religion, speech, and association. These freedoms were based on the rule of law, including due process.

The distinctive character of Western Europe continued its development after the sixteenth century Reformation and the rise of Protestantism. Protestantism emphasized the individual believer's relationship with God, which helped give rise to the individualism that tended to characterize Protestant communities.

THE ROLE OF PROTESTANTISM. Protestantism created procedures of church governance that sharply distinguished it from Catholicism. Protestant church government was generally more democratic than the rigid authoritarianism that characterized Catholicism. Some Protestant congregations learned the art of freely associating together through formal agreements, a process akin to the grouping of states together in federations. They practiced the "federative" principle, rooted in the biblical concept of covenant, or voluntary agreement. By the seventeenth and eighteenth centuries, such free forms of governance carried over into the secular sphere, as democratic ideas spread not only into parts of Western Europe, such as the Netherlands and Britain, but also to the New World's American colonies.

Progress in Protestant communities was advanced by their embrace of modern science, including Copernicanism, which taught that the earth revolves around the Sun, not vice versa. Science tended to favor democratic attitudes, since scientific learning was potentially available to anyone capable of understanding it, not just an established elite. The refusal of Catholicism to bend dogma to new scientific discovery helped to keep Catholic-dominated Eastern and Southern Europe intellectually, economically, and politically backward into the twentieth centuries.

DEVELOPMENT OF LIBERAL DEMOCRACY. By the end of the nineteenth century, Protestant Western Europe had evolved into liberal, if not entirely democratic, societies. Liberal societies tolerated, and sometimes actively promoted, a degree of liberty. Great Britain and the Netherlands stood out as free societies in which liberal ideas gained considerable currency. In Britain, John Stuart Mill was an influential champion of liberalism. France also produced powerful exponents of liberal ideas, including Alexis de Tocqueville, author of the widely read *Democracy in America* (1835-1840), and Benjamin Constant, a leading liberal thinker who identified a key aspect of the modern West's view of liberty in *The Liberty of the Ancients Compared with That of the Moderns* (1816). He described modern liberty as an independent sphere fenced off from unwarranted intrusion by the state.

These ideas, in varying degrees written into law and practice in the cultural life of Western Europe, were joined with ideas and institutions of limited government, guaranteed by written or unwritten constitutions. In Britain, the idea and institutions of the rule of law lay at the heart of the idea of constitutionalism, which had been evolving since the Magna Carta of 1215 first expressed the idea of a rule of law.

From the constitutional reforms of seventeenth century England onward, the powers of monarchs were progressively reduced, until by the end of the nineteenth century they were minimal. Instead, Parliament ruled, though it ruled in the monarch's name. Elsewhere in Western Europe, the idea of limited government gained ground in the Protestant north as well as in Catholic France, with its strong secular traditions stemming from the French Revolution and its rejection of clerical influence. By the close of the nineteenth century, varying degrees of popular government were practiced in Western Europe and the British Isles.

Liberal thinkers in the West championed the free market, both at home and in trade with other countries, as the substance of economic liberty. It was no accident that the Industrial Revolution began in Britain, where both scientific and economic liberty was most advanced. With liberty came economic prosperity; with economic prosperity came the means—economic resources in private hands—for the maintenance of liberty.

POLITICAL ORDER IN THE EAST. Orthodox regions consistently lagged the West in social, political, and economic development. In Russia, serfdom endured until 1863. Half a century later, Russia was still a nation of peasants. Although by 1914 there was a small urban working class, industrialization had hardly begun in Russia when World War I broke out. Democratization had not taken root, as the huge Russian Empire staggered under the weight of an antiquated political system. Russia's attitude to the West was profoundly divided, envying, on one hand, the West's freedom, modernism, and pros-

One of the most famous street addresses in the world is London's 10 Downing Street, the official residence of the prime minister of Great Britain. (R. Kent Rasmussen)

perity, and longing to catch up. On the other hand, Russia believed the West's wealth was soulless, and that Russia possessed a spiritual depth that would atrophy if liberal Western ways were adopted.

When Russia's czarist regime was overthrown in 1917, the new democratic government was weak and inexperienced. Communists, under Vladimir Ilyich Lenin, easily took over in November, 1917. With no democratic background, it was difficult, if not impossible, for Russia to establish genuine democracy after the Soviet Union's collapse in 1991.

THE NORTH-SOUTH AXIS. While the east-west axis played the dominant role in European political affairs, the north-south axis has not been without influence. The crux of this axis was the tension between a wealthy, economically developed north and a poorer, less-developed south. The southern tier of Europe included the small portion of Turkey west of the Bosporus, Bulgaria, Greece, the southern Balkan nations, Albania, southern Italy, and the Iberian Peninsula (Spain and Portugal). There, religion played an important role in maintaining social traditionalism, which translated into the absence of economic development. On the other hand, by the end of the nineteenth century, economic development characterized Protestant-dominated northwest Europe. The political consequence was that Europe's southern tier enjoyed less political liberty than the north.

The religion of southeastern Europe was predominantly Eastern Orthodox Christian. Orthodoxy was the branch of Christianity centered in Constantinople, after the Emperor Constantine divided the Roman Empire into eastern and western portions. Bulgaria, Greece, Romania, and Serbia, which is situated in the Balkan Mountains, lie in the zone of Orthodoxy. Parts of the Balkans, such as Croatia, and southern lands to the west—Italy, Spain, and Portugal—are historically Roman Catholic and therefore culturally part of the West. Turkey is Muslim, as are Albania and portions of Bosnia-Herzegovina, another Balkan country.

Religion was just one factor that delayed the onset of economic development in countries of the southern axis; a relative lack of natural resources was another. For these and other complex reasons, a large,

literate middle class failed to appear, in sharp contrast to the lands of the Protestant north and later in Catholic France, which was independent and nationalist. The development of a literate middle class—versed in a scientific outlook, eager to promote economic progress, and capable of self-organization and therefore of political self-direction—forms the social basis of democracy. Thus democracy gained ground in the Protestant northwest in the nineteenth century and had triumphed by the mid-twentieth century.

AUTHORITARIANISM IN THE SOUTH. By 1950 democracy had not been established in Europe's impoverished southeastern tier. Albania, the Balkans, Bulgaria, and Romania were communist. In the Iberian Peninsula, authoritarian nationalism ruled. By 1950 Greece and Italy were democracies but stood on shaky foundations. In Greece and Turkey in the first years after World War II, communism, aided by Moscow, nearly overcame weak democratic forces. Communism was defeated only through U.S. financial resources and military hardware, provided under the Truman Doctrine, declared by President Harry Truman in 1947 to resist communist subversion of free peoples.

By the mid-twentieth century, Italy had undergone a democratic conversion after its conquest by the U.S. army in 1943, after more than two decades of fascism under Benito Mussolini. However, impoverished southern Italy could scarcely be termed democratic. Grinding poverty, mores that atrophied social cooperation, powerful organized crime, and an education system dominated by obscurantism and social conservatism underwritten by the Catholic Church gravely debilitated the region.

Northern Italy was a different matter, since by midcentury it had progressively industrialized. Industrialization was so successful that by the 1970's, Italy surpassed Britain in per-capita income. Still, the Italian political system was riddled with corruption. Communists were denied national electoral victory in the first decades after World War II by the financial intervention of the United States, which bankrolled democratic Italian political parties to counter Soviet assistance to Italy's communists. So unlike were northern and southern Italy that by the 1990's, a serious separatist movement, the Lombardy League, had arisen in the north.

LATE TWENTIETH CENTURY DEVELOPMENTS. By the start of the twenty-first century, both the north-south and, more especially, the east-west axis of European geography showed signs of flux—even, to

a limited degree, disintegration. A vast change in the east-west axis was undeniable. Until the late twentieth century, Europe was separated into democratic and communist camps, dramatically symbolized by the division of East and West Berlin by the barbed wire-topped Berlin Wall, bordered on the east by minefields, where guards shot numerous would-be escapists.

This division collapsed in 1989 when the Soviet Union withdrew its troops from former satellite nations. Explicitly and publicly, the Soviets told them to develop their own domestic and foreign policies. East Germany, Poland, Czechoslovakia, and Hungary immediately began to democratize, along with other communist nations. Joyful Germans tore down the

Until the reunification of Germany in 1989, Berlin's formidable Brandenburg Gate was the main crossing point between East and West Germany. (PhotoDisc)

East German crew demolishes a section of the Berlin Wall in November, 1989. (Robert McClenaghan)

Berlin Wall, concrete slab by concrete slab. Even Yugoslavia, which had never been under the Soviet thumb but had run a more prosperous and less ruthlessly controlled communist multinational state—authoritarian but not totalitarian—broke up into its national components.

SHIFT IN EAST-WEST POLITICAL GEOGRAPHY. At this historical point, European east-west political geography began to shift according to its cultural roots. Political divisions following cultural fault lines between the Christian Orthodox East and the Catholic and Protestant West forcefully and unmistakably manifested themselves.

The consequence of the differences between Orthodox and Western cultures was that constitutional democracy and a measure of economic prosperity took hold in the West, while varying degrees of authoritarianism and poverty described the East. War repeatedly broke out in the 1990's on the Balkan east-west fault lines, with particularly appalling results where Muslim populations abutted or mingled with Christians, as in Bosnia-Herzegovina. In formerly Muslim Albania, home of the most backward communist dictatorship of the previous era, order degenerated into anarchy as the administrative structures of the state crumbled.

To the west, conditions were dramatically better. East Germany, Poland, Czechoslovakia, and Hungary, located on the western side of the cultural divide, more or less peacefully overthrew their communist regimes and immediately began to democratize. Led by acclaimed Czech playwright Vaclav Havel, Czechoslovakia's change from autocracy to popular government proceeded so smoothly that it was dubbed the Velvet Revolution. Soon, the Czechs and Slovaks had peacefully and democratically consented to a Velvet Divorce, establishing two separate countries.

In 1989 the Soviet-occupied Baltic republics, traditionally Western Christian rather than Orthodox, declared their independence, recognized by the Soviet Union two years later after some bloodshed. All three republics—Lithuania, Latvia, and Estonia—successfully established constitutional democracies. With Soviet approval, West Germany absorbed East Germany in 1990, creating a reunified Germany. The east-west axis thus moved considerably eastward, as lands so recently claimed and dominated by the Soviet/Orthodox east regained their status as integral to Western civilization.

To the east of this great cultural divide, however, conditions were immeasurably worse. Russia struggled valiantly to establish constitutional democracy after its authoritarian, totalitarian past. At the start of the twenty-first century, the question of whether a democratic Russia was possible remained unresolved.

The latter part of the twentieth century also saw a significant breakdown of the north-south axis. In the 1970's, both Portugal and Spain abandoned authoritarian government, embraced democracy, and joined the European Community. Both countries made significant progress in overcoming their legacies of poverty, as commerce and industry grew apace. In the

1990's, Italy made significant strides in overcoming its north-south divide when it exposed the massive corruption that had suffused its political system. In 1999 a symbolically important event occurred when Palermo, the capital city of Sicily and center of the organized crime that historically infested southern Italy, declared its independence of the Mafia crime network. It then attempted to immerse itself in the civic culture of the West by sponsoring a conference on education for democracy.

DYNAMICS OF POLITICAL-GEOGRAPHIC CHANGE. The dynamics of Europe's political geography at the end of the twentieth century were both complex and seemingly contradictory. Western and Central Europe may be thought to have been growing more unified. Europe showed a steady decline of the independence of individual nation-states and the rise of the European Union, but evidence of contrary disunity also continued.

European unification began not long after the end of World War II. The mutual association of separate states evolved from the European Coal and Steel Community (ECSC), a jointly managed market in those two commodities, founded in 1950-1951 at the suggestion of French economist Jean Monnet, often called the "Father of Europe." Prompted by a further proposal of Monnet for a United States of Europe, the ECSC progressed from this limited form of unification to a more inclusive common market, the European Economic Community (EEC), created in 1957 by the Treaty of Rome. This treaty gradually reduced tariffs among six Western nations, the three Low Countries, Germany, France, and Italy.

In 1973 the Common Market was enlarged to include Great Britain, Denmark, and Ireland. The EEC changed its name to the European Community (EC), suggesting a closer stage of association than "market." In 1979 the first direct elections to the first European Parliament were held; in 1986, an agreement was signed to create a fully integrated internal market among the European Community's nine members. It became law on January 1, 1993. The previous year, by the Treaty on European Union, signed at Maastricht, Netherlands, the EC had agreed to become the European Union on November 1, 1993. In 1999 several Union countries, led by Germany and France, adopted a common currency, the euro. Countries that adopted the euro became know, collectively, as Euroland.

FORCES OPPOSING POLITICAL UNIFICATION. Despite this steady march toward unification, Europe remains anything but united. Several nations on the western side of the east-west axis were not members of the European Union. Even within the EU, there were marked fissures. With no common language, all European Union documents had to be translated into twelve languages. A common foreign policy is seldom apparent. Some mem-

bers, led by traditionally insular Britain, either did not want to, or were not eligible to, adopt the euro as the unit of common currency. Adoption of a common currency would restrict the freedom of individual countries to regulate the value of their individual currencies, and therefore to direct their economic destiny.

Unity also was challenged by nationalism, which was proving stubbornly resilient. Separatist national movements within states were active, such as those by Basques and Catalonians in Spain. One response to separatist sentiments was decentralization of government functions, or devolution. In Britain (the United Kingdom of Great Britain and Northern Ireland), where nationalist movements were active, devolution took the form of allowing Scotland and Wales to form their own national parliaments for local affairs. Across the Irish Sea in Northern Ireland, the British allowed a local parliament to reopen its doors after nearly three decades of violent sectarian strife. On the continent of Eu-

---

KEY DATES IN EUROPEAN UNIFICATION

May 9, 1950:	France officially proposes a jointly managed market in two important industrial commodities, the European Coal and Steel Community (ECSC), with six participating nations.
March 25, 1957:	The Treaty of Rome is signed, creating the European Economic Community (EEC).
January 1, 1973:	The first expansion of the EEC takes place as Great Britain, Denmark, and the Republic of Ireland are added.
June 7-10, 1979:	The first direct elections to a European Parliament, sitting in Strasbourg, France, are conducted by universal suffrage.
February 17, 1986:	The Single European Act is signed, committing the EEC to assisting underdeveloped regions of Europe.
November 1, 1993:	The Treaty on European Union, signed in 1992, goes into effect, creating a new level of European integration that transforms the European Community into a new European Union.

rope, northern Italy was still restive although united with the south, and voices advocating independence continued to be heard.

A more protracted and potentially troubling problem lay in the steady arrival of illegal immigrants and asylum-seekers from the developing nations of African and Asia, which might eventually challenge the national identity of the European Union's individual countries. By the 1990's, this phenomenon had energized shrill political disputes between the political left and right.

CONTINUED EAST-WEST SEPARATION. Western and Central Europe, to a significant degree, lacked integration. Various European political and military associations, for example, lacked common membership. NATO was expanded to include the Czech Republic, Hungary, and Poland, but none of the three had joined the European Union. Turkey, with the majority of its territory in Asia, wanted to join the EU, but Western Europe was undecided about admitting Turkey, however valiantly it struggled against Muslim fundamentalists to remain a secular state. As of the year 2000 the European Union had not admitted Turkey.

Finally, the members of Europe's most powerful unifying organizations were not all Western. Orthodox Greece was a member of NATO and the European Union, but could not be counted on for support in all circumstances. In an open display of the tension between Western and Orthodox civilizations, Greece refused to join NATO's attack on nearby Orthodox Serbia in 1999. In the year 2000, when the Greek government, responding to EU policy, proposed removing religion from citizens' identification cards, large numbers of Orthodox Christians vehemently protested.

A further political divide lay in the tension between the principal members of the European Union on the European continent and Britain, with its long, deep association and special relationship with the United States. While France sought successful resistance to U.S. military and economic ascendance and Germans were divided on this question, Britain continued its membership in the English-speaking family of nations, of which the United States was the largest and most powerful. Europe as a whole remained split by the Western-Orthodox civilization divide; an east-west axis in political and cultural geography continued in force.

Charles F. Bahmueller

FOR FURTHER STUDY

Bahmueller, Charles F., ed. *World Conflicts and Confrontations.* Vol. 4. Pasadena, Calif.: Salem Press, 2000.

Derleth, J. William. *The Transition in Central and Eastern European Politics.* Englewood Cliffs, N.J.: Prentice-Hall, 1999.

INFORMATION ON THE WORLD WIDE WEB

Europa, the European Union's server, is a good place to begin Internet research on the European Community. The site contains a great deal of information, including much supplied by the various national agencies. (europa.eu.int/)

Another good starting point for Internet research on European political geography is Links2Go: European Politics, which provides an outline of related Web sites offering detailed information. (www.links2go.com/topic/European_Politics)

Huntington, Samuel. *The Clash of Civilizations and the Remaking of the World Order.* New York: Touchstone Books, 1999.

Sandholtz, Wayne, et al., eds. *European Integration and Supranational Governance.* New York: Oxford University Press, 1998.

Slomp, Hans. *European Politics into the Twenty-First Century: Integration and Division.* Westport, Conn.: Praeger, 2000.

ECONOMIC
GEOGRAPHY

AGRICULTURE

Map
Page 1316

Agriculture in Europe goes back to classical times. The development first of the Greek city-states, then of the Roman Empire, created urban centers that required substantial amounts of food to be imported from as far away as Egypt. Land ownership has varied over time between small peasant holdings and large estates. By the twentieth century, most large estates in Europe had been either broken up into small holdings owned by the peasants who occupied them or taken over by the governments of the countries in which the land was located. The latter properties then were operated either directly by the government or indirectly through cooperatives. Most recently, except in Russia, land largely has been redistributed to those who actually farm it.

In the year 2000 European agriculture was dominated by two major groups: the European Union (EU), with fifteen member states, and those European states outside the EU. The EU, which began with the Common Market created by the Treaty of Rome, signed in 1957 and put in force on January 1, 1958, initially comprised France, West Germany, Italy, Belgium, the Netherlands, and Luxembourg. By the year 2000 it had expanded to include Great Britain, Ireland, Denmark, Greece, Spain, Portugal, Finland, Sweden, and Austria. All fifteen countries participate in the Common Agricultural Policy (CAP) whose objective, as defined in the Rome Treaties, is to make the EU self-sufficient in food.

LAND IN FARMING. Only 11 percent of the land in the world (slightly more than 5 million square miles) is suitable for agri-culture. Among the continents, Europe has the highest percentage of land suitable for farming: 36 percent. (In North America, the comparable figure is 22 percent.) Overall, 80 percent of the land in Europe is usable in some way, either as agricultural land or as forestland.

In the latter half of the twentieth century, the cultivated area of the world dropped from 0.44 hectares to 0.31 hectares per person. (A hectare equals 2.47 acres.) During this same period, fertilizer use increased, in the world as a whole, from 29.3 kilograms per hectare (kg/ha) to 85.3 kg/ha; in North America it about doubled, as it did in Western Europe (124.4 kg/ha to 224.3 kg/ha); in Eastern Europe, it quadrupled (30.4 kg/ha to 122.3 kg/ha). Since agricultural output increased dramatically during this same period, but the land dedicated to agriculture declined, one can infer that the higher output was greatly helped by the addition of fertilizer.

In the EU, the size of agricultural holdings has increased, and most of the increased agricultural output comes from these larger holdings. The EU has special programs to help maintain smaller farms; these are more extensive in the southern countries of the EU than in the northern countries. Some 60 percent of all farms in the EU are less than 5 hectares (12.5 acres) in size. Many of these small farms are either part-time or subsistence farms. Farms that are more than 50 hectares in size (125 acres, a small farm by U.S. standards) constitute only 6 percent of all farms but produce most of the crops.

AVERAGE FARM SIZES IN COUNTRIES OF THE EUROPEAN UNION

Country	Average Farm Size	
	Acres	Hectares
Belgium	42.0	17.0
Denmark	80.3	32.5
France	75.9	30.7
Germany	42.0	17.0
Greece	15.5	5.3
Ireland	56.1	22.7
Italy	19.0	7.7
Luxembourg	82.0	33.2
Netherlands	42.0	17.0
Portugal	20.5	8.3
Spain	42.0	17.0
United Kingdom	170	68.9

The EU has achieved the goal set by the Treaty of Rome, to become self-sufficient in food, and surpassed it. At the beginning of the twenty-first century, the EU was producing 10 percent more food than it consumed; in dairy products, the excess was 20-25 percent.

WORKERS. The percentage of the labor force employed in agriculture is small where the farms are large—in the United Kingdom, it is a mere 2 percent. In the EU, except for some of the more recent members, such as Greece, Spain, and Portugal, the percentages are all in the single digits. Where the farms are small, or in non-EU countries, without the EU's agricultural policy to push production up with high prices, the percentage of the labor force employed in agriculture is much higher. In Poland, 27 percent of the labor force is employed in agriculture; in Romania, 21 percent; and in the Ukraine, 19 percent.

CROPS. Europe produces about 19 per-

Italian Vineyard Page 1314

cent of the world's grains that provide human food directly or indirectly (as food for livestock that in turn feeds humans). Of this, about two-fifths is produced in Russia. About 12 percent of the world's wheat is grown in Europe, most of that in Russia. Almost 24 percent of the world's coarse grains (barley, rye, oats) are grown in Europe, again mostly in Russia. Of the world's tubers, only 20 percent are grown in Europe, but half the world's potatoes are grown there, reflecting the fact that potatoes are mostly a food of the Northern Hemisphere. The Russian Federation grows the largest share of those potatoes.

Europe also grows half of the world's dry peas; about 40 percent are produced in the Russian Federation. Three-quarters of the world's sugar beets are grown in Europe, the Ukraine being the largest European producer. Rapeseed—like sugar beets, a raw product that requires further processing before being used for human consumption, generally as cooking oil—has been increasing as an agricultural product. Germany is its largest producer in Europe, followed closely by France. European production is a bit more than 17 percent of world production.

Europe grows 20 percent of the world's tomatoes, although the tomato is not a native European plant. Spain and Italy are the leading producers of tomatoes in Europe. Overall, Europe grows 16 percent of the world's vegetables, with Italy being the largest European producer, closely followed by the Russian Federation and Spain. Europe produces a quarter of the world's green beans, with the Russian Federation and Italy leading other European nations.

Over half of the world's grapes are grown in Europe—despite the substantial production in California, Chile, South Africa, and Australia. These grapes feed Europe's great wineries, which produce 70 percent of the world's wine, a substantial proportion of which is drunk in Europe, although it remains an important export item. Europe also produces nearly three-quarters of the world's hops, which go into the much-prized European beers. Europe grows more than half the world's olives, almost all of them in Italy, Spain, and Greece. It also produces about 60 percent of the world's olive oil, likewise in Italy, Spain, and Greece.

LIVESTOCK. Europe has a bit more than 8 percent of the world's cattle, most of them in the Russian Federation, but a substantial number in France and Germany. However, Europe produces 14 percent of the world's beef, much of it coming from the Russian Federation. Among other livestock, 18 percent of the world's lambs are raised in Europe, most of them in Spain and the United Kingdom. Europe also produces 18 percent of the world's stock of pigs, mostly in Germany, the Russian Federation, and Poland, but Spain and Romania are not far behind. Only 8 percent of the world's chickens are hatched in Europe. The Russian Federation and France are the principal chicken producers.

Just under 15 percent of the world's milk cows are in Europe, the vast majority in the Russian Federation. Nevertheless, Europe produces half of the world's cheese and 40 percent of the world's dry milk, much of this in the EU—France and Germany lead in the production of dry milk powder. European chickens lay 15

Longhair cattle Page 1317

Olive groves Page 1249

Cheeses Page 1317

Beer brewery in the Netherlands. (PhotoDisc)

Grocery shop in Florence, Italy. (PhotoDisc)

dated, especially in the United Kingdom, but also in France and Germany. As a result, the larger holdings became economic to operate with modern agricultural machinery, such as is used throughout the United States. Now, 44 percent of the world's tractors are owned in Europe, most in France, Italy, and Poland. This circumstance helps to explain why, when French farmers want to express objection to a political proposal, they turn up in Paris with their tractors and bring all traffic to a standstill. It also has helped make European agriculture sufficiently productive that, according to the U.S. Department of Agriculture, Europe's best farms are as efficient as the best in the United States.

European farmers have vastly increased their yields. Between 1960 and 1976, French dairy farmers increased the amount of milk produced per cow by more than 50 percent, and the increase continued in the years following. Most European dairy cows produced about twice as much milk in the 1990's as they did before World War II. Labor in the dairy business has been drastically reduced: In the Netherlands, for example, there is a dairy operation that is entirely automated—it uses no human beings at all in its milk production, which is the highest in Europe. Output of cereal grains has grown almost as much as milk. The United Kingdom's wheat output is up 60 percent over what it was immediately after World War II; the growth in output is nearly as great in

percent of the world's eggs, mostly in France and the Russian Federation.

THE AGRICULTURAL REVOLUTION. Beginning in the 1970's, Europe underwent what has been called a new agricultural "revolution." Ownerships were consoli-

LEADING AGRICULTURAL PRODUCTS OF EUROPEAN COUNTRIES WITH MORE THAN 20 PERCENT OF ARABLE LAND

Country	Products	Percent of Arable Land
Albania	Temperate-zone crops and livestock	21
Belarus	Grain, potatoes, vegetables, meat, milk	29
Belgium	Sugar beets, fresh vegetables, fruits, grain, tobacco, beef, veal, pork, milk	24
Bulgaria	Grain, oilseed, vegetables, fruits, tobacco, livestock	37
Denmark	Grain, potatoes, rapeseed, sugar beets, meat, dairy products, fish	60
France	Wheat, cereals, sugar beets, potatoes, wine grapes, beef, dairy products, fish	33
Germany	Potatoes, wheat, rye, barley, sugar beets, fruit, cabbage, cattle, pigs, poultry	—
Hungary	Wheat, corn, sunflower seed, potatoes, sugar beets, pigs, cattle, poultry, dairy products	51
Italy	Fruits, vegetables, grapes, potatoes, sugar beets, soybeans, grain, olives, meat and dairy products, fish	31
Liechtenstein	Wheat, barley, maize, potatoes, livestock, dairy products	25
Luxembourg	Barley, oats, potatoes, wheat, fruit, wine grapes, livestock	24
Malta	Potatoes, cauliflower, grapes, wheat, barley, tomatoes, citrus, cut flowers, green peppers, pork, milk, poultry, eggs	38
Moldova	Vegetables, fruits, wine, grain, sugar beets, sunflower seed, tobacco, meat, milk	53
The Netherlands	Grains, potatoes, sugar beets, fruits, vegetables, livestock	27
Portugal	Grain, potatoes, olives, grapes, sheep, cattle, goats, poultry, meat, dairy products	26
Romania	Corn, wheat, sugar beets, sunflower seed, potatoes, grapes, milk, eggs, meat	41
Russia	Grain, sugar beets, sunflower seed, vegetables, fruits, meat, milk	—
Spain	Grain, vegetables, olives, wine grapes, sugar beets, citrus, beef, pork, poultry, dairy products, fish	30
United Kingdom	Cereals, oilseed, potatoes, vegetables, cattle, sheep, poultry, fish	25

Source: The Time Almanac 2000. Boston: Infoplease, 1999.

France. In general, European agricultural productivity has grown 5 percent a year between 1960 and 1999.

Productivity has grown much less in Eastern Europe than in Western Europe. This is partly because rainfall there varies so widely from year to year. In some years, Russia was in a position to export grain; in other years, it had to import from the EU. During the last twenty years or so of Soviet domination of Eastern Europe, the EU often sent its excess agricultural products to Russia.

In 1979 the EU moved from being an importer of cereal grains to an exporter, as it did in 1975 for sugar, in 1976 for wine, and in 1979 for beef and veal. Since 1960, the number of workers employed in agriculture has dropped by 50 percent, although the agricultural output remains the same or even higher. Authorities in the United Kingdom have estimated that farms there are at their most efficient when they employ no more than two or three people—a far cry from the dozens or hundreds of people who worked Europe's farms for subsistence wages in earlier centuries.

IRRIGATION AND DRAINAGE. Despite the generally favorable climate, Europe has 10 percent of the world's irrigated acreage. Most of that is in the Russian Federation, but Italy, Spain, and Romania also have significant amounts. Perhaps the most striking feature of European agriculture is the extent to which agricultural lands—some of them former wetlands— have been drained, to ensure uniform moisture conditions for the crops being grown. In Finland, 91 percent of the agricultural land has been drained. The European nation that has seen the second largest percentage of its land drained is Hungary—more than 70 percent. The Netherlands is next with 65 percent; the United Kingdom is fourth, with 60 per-

cent; Germany is fifth with 50 percent. The high value of the land makes such work worthwhile.

AGRICULTURE'S SHARE OF THE ECONOMY. Throughout Western Europe agriculture represents a relatively small part of the value of national economies—about 4 percent in Denmark, Spain, France, and the Netherlands, and as low as 2 percent in the United Kingdom and Germany. In Eastern Europe, it is a different story. Although agriculture is only 6 percent of the gross domestic product of the Russian Federation, it is 30 percent in the Ukraine, 21 percent in Romania, and 16 percent in Greece. The large percentage of the population that still makes its living from agriculture in Eastern Europe explains why the inclusion of these countries poses a significant problem for the European Union, which is already overproducing agricultural goods. Although figures have not been available for many European nations, Denmark derived 19 percent of its export earnings from agricultural products, and Greece 20 percent. For Portugal the figure was 8 percent; for the Netherlands, 4 percent.

THE COMMON AGRICULTURAL POLICY. The dominant factor in European agriculture has been the Common Agricultural Policy (CAP) of the EU. Beginning with the Treaty of Rome, the goal has been to make the members of the EU self-sufficient in food, and they have succeeded admirably, so much so that the EU now has the opposite problem, how to dispose of the agricultural surpluses that have been accumulating. Because the system of agricultural price supports was designed to encourage greater production, the problem has become how to bring prices more into line with world agricultural prices without bankrupting the farmers whose production has been based on the subsidies of the CAP.

ELIMINATING AGRICULTURAL SURPLUSES

During the 1980's, the accumulation of surplus agricultural products began to be a serious problem, as governments were obliged to buy up the excesses. In Germany, the amount of butter piled up in government storehouses became some- thing of a scandal and was referred to by the German public as the "butter mountain." One popular solution has been to send surplus products to developing nations as food aid.

The CAP operates by a system of price supports, not dissimilar to the system in the United States. The EU sets a minimum price for each agricultural commodity, at which farmers are compensated for that commodity by the wholesalers who buy up the commodity directly from the farmer. Unlike the system that prevails in the United States, the government subsidies in the EU are paid to the wholesalers, who pass them on to the farmers in the prices they pay the farmers for the agricultural commodities they produce. This minimum price is about 50 percent above the world price. There are few imports of these supported agricultural commodities into the EU, because the EU also sets a minimum import price that is always above that set for domestically produced commodities. Part of the cost of these subsidies comes from taxation, but part of the cost comes from higher prices for food charged to consumers. In the United States, the cost of agricultural subsidies comes mostly from taxation—only 25 percent comes from higher food prices. In the EU the subsidies are funded 80 percent through higher consumer prices for food.

When it became apparent that the effect of the CAP was to raise agricultural production in the EU above the level of domestic demand, the officials of the EU—under pressure not just from the United States, a major exporter of agricul- tural commodities, but also from Canada, Argentina, Australia, and New Zealand— began to consider ways in which the CAP could be modernized. In 1992 some changes were introduced into the support system, reducing the amount of subsidy provided for some agricultural commodi- ties, chiefly grains. Because there has been strong political support for the mainte- nance of the rural countryside, this reduc- tion was balanced by the introduction of direct subsidies to grain farmers for taking land out of production.

As long as the existing system was in place, there was an incentive for farmers to increase their production to counterbal- ance the lower price for each unit of grain, even if they were receiving a special pay- ment for taking some land out of produc- tion. As the experience of the United States has shown, it is difficult to dismantle a system of government subsidies for agri- cultural production. Although the 1996 U.S. federal Farm Bill, sometimes called the "Freedom to Farm Act," stated as a goal the phasing out of agricultural subsi- dies, in most years since then, as farmers complained of reduced incomes, the gov- ernment came forward with a special sup- port plan, designed generally as income support. The EU has moved very slowly in the same direction.

By the year 2000, although the EU Council of Ministers of Agriculture had promised to move forward on reform of the CAP, no significant progress had been made. In particular, no progress had been made in the reform of the overproduction of dairy products, where the EU produces 20-25 percent above domestic consumption. This sector is particularly difficult to reform, because many of the dairy farmers are smaller farmers who would fail without the support system, and most governments within the EU are committed to the maintenance of the smaller agricultural owners, Europe's family farms. The extent to which dairy farming in the EU is subsidized is shown by the fact that the cost of producing dairy products in Australia and New Zealand determines the world price, but the cost of production in the EU is about twice that in Australia and New Zealand.

One further complication in the reform of the CAP lies with the export subsidies provided the wholesalers or dealers in agricultural produce. Since the farmers of the EU produced more than could be sold within the EU, provision had to be made for the excess. For this, dealers received a special export subsidy to enable them to sell the excess outside the EU at the much lower world price for the product. This subsidy has been particularly criticized by those nations, including the United States, that produce agricultural products for the world market. (The United States

also provides some export subsidies, but not as great as those provided in the EU.) In the year 2000 it appeared that until the EU changed its system of internal price supports so it would no longer provide incentives for farmers to increase output, no solution for this problem was in sight.

One possible solution to the problem of agricultural surpluses has been the development of marketing cooperatives. Cooperatives are popular in Denmark, and an extensive system has existed there for some time. In recent years, cooperatives have spread widely in France, which has both regional cooperatives, embracing all farmers in a region, and national cooperatives for particular crops. In other countries, they have not proved so successful. In the United Kingdom and Germany, the food-processing industries have gained increasing control of markets. Many of these companies contract directly with farmers for the production of agricultural products that they then process before passing them on to the grocery stores.

ENVIRONMENT. One factor that is assuming increasing influence over European agriculture is environmental concerns. The heavy use of fertilizers, pesticides, and herbicides on EU farms has created damaging environmental conditions in some countries. The amount of cow manure generated in the Netherlands

MODERN LIVESTOCK PERILS

Despite technological advances in agriculture, modern European countries are not immune to calamitous problems. In 1996, for example, British beef was banished from European Union (EU) countries after it was reported that bovine spongiform encephalopathy—a cattle ailment popularly known as "mad cow disease"—could be transmitted to humans. Farmers had to slaughter millions of beef cattle infected with this slow-to-develop disease. In early 2001 their problems were compounded by an outbreak of foot-and-mouth disease among several varieties of livestock, and the European Union banned Britain from exporting *any* meat or milk products or live animals.

by its super-efficient dairy industry is more than the land of the entire country could absorb. The Dutch government subsidizes a company that composts some of this manure and sells it abroad as fertilizer for flowers. The Netherlands also introduced a system to compensate pig farmers who reduced the number of pigs they raised. Sweden compensates farmers who reduce the runoff from their farms, a growing problem as the nitrogen content in European water rises from fertilizer runoff. The EU has introduced a program to compensate those who set land aside for environmental protection, but more needs to be done to bring the EU's production levels closer to domestic demand, as well as to reduce the cost to consumers and taxpayers of the subsidies paid to EU farmers.

ORGANIC FARMING AND BIOENGINEERING. Several European countries, including the Czech Republic, France, and the United Kingdom, have introduced programs to encourage organic farming. At the beginning of the twenty-first century, however, a mere 2 percent of European crops were raised organically. Some scientists believe that environmental improvement could be generated if crops were developed that could ward off the insects that attack them, or that provide their own nitrogen, as the leguminous plants (peas and beans) do.

The European environmental movement has strongly opposed genetically modified foods, which some of its members have labeled "Frankenfoods" after Mary Shelley's classic horror story, *Frankenstein* (1818), in which a man-made monster eventually self-destructs. Ways need to be found, however, to reduce the use of chemicals in farming.

Nancy M. Gordon

FOR FURTHER STUDY

Bowler, Ian R. *The Geography of Agriculture in Developed Market Economies.* New York: John Wiley & Sons, 1992.

Food and Agriculture Organization of the United Nations. *Yearbook: Production.* Vol. 50 (1996). Rome: Food and Agriculture Organization of the United Nations, 1997.

Reid, T. R. "Feeding the Planet." *National Geographic* (October, 1998): 56-74.

Stecklow, Steve. "Germination: How a U.S. Gadfly and a Green Activist Started a Food Fight." *The Wall Street Journal* 234 (November 30, 1999): A1, A10.

Thayer, Ann M. "Ag Biotech Food: Risky or Risk Free?" *Chemical and Engineering News* 77, no. 44 (November 1, 1999): 11-20.

Zwingle, Erle. "Olive Oil: Elixir of the Gods." *National Geographic* (September, 1999): 66-81.

INFORMATION ON THE WORLD WIDE WEB

A good site for detailed European agricultural information is that of the United Nations' Food and Agriculture Organization (FAO), which features a searchable database organized by individual country. (www.fao.org)

Tower Bridge, which spans the Thames River in London's East End, was built in the late nineteenth century. It was one of the first modern bridges whose span opened upward to permit ships to pass beneath it. Like London's other bridges, it is named after its location, which is near the Tower of London. (PhotoDisc)

Paris's Pompidou Center, which was completed in 1979, is an art museum with an unusual design feature: All its elevators and escalators are external to the main structure. (PhotoDisc)

The switchbacks on this Tyrolian mountain road in northern Italy are indicative of why tunneling is important in Europe's Alps. (American Stock Photography)

Autobahn in Frankfort, Germany, which began building its national highway network in the early 1930's. (PhotoDisc)

A Eurostar train enters the Channel Tunnel at Calais, in northern France, beginning its journey under the English Channel to Dover in Great Britain. A major development in European transportation links, the tunnel under the channel, known popularly as the "Chunnel," largely replaced ferry traffic. (AP/Wide World Photos)

Train station in Helsinki, Finland. (PhotoDisc)

Gondolas—the classical form of transportation through the canals of Venice, Italy. (PhotoDisc)

Hedged-lined roads are found throughout the English countryside. (PhotoDisc)

Shipping containers. Europe's principal ports have grown in importation along with the widespread adoption of containerization—the creation of large box-carlike containers into which smaller items are packed. The containers themselves are then transported on vessels designed specifically for that purpose, moved by large cranes specially adapted to handling containers. (PhotoDisc)

Interior of the London Stock Exchange, the leading stock exchange in Europe. (PhotoDisc)

Barge in a French canal. Europeans have used natural and artificial waterways for trade for millennia. Trade carried by ship or barge is cost effective and remains preferred for the shipment of such goods as coal, iron ore, and grain. (PhotoDisc)

Amsterdam, the primate city, financial hub, and one of two capitals of the Netherlands. (PhotoDisc)

Aberdeen, Scotland, is at the mouth of two rivers: the Dee—after which it is named—and the Don (pictured). (R. Kent Rasmussen)

Athens, Greece, from the Acropolis. (PhotoDisc)

Barcelona is Spain's second-largest city and the center for the Catalonia region. Located on Spain's northeastern Mediterranean coast, it is a major seaport and manufacturing area. (PhotoDisc)

Neuschwanstein castle built in the Bavarian Alps as a country palace for Bavarian king Louis II in the late nineteenth century. The castle's neo-Romanesque design was inspired by operas of German composer Richard Wagner. (PhotoDisc)

Cork, Ireland. Bridge over the Lee River. (PhotoDisc)

Coastline near Llanes on the Spanish coast of the Bay of Biscay. (PhotoDisc)

Copenhagen, the capital, largest city, and chief seaport of Denmark, was founded as a fishing village and still maintains its ties to the sea. (PhotoDisc)

Cornwall's western tip, Land's End, is the westernmost point in Great Britain. There is nothing between it and North America but water. (PhotoDisc)

Looking west toward America, across Land's End. (R. Kent Rasmussen)

Edinburgh, Scotland, looking across Old Town toward Edinburgh Castle. (PhotoDisc)

Mount Etna is one of Europe's most active, and potentially most dangerous, volcanoes. In this satellite image of Sicily, a faint trail of vapor can be seen escaping from the snowcapped mountain. (Corbis)

The capital of central Italy's Florence provence, the city of Florence is built on the Arno River. Famed for its art treasures, Florence was the center of the Italian Renaissance and was capital of much of Italy through the early nineteenth century. (PhotoDisc)

Hadrian's Wall was built by the Romans in the early second century C.E. to protect England from invasion from the North. (PhotoDisc)

Farms and hedgerows in southwestern Ireland's Kerry County. (American Stock Photography)

INDUSTRIES

Europe is the historical center and birthplace of modern industry. It became an important power that influenced the world both politically and economically. Natural resources found in the region were primarily responsible for Europe's economic expansion and large global influence.

EARLY HISTORY. The Industrial Revolution began in the late eighteenth century and spread rapidly through Great Britain. Life in Europe was transformed as new methods of production were used and machines became power-driven. The use of machines contributed to increased production and lower costs. As a result, European living standards were raised. Transportation and communication improved, and many European countries became world-leading industrial centers.

An abundance of coal and iron ore contributed to Europe's success as an industrialized society. Because these two resources are used together to make steel, they provided the basis for the growth of heavy industry—machinery and equipment needed for mines and factories. Early centers of modern manufacturing began developing in northern and central England as well as the Ruhr and Saxony regions of Germany, northern France, and Silesia in Poland. Heavy industry manufacture continued in Europe in the nineteenth and early twentieth centuries. European products such as iron and steel, textiles, ships, railroad equipment, and motor vehicles have long been important. After World War II, chemicals, electronic equipment, and other high-technology items were the leading growth industries. France and Germany continue to be leaders in manufacturing as a result of the vast deposits of mineral wealth found there.

Major coal deposits exist in Britain, the Ruhr District of Western Germany, Belgium, Poland, the Czech Republic, and northern France. Western Germany, northeastern France, northern Sweden, and the Balkan Peninsula contain major deposits of iron ore. Overall, the greatest concentration of manufacturing occurs in the central part of the continent.

Coal
Page 1318

Some Western European countries do not have the raw materials found in France and Germany. They may specialize in light industry, which is geared more toward making consumer goods than heavy machinery. Denmark and the Netherlands, for example, specialize in textiles or food processing. In most European nations, a large percentage of the workforce is employed in service industries. For instance, Switzerland has enjoyed great success in finance and banking.

OTHER MINERAL AND ENERGY RESOURCES. Potash, an element used in fertilizer, is one of Europe's two major mineral resources. It is found in Spain, France, and Germany. The second resource is bauxite, the source of aluminum, located in the Yugoslav republics, Hungary, and southern France. Uranium, zinc, lead, gold, silver, manganese, nickel, and copper are also mined in substantial amounts in Europe. For economic reasons, transportation and industrial centers have frequently developed near the locations of mineral deposits.

Fuel for homes and factories in Europe is provided by a wide variety of resources. In some Western European homes, a vegetable matter usually composed of mosses, or peat, was burned as fuel. Only in the Republic of Ireland does peat remain a significant source of fuel for generating electricity and for household use.

Nuclear power plant Page 1309

RECENT DEVELOPMENTS. At the start of the twenty-first century, most European countries rely on coal, oil, natural gas, and nuclear and hydroelectric power as energy sources. The production of petroleum and natural gas from offshore fields in the North Sea is a new and important extracting industry. Discovered in the 1960's and 1970's, these oil and natural gas reserves increased energy sources in Western and Eastern Europe. Good sources of power for electricity can be found in the continent's fast-flowing streams and rivers, particularly in Norway, Sweden, France, Switzerland, Austria, Italy, and Spain. Major hydroelectric installations in these countries contribute large portions of the annual output of electricity. In France, Great Britain, Germany, Belgium, Sweden, Switzerland, and Finland, nuclear power is important.

In countries and regions that have become industrialized more recently, coal has not been as significant. Hydroelectricity has played a strong modern-day role in the absence of local supplies of coal. In Italy and Sweden, hydroelectricity has influenced the location of industry. About 75 percent of all manufacturing in Italy takes place in the Po Basin in the north. No single factor accounts for the pattern of industry within that region. Cities with well-developed transportation facilities have a distinct advantage, since most industrial materials must be brought into the area from outside. Those are often old places with rich cultural traditions, such as Milan and Turin. There is more choice in where industries are located, however, because of the availability of inexpensive hydroelectric power over wide areas. In central Sweden, conditions are similar to those on Italy's northern plain.

Wherever they exist in Europe, untapped sources of hydroelectric power are bound to be developed. Coal-fired electricity-generating plants can create international air pollu-

Wooden shoes, or clogs, are closely associated with the Netherlands; however, they are manufactured in many northern European countries. (PhotoDisc)

tion and acid rain; therefore, hydroelectric power is preferred as a source of energy. In addition, inexpensive superconductors have been developed, making the cost of transmitting electricity from remote areas through hydropower cheaper.

MAJOR MANUFACTURING INDUSTRIES. Manufacturing industries include the production of airplanes, automobiles and trucks, pharmaceuticals, and electronic goods. The aerospace industry in Europe remains fragmented, with relatively small, protected markets. This is because each of the major countries wants to maintain control over its own portion for defense-related security. However, Western Europe has attempted some cooperative projects such as the European fighter project, the Ariane rockets, and the Airbus. These projects made Western Europe the world's second-largest plane maker, but the complexities of cooperation led to problems, including additional costs.

The automobile industry is partly owned by foreign companies and partly nationalized, making it difficult to expand further. In the 1950's, some European plants were opened by U.S. companies. A complex set of interrelationships was built throughout Europe among plants, factories specializing in producing engines and transmission systems, and independent parts suppliers. Assembly plants were also built in the United Kingdom by Japanese carmakers. Some European firms, such as Peugot Citroen of France and BMW of Germany, continued to be owned privately.

Western Europe is a strong leader in the global pharmaceutical industry. More than two-thirds of the world's pharmaceutical exports come from Western Europe. One-half the world's total is produced in that subregion, but less than 30 percent is consumed there. In contrast, the United States produces 30 percent and consumes 34 percent. The leading Western European pharmaceutical companies are based in Germany and the United Kingdom.

The spectrum of the electronics industries, which includes computers, consumer goods such as stereo sound systems and televisions, and integrated circuits and microprocessors, has grown since the 1950's. Multinational corporations have played a particularly significant role in the growth of the electronics industry. U.S. and Japanese corporations both invested in Western Europe to make use of scientific and technical labor and to gain access to defense industry customers. By the 1990's, Western Europe produced 20 percent of the world's electronics. The only global electronics companies that originated and are headquartered in Europe are Thomson of France and Philips of the Netherlands. To compete with Japanese dominance in many sectors of the electronics industry, Western European and U.S. firms began linking their resources in the 1990's.

SERVICE SECTOR. Although Western Europe has fallen behind the United States and Japan as a world leader in manufacturing, its service sector nearly equals that of the United States. More than 65 percent of the total workforce in most Western European countries was employed in the service sector in the late 1990's. Where manufacturing dominates, in Germany for example, the service sector is about 50 percent. In recent years, older industries have closed or cut their labor forces, contributing to a deindustrialization phase in Western Europe's industrial countries. As a result, service industries are enjoying greater prominence.

As the population of countries increased, they became wealthier, strong social welfare programs were instituted, and service jobs grew in significance. Providers of service jobs in education, health care, and retailing can be state-controlled or private corporations. The service sector has seen major growth in the areas of tourism and producer services.

TOURISM. More than 320 million foreigners visit Western Europe each year, the most in the international market. In terms of international tourist receipts, eight of the eleven top places were European countries. Receipts in Austria, Great Britain, France, Germany, Italy, and Spain totaled $134 billion in 1997. In comparison, the United States reported $75 billion in international tourist receipts the same year.

From 1970 to the 1990's, the number of incoming and outgoing internal and international tourists in Europe doubled. New lifestyle expectations along with increased leisure time and incomes were largely responsible for the industry's growth. The main receiving areas were the Alpine and Mediterranean countries. Within Western Europe, the coastal, rural, and historical urban areas also saw increased tourism. The largest number of tourists in other European countries came from the United Kingdom and Germany.

Each country's government encourages tourism. It is also promoted by regional investment in infrastructure such as roads and facilities by the European Union, and through agreements on customs, currency regulation, and the sharing of health facilities. Tourist boards promote the facilities within individual countries. Tourism was Europe's largest industry in the mid-1990's and generated one of every eight jobs in the European Union.

Regional development is often encouraged by tourism, since the less populated rural and coastal areas are distant from the urban areas of industrial growth. Further population loss from rural areas is prevented by increasing local economic activity through tourism. Development of tourism in an area may also improve an area's available facilities and attract other forms of employment. However, jobs in the tourism sector tend to be low paying and low skill, lessening the possible benefit to the local economy.

PRODUCER SERVICES. Along with manufacturing and tourism, producer services such as banking, insurance, legal, and advertising are important in generating economic development. Producer services are those involved in the output of goods and services. Since the 1970's, jobs in producer services increased in Western Europe by one-fourth to one-third. Despite gains in productivity from the use of information technology, producer services employ approximately 10 percent of the labor force. Major cities, including Paris, London, Munich, Frankfurt, and Amsterdam, are the centers of these services, as proximity to a highly qualified labor source is necessary.

After the mid-1980's, a series of mergers and takeovers led to a decrease in the number of large producer service firms. The range of services was broadened as insurance, accountancy, banking, and property services industries were combined. The influence of centrally located specialist firms was extended nationwide and internationally as more local firms were taken over. Transactions of world financial significance occur in the region.

WESTERN EUROPEAN COUNTRIES. The countries of Western Europe include France, Belgium, the Netherlands, Luxembourg, Germany, the United Kingdom, and Ireland. France enjoys an abundance of raw materials, including iron ore, bauxite, and uranium. Large deposits of antimony, magnesium, pyrites, tungsten, and

Urban electric car developed in France. (PhotoDisc)

certain radioactive minerals can also be found there. It also boasts well-developed sources of hydroelectric power and is a leader in the peaceful use of nuclear energy. France is a leading manufacturing country, one of the major suppliers of metals and minerals in Western Europe, and competitive in all major branches of industrial activity. Its chemical, aluminum, mechanical, and electrical industries are among the world's largest. The automobile industry in France produces more than three million vehicles per year. The high level of technological development France is experiencing is largely due to the electronics, telecommunications, and aerospace industries. Its first earth-orbit-ing satellite was launched in 1965, and France has continued to pursue an active space research program.

Iron, steel, and metal fabricating are the leading sectors in Belgium. The country's industries contribute 33 percent of the total value of the goods and services produced annually (GNP) and $50 billion in exports. However, Belgium must import most raw materials, fuel, transportation equipment, machinery, and approximately one-fourth of its food because it has no significant stores of natural resources. The highly skilled labor force and managerial expertise among Belgians are largely responsible for the country's development and prosperity.

Luxembourg, a country the size of Rhode Island, boasts the highest per capita GNP in the European Union. Iron and steel account for half of Luxembourg's total industrial production. Financial activities also flourish there. Luxembourg has more than sixty large banks employing a large number of workers and making the country one of the world's most important financial centers.

The Netherlands is unique to Western Europe because it is unusually dependent on foreign trade. This dependency stems from its limited base of natural resources, particularly oil, natural gas, and coal, and the fact that it is located at the mouth of the Rhine River, Western Europe's busiest waterway. An adaptable business community and a highly skilled labor force back the modernized and competitive industry. Although the manufacturing sector has seen a decline, service-related employment continues to rise.

Germany's major industries are steel and iron, electrical equipment, machinery, chemicals, and automobiles. Threats to the continued development of Germany's economy lie in its reliance on imported oil. About one-third of the oil imported is consumed by the industrial sector.

*Copenhagen
Page 1378*

Major industries in the United Kingdom include aircraft, railroad equipment, shipbuilding, motor vehicles and parts, communications and electronic equipment, coal, petroleum, production machinery, electric power equipment, metals, chemicals, paper and paper products, textiles, clothing, and food processing. Britain, the oldest industrialized economy in the world, ranks fourth behind the United States, Germany, and Japan in world trade. The United Kingdom contributes more than 5 percent of the world's exports.

In the late twentieth century, the Republic of Ireland emerged from a mainly rural nation to one with a growing economy, low unemployment, and increasing prosperity. In 1997, 63 percent of the labor force was in services, 27 percent in manufacturing and construction, and 10 percent in agriculture, forestry, and fishing; Ireland's literacy rate was 98 percent. The computer, chemical, and pharmaceutical industries are thriving in Ireland, joining more traditional industries such as food products, brewing, textiles, glass, and crystal. Its exports in 1998 totaled $61 billion, with the European Union and the United States as its major trading partners.

NORTHERN EUROPEAN COUNTRIES. The region of Northern Europe consists of Denmark, Finland, Norway, Sweden, Iceland, the former colonies of Denmark in Greenland, and the Faeroe Islands. Prior to the recent development of manufacturing and service industries in the 1990's, the economies of Northern European countries depended on primary products—those involving the production of natural resources—obtained through farming, fishing, and forestry. However, the small, stable populations in the region made it possible to advance economically.

Much of Denmark's economy is based on high-tech manufacturing. The entrance to the Baltic Sea was controlled by the port at Copenhagen, and it acted as a center for the transshipment of goods. With government officials and financial services, it is now a major manufacturing and service center. Industries include machinery and equipment, electronics, food processing, shipbuilding, construction, furniture and other wood products, and clothing and textiles.

The discovery of oil and natural gas in the North Sea in the 1970's gave Norway a new resource that constitutes half its income. Norway was the second-largest oil exporter in the world in 1995, but production fell after 1997. Encouraging increased tourism and improving infrastructure are a more recent focus.

The largest and most industrialized Scandinavian country is Sweden. In the northern part of the country, large deposits of iron ore are found, as well as smaller deposits of metallic minerals, including copper, lead, manganese, and zinc. Industries including electronics, furniture, glassware, ships, and stainless steel products exist in the zone between Stockholm and Goteborg.

Finland has few mineral resources. Its greatest natural resource is in its forest, which contributes half of its export value annually. Along the southern coast, where most people live, are metal, machinery, and shipbuilding industry centers. A textile industry exists in Tampere. High-tech manufacturing based on the Nokia mobile telephone factory is located in Oulu.

Some mining, carried out by international companies, takes place in Greenland. The minerals, however, are largely shipped to the United States directly. A tourist industry is growing in Iceland.

ALPINE EUROPEA. The Alpine countries of Austria and Switzerland lack natural resources. Products that require high-skill inputs and labor are produced in Switzerland, since most raw materials for industry must be imported. Items that do not lend themselves to mass production, such as turbines and power generators; specialized quality products such as cheese and chocolate; pharmaceuticals; and chemicals are also made there. Switzerland has one of the world's highest levels of living, but it depends on the world economy for its prosperity. Exports, international banking, the insurance and transportation industries, and a highly developed tourist industry are the basis of the country's economic success.

Tourism in Austria, based in the mountains and in towns associated with classical music, is also promising. With more than seventeen million visitors in 1996, Austria's income from tourism exceeded that of Switzerland. Manufacturing industries are located near small deposits of metal ores, specifically in Vienna and in towns along the southern flank of the Alps.

MEDITERRANEAN EUROPEAN COUNTRIES. The four main countries of Mediterranean Europe are Italy, Spain, Greece, and Portugal.

Italy contains no significant deposits of iron ore or coal. Its most important mineral resource is natural gas deposits. The gas supply is rapidly being depleted, and therefore is not a long-term source of energy.

The main industrial area of Spain is around Barcelona. There, recent automobile production and high-tech industries are mixed with established textile industries. A Volkswagen car plant is located in Pamplona, and metal-based and machine-making industries can be found in the Bilbao area on the northern coast.

Barcelona
Page 1375

Athens remains the main industrial center of Greece. Despite its air pollution, the capital city attracts many tourists. In 1996 the sunny climate, historic relics, and islands attracted nine million visitors.

Athens
Page 1375

Portugal is less industrialized than Spain or Italy. The joint Ford-Volkswagen project to manufacture multipurpose vehicles was the largest industrial development in the 1990's. A 15 percent addition to Portugal's export income is expected when full production is achieved. Tourism is also a major industry in Portugal.

BALKAN AND EASTERN EUROPEAN COUNTRIES. In contrast to Western Europe, Eastern Europe—which includes Poland, Romania, the Czech Republic, Hungary, Serbia and Montenegro, Bulgaria, Slovakia, Croatia, Bosnia-Herzegovina, Albania, Macedonia, and Slovenia—is deficient in industrial resources. Energy

Columns of the ancient Parthenon building show the black crusts caused by modern Athens's industrial air pollution. (U.S. Geological Survey)

resources, iron ore, and other minerals are scarce. The few resources that exist are distributed unequally, may be of poor quality, and are costly to use.

Most of the only substantial deposit of high-quality coal in the region lies in the Silesian-Moravian field in Poland and the Czech Republic. Thus, more coal is produced in Poland than in any other Eastern European country. The Czech Republic has a high-quality coal field of secondary importance. Bosnia, eastern Serbia, and northwestern Croatia are dotted with small deposits of high-quality hard coal, and Europe's largest lignite field is located in the Serbian province of Kosovo. Used for both domestic heating and the production of electricity, low-quality coals are widely scattered throughout Eastern Europe.

A shortage of natural gas and oil also exists in Eastern Europe. At present rates of production, the total reserves will last only a few years. Therefore, most European countries are dependent on imported natural gas and petroleum. As oil and gas consumption increase, dependence on foreign sources will continue to increase, contributing to a rise in prices. The problem of more money leaving than coming in is therefore made worse.

With the exception of the Balkan countries, hydroelectric potential in Eastern Europe is also limited. Little developed hydroelectric power exists presently, and existing plants are small. The countries of the former Yugoslavia have the greatest potential for development, because extensive construction to greatly increase electrical output has begun.

Because of the scarcity of good-quality energy resources, nuclear power is of interest to leaders of Eastern European countries. Nuclear generation of electricity is limited at present but is expected to increase. Uranium, used in nuclear power plants, is mined in much of the region.

Another concern for Eastern Europeans is the short supply of ferrous and nonferrous metals, including iron ore. Poland contains Eastern Europe's largest iron and steel industry but still relies on Russia and the Ukraine for iron ore. Although deposits of metal are relatively small and their production is limited, throughout the former Yugoslavia a variety of ferrous and nonferrous metals can be found. Other resources found in Eastern Europe include major mercury deposits in Slovenia; lead and zinc ores, copper, and chromium in Serbia; bauxite and iron ore in Bosnia-Herzegovina; and manganese, uranium, and chromium in Macedonia. The most important metallic ores and metals in other Eastern European countries are bauxite in Hungary and chromium in Albania. Sulfur, mined in Poland, is the region's most notable nonmetallic mineral since it is used as a raw material for chemical industries.

The area that extends across the northern part of the continent from Western Europe to the western Czech Republic and western Poland is highly industrialized. The Silesian-Moravian district of Poland, the Czech Republic, and the Czech Bohemian Basin contain the greatest concentration of industry there. After World War II, Poland acquired the Silesian-Moravian district, which had been Germany's second-largest region of heavy industry. A small section of Silesia was given to what was then Czechoslovakia. Because of the local resources of coal, Silesia is now Poland's main heavy-industrial district. Along with the coal mining and production of iron and steel occurring in the region, agricultural machinery, machine tools, and a variety of chemicals are also

manufactured. Ostrava, the Czech Republic's iron and steel center, dominates the Czech section of Silesia.

Prague, the capital and largest city of the Czech Republic, is located within the western part of the country in the Bohemian Basin. The basin is an iron- and steel-producing district but also has industries such as foods, machinery, and chemicals. Prague is considered the country's industrial production center.

*Prague
Page 1439*

Outside the primary industrial areas, most manufacturing occurs in the large cities. Diverse industries are found in Belgrade, Budapest, and Warsaw. The smaller centers of production are typically found near the location of a specific raw material.

ENVIRONMENTAL DEGRADATION. Under the Soviet model for economic development, the output of goods was the measure of success. However, in attempting to achieve high output, little concern was given to the environment. Natural resources were undervalued and usually wasted. In Romania, Bulgaria, the Czech Republic, Hungary, and Poland, for example, the water consumption rates are twice those in Western Europe. Furthermore, no money was available for environmental safety because of limited capital. As a result, toxic wastes were dumped into major rivers or on patches of land.

In 2000 no plant or animal life could be found in the Sava River or in 90 percent of Poland's rivers. Poland was named the most polluted country in the world by the Polish Academy of Sciences. This is understandable given that only 5 percent of the sewage in Warsaw was being treated, while the rest was dumped into the Vistula River. In addition, 25 percent of Poland's land was rated as unfit to grow food that humans or animals could consume safely. Environmentally induced diseases, such as respiratory illness or cancer, were expected to afflict one-third of Poland's population.

In much of Eastern Europe, pollution of the environment remains a major problem. The bulk of the responsibility falls upon industry. Sulfur dioxide from the burning of low-grade lignite and coals is air pollution's major source. It has been estimated that in Prague and Bohemia, the levels of sulfur dioxide are twenty times the country's average. In that part of the Czech Republic, life expectancy is eleven years less than in the rest of the country. Acid rain is another problem: 71 percent of forests in Czech and Slovak lands, 48 percent of those in Poland, and 43 percent in Bulgaria are estimated to have been damaged.

Solving the problems of environmental pollution will not be easy. Although signs of increased international cooperation exist, it is expensive to create safe dumps for hazardous waste, build treatment facilities for sewage, and install desulfurization equipment. Western capital will likely be needed for the complex task of halting the damage and beginning the cleanup.

Anne Galantowicz

FOR FURTHER STUDY

Bonomi, Kathryn. *Major World Nations: Italy*. Philadelphia: Chelsea House, 1999.

Bryson, Bill. "A Jolly Good Time in Blackpool, England." *National Geographic* (January, 1998): 34-51.

Hargrove, Jim. *Enchantment of the World: Germany*. Chicago: Childrens Press, 1991.

Lace, William M. *Modern Nations of the World: England*. San Diego, Calif.: Lucent Books, 1997.

Marshall, Bruce, ed. *The Real World: Understanding the Modern World Through the New Geography*. London, England: Marshall Editions, 1991.

Rodgers, Mary, et al., eds. *Spain . . . in Pictures*. Minneapolis: Lerner, 1995.

Sookram, Brian. *Major World Nations: France*. Philadelphia: Chelsea House, 1999.

ENGINEERING PROJECTS

Modern European engineering generally is dated from about 1750, when the kind of thinking promoted during the Enlightenment began to dominate Western thought. This thinking involved the idea that all problems could be solved by the application of reason, and that there were natural laws governing all phenomena that could be discovered through the application of reason.

STEAM POWER. The first steam engines used the weight of the atmosphere to perform work and were devised in large part to aid in removing water from mines. The deep mining of metals and coal was difficult, and impossible in many places, because mine shafts tended to fill with water after a certain depth had been reached. The first engine capable of doing work was that of Thomas Savery, who devised a machine called the "miner's friend" in 1698. This device used a series of valves and containers that permitted the weight of the atmosphere to push water in mines upward into a container that had been evacuated by steam, then other valves were opened to let it drain out.

Credit for the first real steam engine goes to Thomas Newcomen, who devised a working engine in about 1712 that used the principle of a moving piston inside a cylinder to perform work. It operated a pump by evacuating air from the inside of the cylinder using steam, then the weight of the atmosphere pushed down the piston. This was the first machine to translate heat energy into motion. James Watt, a Scot, devised the first efficient engine and the first that could be made small enough

to be used for transportation and general power supply. Watt's major advances involved attaching an external condenser so that the entire piston and cylinder could remain hot, and devising servo mechanisms so that valves could be opened and closed mechanically. Watt's first engine went into service in 1776; between 1840 and 1880, the steam power in use rose from 2 million horsepower to 28 million.

Invented by J. M. Jacquard in 1801, the Jacquard loom revolutionized the weaving of fabric by mechanizing the process and eventually eliminating the need for hand-loom weavers. Since it operated by using punched paper cards to program its operations, some view it as the forerunner of the computer.

AGRICULTURE. Throughout history, food has been produced by a combination of human and animal muscle power working with simple tools. The basic implement was the "scratch plow," which loosened the soil so that seeds flung by hand could sprout. Fields were weeded by hand and crops harvested by the armful, then seeds were freed by trampling them or by using a flail. In the late eighteenth century, technology began to change agriculture. The moldboard plow was invented in the late eighteenth century, and Jethro Tull's seed drill planted seeds evenly and at a uniform depth.

A Scotsman, Patrick Bell, devised the first reaper in the early nineteenth century. A machine that was the forerunner of the modern combine, because it used a rotating cylinder to thresh grain, was invented in 1784 by Andrew Meikle. Although the early machines were powered by animals, steam power soon was used to operate them. These applications of engineering to agriculture helped to dramatically increase the supply of food in the nineteenth century, which made the Industrial Revolution possible by freeing millions of people from the task of growing food.

TRANSPORTATION. The earliest form of engineered transportation was the sailing ship. Early sailing ships had fairly flat bottoms. They were slow, but relatively safe. In Europe, they generally were made from oak beams and planks. By the mid-nineteenth century, iron began to be used for bracing and for making chains. The sailing ship was epitomized by the clipper ship, a ship based on traditional design but which could carry much more sail, thus increasing speed. Iron ships powered by steam were first developed in Great Britain in the 1850's but were hampered by the huge amounts of coal they required. Steel ships appeared in the late nineteenth century.

The rapid expansion of the iron industry in the nineteenth century led engineers to contemplate the construction of ships made of iron instead of wood. Isambard Kingdom Brunel, a successful designer of railways and bridges, agreed in 1853 to build a huge iron steamship that, in principle, could make the trip from England to Australia without taking on new supplies of coal. The *Great Eastern* went into service several years later, and, although its engines were too inefficient to perform its original purpose, it remained in trans-Atlantic service for thirty years.

Rail transportation also largely related to the introduction of lightweight steam engines. The idea of having wagons based on rails was an old one and had been used in mines for centuries. The wagons were pulled by horses and rested on wooden rails that sometimes had iron surfaces. The first underground railway was put into service in London in 1863 and, although extremely expensive, became common in major cities toward the end of the century.

Completed in the fourteenth century, Italy's 179-foot-tall (54.5 meters) Leaning Tower of Pisa has gradually moved to a position more than 16.5 feet (5 meters) out of perpendicular. Preventing it from toppling over has became a major modern engineering project in itself. (PhotoDisc)

The automobile came into existence during the late nineteenth century. Karl Benz is generally regarded as the father of the automobile, having constructed a three-wheeled machine that could reach the speed of eight miles per hour. A fellow German, Gottlieb Daimler, devised the first high-speed engine and produced four-wheeled machines in a factory near Stuttgart.

AIRCRAFT. Humans have always dreamed of flying. Throughout European history, many designs were produced based on the ornithopter principle, that is, machines with flapping wings that resembled the flight of birds. Such machines always failed. The first manned flights took place in France in the 1780's when the concept of the hot-air balloon appeared. Hydrogen had been isolated and was quickly applied to balloon lifting. German engineers developed the rigid body air frame that is most closely associated with the name of Count F. von Zeppelin, who launched his first airship in 1900. These rigid-frame airships were powered by internal combustion engines. One of the most important modern European engineering achievements was the building of the supersonic airplane, the Concorde. It was built by a consortium established by Great Britain and France. It was the only supersonic passenger aircraft in operation at the end of the twentieth century.

IRON AND STEEL. Throughout history, the main building material has been wood, although in Europe, limestone and marble often were used for expensive and elaborate buildings. In the mid-nineteenth century, however, cast iron became a popular building material. The great exposition building known as the Crystal Pal-

Paris's Eiffel Tower is the world's most famous wrought-iron edifice. (PhotoDisc)

ace in London's 1850's exposition is the best example of this kind of construction.

Construction using wrought iron increased during the nineteenth century as well. The best-known example is the famous Eiffel Tower in Paris, created by one of the most outstanding engineers of the nineteenth century, Alexandre Gustave Eiffel. It was originally built as a temporary monument to commemorate the one hundredth anniversary of the French Rev-

Tower Bridge Page 1367

olution in 1889. The tower is 984 feet (300 meters) tall and uses twelve thousand iron beams with a weight of about 7,000 tons (6,300 metric tons) of iron. It symbolized the new industrial age, because until its construction the highest structures in the world were the pyramids of Egypt and the cathedrals. By the year 2000 the highest structures were skyscrapers and transmission towers that symbolized the primacy of business and communication.

Canals
Page 1241

Henry Bessemer's name is closely linked to the production of inexpensive steel, a major engineering achievement. His method raised the annual production of steel in England greatly by making an excellent grade of steel available at a fraction of the former cost. The availability of inexpensive steel was crucial to the introduction of the high-rise buildings that revolutionized urban construction. Bessemer received many honors, including knighthood and a fellowship in the Royal Society, both awarded in 1879.

ROADS. Travelers continually seek better roads, and engineering is critical. Throughout most of human history, roads have been impassible for much of the year. That is because as horses and wagons passed over them, the hooves and wheels displaced earth, and the road would become an indentation in the soil. This indentation collected water, which made the road's condition worse. Until modern times, the best roads were built by the Romans, who used large blocks of stone to create their roads.

Alpine
roads
Page 1368

Modern road building dates from the early nineteenth century and the work of the great civil engineer John Loudon McAdam. A Scot, McAdam developed a fundamental insight that became the key to road building. He realized that the surface of a road matters little, but the firmness and dryness of the underlying bed is critical—if this underlying material can be kept dry and hard, the road will remain serviceable for a long time. He also understood that if a roadbed is kept above grade and water is prevented from infiltrating the soil, the road will remain strong. The word "tarmac," which is often used to describe an airport runway, means that there is a roadbed using McAdam principles that has been given an asphalt surface.

CANALS. The construction of canals is an ancient engineering technology that was perfected in the mid-eighteenth century. Before modern engines, a canal was a waterbed of a uniform width and depth bordered by a towpath on which animals or men could tow barges. Locks are required to enable barges to move to different levels. The most famous European-built canal was the Suez Canal in Egypt. It originally was 92 miles (148 km.) long, 26 feet (8 meters) deep, and 72 feet (22 meters) wide. Its construction was fairly straightforward, mainly involving the massive excavation of sand and clay. By the time it opened in 1867, more than 25 million cubic feet of earth had been moved.

Canal building reached its high point around 1860 when railways began to take over the movement of goods. Many railways were constructed on the rights-of-way of canals that had been filled in. The St. Quentin Canal was opened in 1810 under the regime of Napoleon Bonaparte, linking Belgium and Holland with the French Somme, Oise, and Seine River systems. It allowed water access to Paris and the Channel ports.

TUNNELS. Tunneling was not an important engineering art until the widespread introduction of the railway. Early tunnels, such as those used for canals, were built using the age-old techniques of the miner, which involved sinking shafts and bringing earth out through the shafts. Tunnels designed to accommodate the height of railway cars required new techniques in excavation and shoring, steam-powered equipment, and powerful explosives. The most important European tunnels were those built through the Alps: the Mont Cenis (8 miles/13 km. long), the St. Gotthard (9.5 miles/15 km.), and the Simplon (12 miles/19 km.). These three tunnels were completed between 1870 and 1914.

The Channel Tunnel, or "Chunnel," was completed in 1993, providing a new link between Europe and Great Britain. Although the English Channel separates Great Britain from Europe by only 21 miles (34 km.), it had been a major barrier. In 1987 the United Kingdom and France signed a treaty to build a fixed link between the two countries. The plan was to build a tunnel under the English Channel from Folkstone in the United Kingdom to Calais in France. The "Chunnel" is really three separate tunnels, one for service and ventilation, and two for high-speed trains going different directions. The engineering problems were immense but were overcome by using state-of-the-art continuous mining equipment. Although there have been accidents within the Channel Tunnel, it has been an engineering success. It suffered from massive cost overruns, however, and its financial success remains to be seen.

WATER SUPPLY. Traditionally, humans have drawn their water from rivers, streams, or shallow wells. With the rapid urbanization of Europe, that system rapidly became unsatisfactory because of the extensive pollution of shallow water sources and the accompanying spread of water-borne diseases. Gradually, the cities of Europe developed new systems of water supply and waste disposal. Led by such visionary French engineers as Adolph Alphand and Alfred Durand-Claye in Paris and Joseph Bazalgette in London, engi-

neers also began to build efficient sewers to dispose of human waste and runoff water, and to establish piping systems to provide fresh water from distant sources. By 1885 the work of Louis Pasteur, Robert Koch, and others made it possible to test water for the presence of disease-causing organisms.

Alpine tunnels Page 1436

HIGH EXPLOSIVE. Some engineers think that one good way to measure the modernization of a nation is to measure the amount of high explosive used within its borders. That is because high explosive is used in all aspects of mining and transportation. The first high explosive was nitrocellulose, which was invented by C. F. Schönbein in 1846. Nitroglycerine was discovered in the same year by an Italian, A. Sobrero. The key figure, however, was Alfred Nobel, the inventor of dynamite, which was nitroglycerine that had been absorbed into a special clay that was safe to handle until exploded by a detonator.

Chunnel Page 1369

TELEGRAPHY. The electrical telegraph was invented in Europe in the late eighteenth century. It operated on static electricity. The invention of the storage battery around 1800 and the almost simultaneous discovery of electromagnetism made electrical telegraphy more practical. The first practical use of the telegraph was on the Liverpool-Manchester railway. By 1846 engineers put forth the possibility of laying underwater cables, and the first successful cable linked Great Britain and France in 1851. Almost immediately, engineers began thinking of the possibility of linking Europe and the United States by cable. After several expensive failures, a successful telegraphic cable was completed in 1866. Rapid communication over long distances became possible for the first time.

RADIO. The impact of electrical transmission of information through the air is one of the most important achievements of the modern age. In 1873 James Clerk Maxwell published a treatise in which he mathematically demonstrated that electricity and light are part of the same phenomenon. The theory was experimentally proved by a German physics professor, Heinrich Hertz, in 1885.

The first person to actually transmit messages over a distance was the Englishman Ernest (later Lord) Rutherford. Later, the Italian Guglielmo Marconi made "wireless telegraphy" practical. In 1901 Marconi stunned the world by sending an electrical signal from Europe to the United States.

C. James Haug

FOR FURTHER STUDY

Derry, T. K., and Trevor I. Williams. *A Short History of Technology from the Earliest Times to A.D. 1900.* Oxford, England: Oxford University Press, 1960.

Hankins, Thomas L., and Robert J. Silverman. *Instruments and the Imagination.* Princeton, N.J.: Princeton University Press, 1995.

Landes, David S. *The Unbound Prometheus: Technological Change and Industrial Development in Western Europe from 1750 to the Present.* Cambridge, England: Cambridge University Press, 1969.

Volti, Rudi. *Society and Technological Change.* New York: St. Martin's Press, 1995.

Transportation

The unique geography of the European continent has been critical to the nature of its transportation systems. Not only the seas that surround the continent—the Mediterranean, the North Atlantic, and the North Sea—but also those that intrude into it—the Baltic Sea, the Black Sea, the Irish Sea, and the English Channel—have profoundly affected the system, forcing Europeans to use what has been dubbed "intermodal" transport—transport that uses more than one means of travel between the starting point and the goal.

INFLUENCE OF TERRAIN. Mountain chains on the continent have also shaped Europe's transportation system. The Alps, in the center of the continent, are the most important mountains affecting European transport: Moving goods or people from one side of the Alps to the other requires going either around or through the mountains. The development of mountain passes and tunnels has been critical.

Other mountain ranges have had a defining effect on European transport systems as well. The Pyrenees, which separate the Iberian Peninsula from the rest of the continent, continue to pose a barrier to the integration of the economy of that region with the rest of Europe. The mountains that run from south to north all along the coast of Norway have made it necessary for people of that region to travel by sea. The mountain ranges of the Balkan Peninsula have impeded transport in that area for centuries and still do. The mountains that run down the Italian "boot" make east-west transport in Italy difficult.

The European continent contains several peninsulas—Greece, Italy, the Iberian Peninsula, Denmark, and Scandinavia—and also includes a great many islands. The Greek islands have been politically a part of Greece for at least three thousand years. Sardinia and Corsica have been part of the Italian sphere for almost as long. Probably the most important islands in Europe at the start of the twenty-first century were Britain and Ireland. Numerous small islands are scattered along the coast of Europe as well.

THE INFLUENCE OF HISTORY. History as well as geography has defined Europe's transportation systems. In the modern era, the continent has been organized politically into national groups or countries. National governments have tended to see transport as a means of uniting a country and separating it from other countries. The military uses of transport also have profoundly affected how and where it has been developed. Although much of Europe is in the process of integrating itself into a single political system—the European Union—its transport system still largely reflects the national interests that governed the original layout.

Even ancient history had an important effect on Europe's transport system. The most integrated political system in Europe prior to the European Union, the Roman Empire, designed a transport system to serve its military needs, known as the Roman roads or ways. Many of the modern transport corridors are located in the same place as the Roman ways.

The evolution of technology has pro-

Shipping containers Page 1372

Venice canals Pages 1313, 1370

foundly affected Europe's transport system. As technological advances were made in different sectors, they propelled the development of the transportation system, emphasizing that sector that was best able to provide speedy passage from one point to another. From ancient times until the nineteenth century, travel on water—whether on inland waters, including rivers, or on the open sea—had the technological advantage. From the middle of the nineteenth century, great leaps were made in the technology of land transport, first with railroads and streetcars, then with the automobile.

In the mid-twentieth century, travel by air surpassed all other forms in the speed with which people and products could be moved from one place to another. Despite the great technological advances that have been made in the last century and a half, people still spend about the same amount of time moving from one place to another as they did at the dawn of civilization, about one hour every day.

MARINE TRANSPORTATION. Transportation over water, the oldest method, is still an important part of the European transport system, although its viability has declined in recent years. Within the borders of the separate European countries it is statistically insignificant, but when crossing traditional borders, it assumes a far more important role. One-third of freight traveling from one country within the European continent to another goes by water.

In 1986, 60 percent of freight traffic in Europe went by water, divided about equally between oceangoing vessels traveling the European coastline and barges going along the many European rivers. Of the latter, the most important has been the Rhine, which has been an avenue to the center of the continent for at least two millennia. The Danube, going eastward from

the center of the continent, is next in importance. Since the nineteenth century, vessels have been able to connect via the Main River and a canal between these two major river systems of Europe.

The principal European ports are Rotterdam, Antwerp, Bremen, and Hamburg. Their influence grew with the widespread adoption of containerization—the creation of large boxcar-like containers into which smaller items are packed. The containers themselves are then transported on vessels designed specifically for that purpose, moved by large cranes specially adapted to handling containers. The dominance of Rotterdam, Antwerp, Bremen, and Hamburg, and the decline of lesser European ports, resulted in large part because those four major ports installed facilities capable of handling large numbers of containers. The containers are moved directly to rail cars or trucks for transport to their final destination.

One modern development that has also played a part in Europe's transportation system has been the development of pipelines. The major ports are equipped to handle huge vessels transporting oil and can transfer that oil directly to pipelines that deliver it at low cost to inland distribution points. Forty-four percent of the total tonnage coming into European ports consists of oil.

Two small European countries are major players in maritime transportation: Greece and Norway. Fifty-three percent of Europe's shipping fleet is nominally owned by Greece—including a number of large tankers—some 16 percent of the world's total. Although Europe's share of the shipbuilding industry shrank dramatically in the late twentieth century, it still plays a modest part. Norway's fleet is the fifth-largest in the world, and Norway still builds many ships. Britain, which has for years specialized in shipbrokering, also plays an important role in marine transportation.

RAILROADS. The great transportation innovation of the nineteenth century was the development of railroads. The railroad revolutionized transportation by land, and the national states of Europe, often motivated by military needs, hastened to build railroad systems that linked the parts of the country that could not be reached by water. Between 1850 and 1950, railroads—and their adaptations to local needs, streetcars and subway systems in larger cities—were the major means by which both people and products were moved from place to place. In Russia, where the road system is less well developed, railroads remain the principal means of moving goods long distances.

Europe's railroad system continues to be heavily influenced by the fact that much of it was built by the governments of the various nations. As a result, the connection between the lines of one country and those of another country is often poor. European railroads were generally state-run enterprises, and they were often used for other purposes than economical transport: for defense purposes, or as an income-distribution scheme, providing jobs that were not justified by the economic return. The railroads in Spain and Russia are built to a different gauge; that is, the tracks are wider apart than those in other countries, which makes it difficult or impossible for a single freight car to cross their borders. When goods have to be moved from one car to another, labor costs increase to the point that rail shipment is not economical.

In passenger transport, railroads have been aided by new technology, the high-speed train. The first major high-speed train was created by the French national railway system, running between the capital, Paris, and the city of Lyons in south central France. The trains on this line run at up to 300 miles (500 km.) per hour, and the reduced time needed to travel between Lyons and Paris has drawn many travelers. This line opened in stages between 1981 and 1983 and quickly became profitable. It has

Helsinki train station Page 1369

Entrance to a Paris Metro station. Most of Europe's major cities move large numbers of commuters, shoppers, and travelers through underground subway systems. (PhotoDisc)

*Autobahn
Page 1368*

*Dutch
streetcar
Page 1314*

*Chunnel
Page 1369*

been a model for other high-speed lines that are being constructed. The higher speeds are possible because of new developments in train technology—new electric motors, magnetic guidance systems, and braking systems—as well as changes in the gradient, or slope, of the tracks. A competing technology developed in Germany, magnetic levitation, has not won over large numbers of adherents because its costs are greater. The rapidly expanding lines of high-speed trains in Europe still run on conventional railroad tracks.

The success of the high-speed trains in capturing passengers has led the French national railway, in particular, to begin developing connections between this interurban mode and tracked travel within cities and metropolitan areas. The streetcar, one nineteenth century adaptation of railroads to local travel, has been modified for the suburban-urban structure of modern cities. In Europe, ring lines around the metropolitan core are being designed to connect with the intercity high-speed lines. Modernization of the subway lines that have existed for much of the twentieth century in the major cities of Europe has helped move people from one place to another in record time.

Another new development in the rail sector is the completion of the tunnel underneath the English Channel, known popularly as the "Chunnel." The Chunnel has replaced ferry traffic between Dover, England, and Calais, France, but ferry traffic between Britain and the continent has increased elsewhere. Traffic is carried through the Chunnel by double-track rail, but there are so-called shuttle trains, on which autos can be driven on, carried through the tunnel by rail, and driven off on the other side. It is a striking example of intermodality, that is, the use of two or more modes of travel during a single trip, whether of passengers or goods.

HIGHWAYS AND ROADS. The most startling change in European transportation systems has been the growth in road use. This was made possible by the vast increase in the number of road-using vehicles after 1950. The number of cars per one thousand inhabitants of Europe grew from 22 in 1950 to 353 in 1985; during the same period, the number of commercial vehicles multiplied four times. The increase of truck sizes, from twenty-eight to forty-four tons, largely accounts for the growth in tons-per-mile moved by road.

The volume of freight traffic by road has run up against one of Europe's geographic barriers: the Alps. Switzerland, whose voters have declined to join the European Union, has become alarmed at the heavy volume of freight traffic moving through it. An agreement reached between Switzerland and the European Union in the early 1990's limited trucks of forty-ton capacity to fifty per day, unless all rail capacity was being used. The Swiss also voted to phase out all long-distance truck movement through the country by 2004. In an attempt to mitigate the severity of this ban, Swiss voters approved the construction of two new rail tunnels.

The extremely heavy growth in the use of passenger cars in Europe has been marked by huge traffic bottlenecks, despite the steady growth in the construction of motorways, equivalent to the interstate highways of the United States. There are groups, mostly associated with the environmental movement, that oppose the construction of any more roads on the grounds that it merely spurs more people to use their cars to travel. There can be no doubt that the heavy use of cars has an environmental impact: carbon dioxide emissions have grown since the early 1970's by 76 percent, nitrogen oxide emissions by 68 percent, and hydrocarbons by 41 percent, despite technological improvements in auto engines and the adoption of catalytic converters.

Pressure exists for the increased use of other modes of travel, especially for the movement of freight. Progress in this area may be difficult to achieve, as surveys have shown that most road use, whether for the movement of freight or of passengers, is local. The most heavily traveled roads in Europe are the ring roads that circle most large European cities. In this respect, Europe is no different from the United States, where the most heavily traveled roads are those that carry commuters between home in suburbia and work in the city.

Although there are moves to avoid the construction of additional roads, where political pressure is strong, European countries have tended to move ahead. Ferry service has been expanded in both the south and the north: across parts of the Baltic Sea, between Finland and its neighbors, and between Italy and the Balkans. Some transportation experts see increased use of ferries as a form of intermodal transport. Perhaps the most dramatic innovation is the combination bridge-tunnel at Oresund, linking Sweden and Denmark. This project was promoted heavily by the residents of southern Sweden who will be its primary beneficiaries.

AIR TRANSPORTATION. Transportation by air is uniquely a product of the twentieth century, primarily of the last half of the twentieth century. Between 1960 and 1985, airline passenger growth increased

German road signs. (PhotoDisc)

by a factor of nine. Although originally most airlines were national enterprises, a decision by the European Court of Justice in 1974 that favored competitive airlines sparked the emergence of many smaller lines connecting various European cities. The United States' deregulation of air travel and opening of the air passenger market to competition spurred the Europeans to do the same. The general endorsement of market forces contained in

*English country road
Page 1371*

SHIFTING USE OF SURFACE TRANSPORT MODE IN EUROPE

Between 1950 and 1990 the amount of freight moved by rail in Europe declined dramatically. In 1950 more than half the freight hauled in Europe went by rail; by 1990 that percentage had decreased to less than 20. The rail network, or the railroad infrastructure, declined by 20 percent. The number of freight cars had decreased by 30 percent, even though containerization, to which the railroads were well adapted, had simplified the movement of large quantities of goods.

As shown in the table below, European surface transport modes have been shifting since 1970 from the use of railways and inland waterways to the use of roads.

Year	Roads	Rail	Inland Waterway
1970	50.6	27.8	13.6
1980	60.6	20.2	9.8
1990	69.9	15.4	9.2

the Treaty of Rome of 1957, the founding treaty that led to the European Union in the 1990's, was applied by the European Court of Justice to civil aviation in 1986. As a result, most of the national airlines of Europe were privatized, and the resulting intense competition led to lower fares and a dramatic growth in airline use. In April, 1997, air traffic was fully opened to competitive pressures, and although a few national airlines still exist, they no longer enjoy monopolies.

European airlines have copied the U.S. model of a hub in which a limited number of major airports receive long-haul flights, and passengers are transferred to shorter connecting flights to reach secondary cities. London, Paris, Amsterdam, and Frankfort are Europe's major hubs, and these are the origin and destination of most transcontinental flights. The European reservation system has also followed the American model, adopting its version of the computerized system used by U.S. airlines.

COMMON TRANSPORT POLICY. The Treaty of Rome that created the European Economic Community in 1956, comprising six nations in Central and Western Europe, contained vague references to the creation of a common transport policy as part of the economic integration that was seen as a goal of the treaty. The treaty referred to three areas of commonality: a common market, common policies, and common institutions. However, perhaps in part because of the emphasis on the development of common institutions (the European Parliament, the European Commission, the European Court of Justice, the Council of Ministers), for many years a common transport policy remained largely a long-term goal. Moreover, the action of the various European institutions was constrained by the facts that maritime trade was largely governed by international law and that many transport areas were controlled by bilateral agreements between member and nonmember states.

The development of the European Community, and its conversion into the European Union in 1992, gave new impetus to the development of a common transport policy. The mandate of the treaties establishing the European Union, including the Maastricht treaty of 1993, made the development of an active common transport policy both easier and more necessary. When the borders of the member countries were opened up to free movement of people and goods, decisions came before the various European institutions that affected transport in vital ways.

Institutional changes, such as the growing authority of the European Parliament and the arrival of Neal Kinnock, the former leader of the British Labor Party, as the Minister for Transport of the European Union, also led to significant forward motion on common transport issues. A decision of the European Court of Justice in 1985, taking the Council of Ministers to task for failing to move a common transport policy forward, gave added impetus in the 1990's.

Three major policy areas are the focus of the common transport policy: harmonization of the infrastructure (rail lines, roads, border crossing points, air traffic control systems) and its management; liberalization of the transport market, which means opening the market up to competition; and structural policies, such as common tariffs and tolls at all points in the transport system. There has been a shift from pure efficiency in objectives to at least some recognition of the environmental impact of transport. Transport is only 7 to 8 percent of the gross domestic product

of Europe, but its environmental stresses are large.

Responding to popular pressure in 1996, the European Parliament adopted the Transeuropean Transport Networks (TEN) plan for the European Union. TEN was intended to embrace not just transportation but also communications and energy. The object was to maximize the efficient use of all those resources. One way to do that is through the use of logistics, that is, careful planning of the entire transport sequence of any commodity through the use of computer strategies that correlate the different modes. The aim is intermodality, that is, for each stage of the journey of goods or people to use the most efficient and cost-effective transport mode: road, rail, water transport, air transport, or even pipeline. The goal, made vital by the adoption by industry (for cost and efficiency reasons) of just-in-time manufacturing, was to provide transportation in smaller units over longer distances, with

Motorscooters in Italy, the birthplace of this mode of transport. (PhotoDisc)

less lead time and a high degree of reliability.

The geographic diversity of Europe both assists and complicates this task. A high proportion of the European population lives in a central core of the continent embracing the Low Countries, northern France, southern England, and western Germany. The farther one goes from this core, the sparser the population, especially in the far north of Scandinavia, but also in the Iberian Peninsula and in eastern Europe. The richer countries at the core have agreed to dedicate special funds to enhance the cohesion of these fringe areas, and transport infrastructure is an area where the cohesion funds can be spent. This policy explains the decision to build a motorway through the Balkans to Greece.

One major problem the common transport policy tackled in the 1990's was that of differing national laws. Under restrictive national rules, many carriers were prohibited from picking up freight in countries other than the one in which they were registered, so that many large trucks returned home empty. These restrictions were gradually lifted during the 1990's, so that, in theory, all carriers will be able to carry maximum loads in both directions in the twenty-first century.

Obstacles remain, however, to achieving full efficiency in Europe's transport system. The continued existence of public subsidy for some transport modes that enjoy strong political support, the lack of a system that forces users to pay for the social and environmental costs of transport usage, and the continued application of international law to some transport modes, notably shipping, must be dealt with if a true common transport policy is to be implemented. The prospect of the further loss of land to transport infrastructure—in Los Angeles, 40 percent of the land is used for such a purpose—helps to motivate the administrators of Europe's transport policy, especially when they sit in long lines of passenger cars immobilized by too many vehicles on the existing road system. Until these problems are solved, the system will suffer from economic inefficiency and physical congestion at many places.

Nancy M. Gordon

FOR FURTHER STUDY

Banister, David, et al. *European Transport and Communication Networks.* New York: Wiley, 1995.

Giannopoulos, G., and A. Gillespie. *Transport and Communications Innovation in Europe.* New York: Belhaven, 1993.

Milich, L. V., and R. G. Vanady. "Managing Transboundary Resources." *Environment* 40, no. 2 (October, 1998): 10-15.

Ross, John F. L. *Linking Europe: Transport Policies and Politics in the European Union.* Westport, Conn.: Praeger, 1998.

Sparaco, P. "French Panel Says EU Far from Transport Policy." *Aviation Week and Space Technology* 142 (May 8, 1995): 28-29.

Turró, Mateu. *Going Trans-European.* Amsterdam: Pergamon, 1999.

INFORMATION ON THE WORLD WIDE WEB

Europa, the European Union's server, is a good place to begin Internet research on the European Community in general, and on the European Transportation System in particular. (europa.eu.int/pol/trans/index_en.htm)

TRADE

Trade has been important in European communities for more than twenty-five hundred years. From the early Greeks and Romans who traded throughout the Mediterranean region, to the Venetians, Florentines, and other Italians of the High Middle Ages, Europeans demonstrated a continuing interest in trading. In the late Middle Ages, traders in northern Germany organized the Hanseatic League as a Baltic-North Sea trading organization that exploited the river systems of northern Europe. While these pre-Renaissance traders were involved in trade focused on the Mediterranean, North, and Baltic Seas; a few rivers; and the county fair circuits, trade expanded significantly with the emergence of modern society in the sixteenth century.

HISTORICAL BACKGROUND. Urban centers developed and grew in population, the Atlantic Ocean became a gateway to world trade as a result of new technology and a new worldview, and mercantilism emerged in the seventeenth century. The mercantilist view of the economy argues that there is a static amount of wealth in the world and that it is essential to maintain a favorable balance of trade; that is, exports should exceed imports. This approach to trade led to governmental invention in the economy in two major ways: state efforts to enhance national self-sufficiency to minimize the need for imports, and the deployment of tariff barriers to protect native industries against foreign competition.

In the eighteenth century, capitalism became fully developed and manifested its four major characteristics: private property, the profit motive, competition, and the institution of bank credit. Under the capitalist model, trade would be affected by the freedom under which the economy operates and by any restrictions resulting from the prevailing conditions of the European economies and the relations among the European states. The European acceptance of material culture accelerated the process of imperialism throughout the world.

TWENTIETH CENTURY DEVELOPMENTS. By the start of the twentieth century, the major European powers had established a network of colonies throughout the world; while this development was justified as an extension of cultural and religious values, the ultimate motive was to achieve a predominant position in trade. Access to raw materials and new markets was the goal of European imperialism. Imperial commercial issues contributed to the alignment of the European powers prior to the outbreak of World War I and served in part to justify the outbreak of the war in 1914.

With the defeat of Germany in 1918 and the emergence of the ideologies of fascism and communism, trade was restricted by those controlled economies: the fascist German, Italian, and Spanish governments and the communist Soviet Union and its Eastern European satellites from 1945 to 1989. By the middle of the twentieth century, U.S. capitalism and Soviet communism were at odds and the Cold War began; while national aspirations were the predominant cause of the rivalry, economics and economic theories

London Stock Exchange Page 1372

Shipyard in Hamburg, Germany. (PhotoDisc)

After the collapse of the Soviet Union in 1991 and the expansion of democratic, capitalist economies in Eastern Europe, European trade patterns shifted dramatically. Access to the new markets in Russia and Eastern Europe resulted in an initial flood of investment from Europe and the United States. While the movement to Western capitalism has been slowed, the Western openness of trade with the East has been sustained. This process has been accelerated by the impact of the Internet and the accompanying openness in communications. With the possible exception of Russia, it appeared in the year 2000 that the European Union movement toward a single market was gaining support throughout most of Eastern Europe.

INTERNAL AND EXTERNAL TRADE. European nations are the world's major trading partners, involved in more than 50 percent of all international trade. This volume of trade is based on Europe's dependency on many products, especially energy and food, and Europe's historic international trading patterns. The Western European states are the principal traders and collectively control more than one-fourth of the oceangoing shipping. The inherent connections between internal and external trade in Europe have resulted in the ascendancy of European finance-related industries such as banking and insurance. At the same time, they are vulnerable to rapid fluctuations in exchange rates that cannot be controlled.

contributed to shaping the national agendas. During most of the second half of the twentieth century, Europe was subjected to the external pressures resulting from the U.S.-Soviet struggle; however, during the same period, Europeans seized opportunities to control their own political and economic futures.

Internal trade in Europe is the lifeline of the economy. Domestic and imported goods are continually transported to the distribution and retail outlets of the urban centers. Goods produced within European Union states are distributed without barriers or intervention; these external goods primarily consist of fuels, food and drinks, raw materials, metals, and manufactured goods. In addition to the Common Market and the European Union, a European Free Trade Association has been established to facilitate trade among all European economies. During the 1990's, trade between Russia and other Eastern European countries and the rest of Europe developed rapidly. Russian natural gas supports energy requirements in France, Germany, and Italy. Other Eastern products that are sold to Western and Central Europe include glass, wine, timber, and food.

Trade outside Europe is critical in supporting the quality of life for Europeans. Significant exports from Europe include machinery, aircraft, automobiles, and chemicals. Other important sources of foreign currency are books, professional services, and art. The number of international students studying at European schools and universities increased dramatically during the 1990's; European institutions aggressively marketed their services and realized significant external trade receipts.

TRANSPORTATION. Internal trade within individual European states is conducted mainly by the trucking and barge industries. Western European roads are high quality and designed to handle the volume of automobiles and trucks that are in use; road systems are in a constant state of expansion, maintenance, and repair. To facilitate trade and movement in many densely populated metropolitan areas, beltways around the cities have been constructed. Eastern Europe's roadways, however, have been substandard and in need of major investment.

In the 1990's, France and Great Britain opened the English Channel tunnel. The tunnel provides access for trains and automobiles; it has stimulated trade between Britain and the rest of Western Europe. Tunnels through the Alps have promoted trade in that region. There have been notable improvements in roads in Ireland, Poland, and Italy. Throughout Western and Central Europe, trucking has expanded greatly because of the demands of the marketplace and the level of competition. In Eastern Europe, transport at the start of the twenty-first century is rather primitive and underdeveloped; horses and oxen are still used on the roads, and petroleum retail centers are limited. A poor road system cannot support a vibrant trading economy.

Other major means of conducting trade are the railroad and aircraft. Europe en-

EUROPE'S ROLE IN INTERNATIONAL TRADE

The European Union is the biggest single player in international trade; a large percentage of all international trade in goods consists of items imported into or exported from Europe. The imports are largely bulk commodities, such as oil, but the exports are largely manufactured items. As trade in basic commodities shifted around the world in the latter decades of the twentieth century, Europe lost much of its manufacturing capacity in the conversion of raw materials into basic commodities, but it maintains a positive trade balance because the manufactured goods it exports are of much higher value. Almost all of Europe's international trade goes by sea.

joys a new railroad system that was developed during the post-World War II reconstruction. In the 1990's, railroads, although still significant, declined in both freight and passenger volume because of the increased use of trucks and automobiles. However, if one considers the underground railway system in major metropolitan areas (for example, the Underground in London and the Metro in Paris) in the railroad equation, then passenger volume has increased.

Amsterdam canals Pages 1241, 1373

The volume of air traffic within and to Europe has continued to increase; London, Paris, Rome, Berlin, and Moscow are among the principal air traffic centers in Europe. From the perspective of trade, aircraft are cost effective when transported goods are extremely valuable or perishable; precious metals, art works, and expensive foodstuffs and flowers are examples of products that are effectively traded using aircraft.

Another means of trade are the pipelines used to distribute petroleum and natural gas. World-class tankers, in excess of 300,000 gross tons, pull into ports, some with connections at sea, and download their products into pipelines that distribute them to refineries or distribution centers. Major pipeline networks exist in Great Britain to capitalize on the North Sea oil field; in Italy, France, and Spain; and in Russia and the Ukraine for transporting natural gas and petroleum internally and to Western and Central Europe. An ambitious project has been proposed to transport these raw materials from the Caucasus, through Russia and Turkey, to the Mediterranean Sea.

PORTS AND CANALS. Europeans have used waterways for trade for millennia. During the modern era, engineers have enabled trade to increase by expanding port facilities, developing deeper channels in some rivers, and constructing canals that link existing bodies of water or extend a waterway. While trade is slow when carried by ship or barge, it is cost effective and remains preferred for the shipment of such goods as coal, iron ore, and grain. From the standpoint of trade, the three most important internal waterways are the Rhine, Danube, and Volga Rivers. These large, deep rivers support large barges (in excess of twelve hundred tons) and provide essential support for European trade.

Other canals, such as the Manchester Ship Canal and the Volga-Don Shipping Canal, connect manufacturing centers to access raw materials and external markets. The network of European canals makes it possible to move goods by barges from southwestern France to Poland and from Germany to the Black Sea. In Northern Europe, the Kiel Canal connects the Baltic and North Seas and has contributed to the economic development of Denmark, Germany, Finland, Sweden, and Poland.

SUPRANATIONAL ORGANIZATIONS. Since the close of World War II, trade patterns within Europe have been drastically affected by the emergence of integrated and cross-national economic and political institutions. Responding to the predominant positions of the United States and the Soviet Union in the 1950's and the arguments advanced by Jean Monnet on the need for European unity, France, Italy, West Germany (the Federal Republic of Germany), the Netherlands, Belgium, and Luxembourg formed the European Economic Community (EEC or Common Market) through the Treaty of Rome in 1957. The U.S. government encouraged this development and considered internal European economic cooperation as essential to Europe's postwar recovery and important in the United States' policy of containing Soviet expansion.

The EEC was expanded in 1973 with

Headquarters of the European Economic Community (EEC) in Brussels. (PhotoDisc)

the entrance of Great Britain, Ireland, and Denmark; in 1981 with the admission of Greece; in 1986 with the addition of Spain and Portugal; and in 1995 with the admission of Finland and Sweden. The unification of Germany resulted in the Schengen Agreement in 1990; this agreement between France, Germany, Belgium, Luxembourg, and the Netherlands revised the previous agreement on border controls, becoming the basis for the success at Maastricht and part of the EU system in 1999. The Treaty of Rome (1957) and the Maastricht treaty (1992) were amended by the Treaty of Amsterdam in 1999, which clarified the power of a qualified majority in the European Parliament.

After political revolutions in Eastern Europe in 1989 and the collapse of the Soviet Union in 1991, many states applied for admission to the EEC. Its success has been notable: establishment of common price levels for agricultural products, the elimi-

nation of internal tariffs, and the establishment of a joint external tariff. During the 1980's, prolonged negotiations were conducted to expand the economic union and to begin the process of political and social integration. At that time, Europeans were motivated by the fear that they would not be competitive in trade because of the strength of the United States and Japan. The result was the Maastricht Treaty of European Union (EU) in 1992; its essential components were the establishment of a central banking system and the introduction of a common currency.

In spite of serious opposition, the Maastricht treaty was adopted, although Great Britain has declined to join the currency union. The passage of the Maastricht accord formally established the European Union and advanced the four freedoms that have been at the core of the European integration movement—free movement of people, goods, services, and capital in a single market. The trading impact of the success of this strategy is staggering. The Europeans have established a unified market in which all barriers to internal trade have been or will be eliminated; thus, they have gained control over a marketplace of almost 400 million people. At the same time, the European Union has imposed limitations on trade within the member states by all external economies.

The European Economic Area (EEA) was formed in 1996 as a mechanism to bring together the EU and non-EU states that are members of the European Free Trade Association (EFTA). In addition to single-market trade issues, the EEA has considered the specific issues of education, research and development, tourism, and consumer rights. The direct impact on European businesses has been to reduce the costs previously associated with border controls and, through the adoption of uniform standards of weights and measures, savings through economies of scale are evident. The new trading system has enhanced competition and forced some firms to focus on particular products rather than a wide range of goods; specialization in services and goods has resulted.

The proactive components of the new trading system are based on two strategies designed to realize the common market. One strategy is to develop a minimum number of laws that are focused on safety standards relating to public health, consumer rights, and the environment. The second strategy is directed at enhancing functional harmonization based on mutual recognition. In practice, these two catalysts are contradictory to realizing the single market: local, regional, and national interests have resulted in the interpretation of the new laws in such a way that they restrict open trade among the member states. The European Union Court of Justice has rendered a series of decisions that have sustained the original intent of the laws resulting from this strategy; however, the number of reported violations continued to increase.

One of the greatest concerns of the EU has been agriculture; the need to sustain and expand agricultural production among the member states and the establishment of trading standards were early issues that the EU confronted. The result was the Common Agricultural Policy (CAP), directed at increased production, providing an equitable standard of living for producers, and ensuring the availability and distribution of food at moderate prices. Key components of the CAP are import tariffs, which limit or eliminate foreign competition; EC purchasing, which supports internal pricing; and export subsidies, which make European foodstuffs more competitive in the international market. The Common Agricultural Policy consumes more than 40 percent of EC budget for fiscal year 2001.

Perhaps the boldest step in unifying trade in the European Union, and without doubt the most controversial provision of the Maastricht treaty, is the establishment of a common European currency. This initially was discussed in 1979 in the context of the new European Monetary System, which called for the European Currency Unit (ECU). Maastricht specified that the process to establish a uniform currency would begin on January 1, 1999, for those nations that qualified based on criteria relating to national debt, budget deficits, inflation rate, long-term interest rates, and the valuation of currency. The new euro currency was supported by national referenda of qualified nations except the United Kingdom; the British have been reluctant to abandon the pound sterling. The introduction of the euro is a multiphase step over four or five years.

During its initial year, the euro did not perform well in the exchange rate with the U.S. dollar. Nevertheless, the plan has not been abandoned nor seriously adjusted. The arguments that justify the euro view the trading world of the twenty-first century as consisting of major trading blocs—the European Union, the North American Free Trade Association (and its potential to evolve into a Western Hemisphere trading bloc), Japan leading an East Asia bloc, a Mideast bloc, China, India, and Russia. These huge markets would have uniform internal standards and approach the other blocs from positions of strength.

While perhaps exciting to a highly nationalized Europe, the European Union movement is steeped in historical considerations that may be sustained for much longer. Specifically, this neo-mercantilist view of trade is being challenged by globalization and the rapid expansion of multinational companies.

GLOBALIZATION AND MULTINATIONAL COMPANIES. At the same time that momentum was accelerating the realization of the goals and objectives of the European Union, a significant new force emerged that was more encompassing and ambitious than the EU—globalization. Global economics is a direct result of the communications revolution based on the Internet; this technology-based revolution does not factor in either national or bloc boundaries. It has the capacity to create a global trading pattern that directly links the consumer with the supplier. Within the 1990's, previously held principles of trade were abandoned or transformed by the application of this technology. It has been abetted by the emergence of multinational corporations that transgress national boundaries and have no national identity.

Globalization and the rise of the multinationals have been applauded as conditions that should contribute to minimizing conflicts between nations. Some supporters anticipate that these forces will result in the end of nation-states; others fear that individual liberties and democracy will be at risk. Still others look at the rise of the new right wing throughout Europe and fear the resurgence of nationalism and xenophobia.

In February, 2000, the electoral success of a right-wing party in Austria sent shock waves throughout the European Union and resulted in limited isolation of the Austrian government. While the Austrians followed democratic processes, the EU objected to the results; this crisis pointed to a problem with the EU that needed to be addressed. From the per-

THE EUROPEAN EURO

On December 31, 1998, the Council of the European Union fixed the following conversion/exchange rates between the euro and the currencies of participating countries.

Currency	Units per euro
Austrian schillings	13.7603
Belgian francs	40.3399
Dutch gulden	2.20371
Finnish markka	5.94573
French francs	6.55957
German marks	1.95583
Irish punts	0.787564
Italian lire	1,936.27
Luxembourg francs	40.3399
Portuguese escudos	200.482
Spanish pesetas	166.386

spective of the European Union, Europe would be well positioned, at least in the short term, by adjusting its goals to the new circumstances. E-commerce (electronically based commerce) in Europe and elsewhere reduces the costs of global marketing and some internal processes such as purchasing, inventory, and product support; accelerates the transaction rate; and enhances cash flow.

While the prospects for European trade in the twenty-first century appeared bright in 2000, the vulnerability of Europe was also evident. The foremost threats to Europe's economy and trade are the potential for an oil embargo by the Organization of Petroleum Exporting Countries, the resumption of external national agendas that threaten world stability, and the political stability of Russia and Eastern Europe. The oil stoppages of the 1970's and the interruptions associated with the Persian Gulf War of 1991 have remained in the European memory; Europe's dependency on imported oil is substantial and will continue for the foreseeable future.

The rise of international tensions and the potential for conflicts between India and Pakistan, the United States and China, or Russia and China could result in a world economic collapse from which Europe would not be exempted. It is in Europe's interest to maintain a condition of normalcy in international affairs; recognizing that need, Europeans have been in the forefront in attempting to resolve disputes. Europe's economic and political future also is dependent upon the stability and development of Russia and the nations of Eastern Europe.

Russia's use of overwhelming force to suppress the independence movement in Chechnya in the late 1990's engendered anxiety over Russia's possible use of force in the resolution of conflicts. The Russian economy has been in a precarious position and must continue to evolve rapidly toward the Western model and eliminate corruption in government. During the 1990's, the armed conflicts in Bosnia and Serbia shook Europeans into recognizing that their own continent was not free from the prospect of war. These conflicts have disrupted trade and trade routes and slowed the economic development of the region. The costs of military action and occupation has taken a toll on European economies.

William T. Walker

FOR FURTHER STUDY

Buchan, David. *The Single Market and Tomorrow's Europe.* Dover, N.H.: Kogan Page, 1997.

Dawson, Andrew H. *A Geography of European Integration.* New York: Halstead Press, 1993.

Fontagne, Lionel. G. *Trade Patterns Inside the Single Market.* Dover, N.H.: Kogan Page, 1998.

Gottman, Jean. *A Geography of Europe.* 4th ed. New York: Holt, Rinehart and Winston, 1969.

Grimwade, N. *New Patterns of International Trade.* Beckenham, England: Croom Helm, 1988.

Kinnock, Neil, et al. *The European Union in 2000.* Brussels: European Voice in Association with Adamson/BSMG Worldwide, 2000.

Nelsen, Brent F., and Alexander C-G. Stubb, eds. *The European Union: Readings on the Theory and Practice of European Integration.* 2d ed. Boulder, Colo.: Lynne Rienner, 1998.

Thomas, Kenneth P., and Mary Ann Tétreault, eds. *Racing to Regionalize: Democracy, Capitalism, and Regional Political Economy.* Boulder, Colo.: Lynne Rienner, 1999.

COMMUNICATIONS

The communication systems of Europe are wide and varied. Much of mainstream American culture derives directly from European culture, so it is possible to find predecessors and analogues to almost every U.S. communication system in Europe. Because of Europe's long history of advanced civilization, many of its communications systems have roots dating back to ancient times. This long history also has its downside in that antiquated and inefficient methods and systems often have lingered, particularly in Great Britain and areas that were not devastated by World War II.

Europe, particularly Western Europe, enjoys modern systems of both interpersonal and mass communications. Interpersonal communications systems (such as telephone exchanges and post offices) transmit information between individuals; mass communications systems (such as newspapers, radio, and television) broadcast information from central sources to large numbers of people. The Internet has blurred this distinction, containing elements of both interpersonal (e-mail and chat rooms) and mass (USEnet and the World Wide Web) communications

There are notable differences in communications systems between Western Europe and Eastern Europe. In general, the free-market economies of the West produced communications systems that are varied and vibrant, while the state-controlled communications systems of the East generally were stultified and less reliable. Although this difference has become less since the 1989 fall of the Iron Curtain, the nations of Eastern Europe have gener-

ally lagged behind those of the West in the development of multiple providers of mass communications.

POSTAL SYSTEMS. European postal systems can be traced back to antiquity, to Greek systems of message runners and Roman emperor Augustus Caesar's Roman postal systems. However, these ancient postal systems were primarily networks of government messengers. The first truly modern postal systems, available to the general public, developed during the commercial revolution that followed the Renaissance, particularly in the Northern European countries, such as the Netherlands and England, that had a strong independent merchant class.

The London Penny Post was begun in 1680 by William Dockwra, a merchant who recognized the need for a reliable method of transporting letters and messages. This organization introduced the first postmarks, identifying the location from which a letter was mailed. The London Penny Post was so successful that the government took it over two years later and subsequently expanded regular postal delivery throughout England.

However, difficulties remained. Until 1840, the normal practice was for the cost of mailing to be paid by the recipient. A person who did not want to pay the price could refuse to accept the item in question, leaving the postal system to absorb the cost. In addition, charging according to the distance mail was sent resulted in a confusing system of multiple rates. In 1840 the British postal system introduced the first postage stamp, shifting to the modern

French mailbox. (PhotoDisc)

system by which the sender pays for delivery.

During the twentieth century, many European countries experienced difficulties with their postal systems, particularly as other communications systems such as telephones began to fill the need for casual interpersonal communication. In the last decades of the twentieth century, some European nations began experimenting with privatized postal services.

POSTAGE STAMPS. The 1840 issue of the first postage stamps by Great Britain was the result of reforms proposed by Rowland Hill. The price of a penny for a half ounce letter was made the basic rate throughout the United Kingdom. The "Penny Black" stamp, based upon the Guildhall Medal likeness of Queen Victoria, was the first postage stamp ever issued. Although it lasted only briefly before being replaced by a more attractive red color,

the same basic design continued to be used for more than sixty years. Because Great Britain was the first nation to use postage stamps, it has traditionally not printed its name on its stamps, only a portrait (sometimes much reduced and stylized) of the current reigning monarch.

Early stamps were made without perforations, and users had to cut them apart with a scissors or other implement. In 1854 the first perforated stamps were introduced, allowing users to separate individual stamps from a sheet with little effort. Various devices for mechanically cutting perforations quickly and accurately were soon introduced.

TELEGRAPHS AND TELEPHONES. The telegraph, the first telecommunications system, has had a presence in the European communications scene from its beginning. Both English and French inventors experimented with various schemes for sending electrical signals across distances through wires. After Samuel F. B. Morse invented the first practical telegraph, it quickly spread to Europe. After the invention of the telephone, the role of the telegraph diminished. However, telegraph communications have remained important for certain kinds of communication, such as sending money by wire.

The telephone, an outgrowth of the telegraph that allowed the transmission of sound and thus was usable with little or no specialized training, spread to Europe soon after its invention in the United States. In Europe, telephone systems typically have been run by national governments. However, this has begun to change as many nations have sold parts or all of their telephone systems to private investors.

The earliest transatlantic telephone links were via radio. The Eiffel Tower in Paris was used as a receiving antenna for one of the early experiments. These later were supplemented by trans-Atlantic telephone cables. By the 1930's, these links had moved beyond the experimental stage, to the point where people would find believable a story that an American had telephoned German dictator Adolf Hitler and told him to stop the fighting in Spain so that elections could be heard.

NEWSPAPERS. Newspapers, the oldest form of mass communications, have their origin in the various forms of public announcements produced and posted by Imperial Roman authorities. However, the beginning of the true modern newspaper dates to the invention of movable-type printing by Johannes Gutenberg in the fifteenth century. This was soon followed by the development of broadsheets, which often were publicly posted but also were sold to individual readers, generally for a penny.

As printing technologies developed, newspapers grew steadily larger. In 1811 the first steam-driven press enabled much more rapid production of printed material with much less labor. The need for quick and reliable international news led to the development of news agencies to which individual newspapers could subscribe. Reuters news agency was founded by Paul Julius Reuter in 1848 and remained a private company until 1925. It became a cooperative trust in 1941 and has become international in scope.

Europe accounts for as much as half of the world's newspaper circulation. Notable European newspapers include *Le Monde* in France, *Die Welt* in Germany, *L'Osservatore Romano* of the Vatican, and the *Times* of London. The highest newspaper readerships are in the United Kingdom, Norway, Denmark, and Sweden. However, many small newspapers have closed due to lack of readership. Many of the larger ones, particularly in Great Britain, struggle with problems of "featherbedding" (employing more people than necessary, generally because of obsolete equipment and restric-

tive union contracts). Fleet Street, London's famous newspaper district, has been hit especially hard.

RADIO. The first light-speed mass communications system, radio has remained a relatively popular information medium throughout the world for much the same purposes that it is used in the United States—news, sports, and music. During the Cold War, radio broadcasts from the free world were beamed into communist

Newspapers representing all the languages and countries of Western Europe are sold throughout the region. (PhotoDisc)

countries under the auspices of Radio Free Europe and Radio Liberty.

The radio systems of the free world were not necessarily all that free. During the 1950's, many Western European radio stations were under tight control by government bureaucrats who thought that popular youth culture was inferior. Therefore, much of Europe's popular music radio was broadcast from ships offshore. These unlicensed stations were soon given the nickname of "pirate radio." Because of their great popularity, particularly among young people, land-based pirate stations soon joined them on the airwaves. Because land-based stations were much easier to locate and raid, they were less likely to last for any length of time.

In addition to pirate stations, which were primarily intended to circumvent bureaucratic control and provide listeners with material that had been dismissed as trivial, there are also clandestine stations, which generally have an overt political agenda. They typically represent unpopular or opposition political groups, and often broadcast materials regarded as subversive by the government in power.

In the late 1990's, digital audio broadcasting (DAB) was introduced in the United Kingdom. DAB provides sound quality close to that of a compact disc and enables broadcasters to supplement their transmissions with pictures and other data.

TELEVISION. Television, which transmits moving images over radio waves, was developed almost simultaneously in the United States and various European countries, particularly the United Kingdom. Various inventors experimented with television throughout the 1920's and 1930's. In 1936 the British Broadcasting Corporation (BBC) transmitted the first open-circuit television broadcast. However, World War II stifled research on television, and the real development of television as a com-

munication system took off in the 1950's.

In the 1920's John Logie Baird, a Scottish inventor working in London, developed some of the earliest working television equipment. Unlike modern television systems, which are all-electronic, Baird's system depended on mechanical devices to scan the image, that is, break it down into information that can be transmitted via radio waves.

The heart of Baird's system was a Nipkow disk, a device that was first developed by German scientist Paul Nipkow in 1883 but was not practical until the development of the triode by Lee De Forrest enabled signals to be amplified. This disk had a set of holes or lenses set in a spiral, such that each passed over a successive arc of the picture. In this manner, the image could be scanned.

Baird held the first public demonstration of his system in 1926, and by 1928 he had developed methods of transmitting color and stereoscopic television. He also did successful outdoor shoots and even had a primitive telecine (transmitting film via television) system. However, his early successes were soon eclipsed by the development of all-electronic scanning systems. The moving parts of a mechanical system were more prone to breakdown, and technical limits made it impossible to provide enough light for more than about a hundred scanning lines on a mechanical system. By World War II, Baird's mechanically scanned system had been abandoned by the BBC in favor of all-electronic television.

Most European countries have both public and private television stations, although Western Europe has more stations than Eastern Europe, and more Western European stations are independent. In the United Kingdom, the government-run system is the BBC, while the independent system is the Independent Television Commission (ITC). Ireland's television system is Radio Telefis Eireann (RTE). Many nations fund their public television systems through a tax on television receivers.

European television systems use different scanning systems than the National Television Standards Committee (NTSC) standard familiar in the United States. Most Western European nations use the Phase Alternating Line (PAL) standard, while France and Eastern Europe use a system known as SECAM (*SEquential Couleur Avec Memoire*, French for "sequential color with memory"). Both PAL and SECAM are based upon the 50-hertz alternating current line frequency generally used in European electrical grids (as opposed to the 60-hertz standard on the U.S. grid) but differ in certain technical essentials. SECAM was originally developed by the French as a political move to protect local manufacturers. Subsequently, it was adopted by Eastern European countries to make it difficult for their citizens to pick up Western broadcasts and thus objectionable Western political ideologies and information.

COMMUNICATIONS SATELLITES. The theory that makes artificial satellites possible dates back to the work in orbital mechanics done by Johannes Keppler and Sir Isaac Newton in the seventeenth century. In 1945 a young Royal Air Force officer by the name of Arthur C. Clarke outlined the idea of using satellites positioned in geostationary orbits (orbits that rotate at the same rate as the ground below them is rotating around the earth's axis, having the effect of remaining in the same place overhead) for a worldwide communication network. Although the practical application of this theory could not be realized until rocketry advanced to the point of being able to lift delicate electronic systems to the required altitude, the region of space where geostationary satellites would orbit was named the Clarke Belt.

As soon as the technology was practical,

European nations joined in the international drive to develop telecommunications satellites, carrying telephone, television, and other signals to bridge or cover wide distances. Many European concerns have rented transponder space on international satellites such as the Intelsat system, while other nations have launched their own satellites. For instance, the French TELECOM satellites provide service to France and its dependencies.

Because so much of Russia is at high northern latitudes, it receives only limited benefit from satellites in the Clarke Belt. In order to provide coverage for its northern territories, Russia uses another aspect of orbital mechanics to create a satellite that will move slowly over the necessary region. Known as a molniya orbit, it is inclined and highly elliptical, with a perigee (closest approach to the earth's surface) of only 311 miles (500 km.) in the southern hemisphere and apogee (farthest distance from the earth's surface) of 24,850 miles (40,000 km.) over northern Russia.

Because any given satellite is in service during only a limited time, a working molniya satellite system is a constellation of several satellites, their orbits timed so that one will be near apogee and thus useful at all times. A receiver for molniya satellites is more complex than that for Clarke Belt satellites, because it must be able to track the slow movement of the satellite and switch between the different satellites in the constellation.

THE INTERNET. Although the Internet has its roots in the U.S. government's Advanced Research Projects Agency Network, the need of European scientists for rapid communications between computers quickly led to its spread to European institutions. By the 1990's, use of the Internet had moved beyond the confines of the academic community on both sides of the Atlantic, as the use of personal computers and modems spread among ordinary people.

The Internet has profoundly changed the communications landscape in Europe. The Internet makes it easy to find information from computers located in other countries and to exchange electronic mail or to chat with people around the world. In many ways, the Internet has been as important as political agreements in lowering the boundaries between the various countries of Europe.

THE WORLD WIDE WEB. Tim Berners-Lee, a British computer scientist working at the European Center for Nuclear Research (CERN), headquartered near Geneva, Switzerland, originally wrote the software for the World Wide Web in 1990. It was intended to allow scientists to exchange hyperlinked data over the Internet. Hyperlinks are internal links between documents, allowing people to see connections between information in unique ways. Its implementation in 1991 had far-reaching consequences.

In 1993 the first browser (software designed specifically to ease use of the Web) was developed, bringing multimedia to the Internet. The Web led to the popularization of the Internet throughout the 1990's, making it a medium accessible to people who were not technically oriented and not interested in the details of how their computers worked. It also opened the world of publishing to ordinary people in a way no other medium could. People anywhere could set up their own Web pages and reach a worldwide audience. A computer user in one country can easily find Web pages constructed by people all over the world.

This has not been without its downside, however. There is little or no quality control over Web page content. People putting up their own personal Web pages can repeat misinformation they have learned from others. It is therefore essential that persons using the Web examine their sources in a way that is generally not necessary for print sources. Is the person or organization creating the Web page generally reliable? Do they write from personal experience, or from reliable scholarly sources?

Leigh Husband Kimmel

FOR FURTHER STUDY

Ducatel, Ken, Juliet Webster, and Werner Herrmann, eds. *The Information Society in Europe: Work and Life in an Age of Globalization.* Lanham, Md.: Rowman & Littlefield, 2000.

Kaid, Lynda Lee, ed. *Television and Politics in Evolving European Democracies.* Commack, N.Y.: Nova Science, 1999.

McLuhan, Marshall, and Bruce R Powers. *The Global Village: Transformations in World Life and Media in the Twenty-first Century.* Oxford, England: Oxford University Press, 1992.

Nelson, Michael. *War of the Black Heavens: The Battles of Western Broadcasting in the Cold War.* Syracuse, N.Y.: Syracuse University Press, 1997.

Price, Monroe Edwin. *Television, the Public Sphere, and National Identity.* Oxford, England: Oxford University Press, 1995.

Richardson, Kay. *Worlds in Common?: Television Discourse in a Changing Europe.* New York: Routledge, 1999.

Schenk, Karl-Ernst, Jürgen Müller, and Thomas Schnöring, eds. *Mobile Telecommunications: Emerging European Markets.* Boston: Artech House, 1995.

Tuttlebee, Wally H. W., ed. *Cordless Telecommunications in Europe: The Evolution of Personal Communications.* New York: Springer-Verlag, 1990.

Urban, G. R. *1921—Radio Free Europe and the Pursuit of Democracy: My War Within the Cold War.* New Haven, Conn.: Yale University Press, 1997.

GAZETTEER

Places whose names are printed in SMALL CAPS *are subjects of their own entries in this gazetteer.*

Aarhus. See ÅRHUS.

Aberdeen. Largest city in northeast SCOTLAND, often considered the capital of the Scottish HIGHLANDS. Population was 216,000 in 1997. Seat of an ancient university. With an important harbor on the NORTH SEA, it has long been one of the centers of the Scottish fishing industry. Discovery of oil in the North Sea in the 1960's brought an economic boom. Named after the mouth (*aber*) of the Dee River.

Adriatic Sea. Arm of the MEDITERRANEAN SEA separating ITALY from the BALKAN PENINSULA. Total area is about 61,776 square miles (160,000 sq. km.); about 497 miles (800 km.) long, 140 miles (225 km.) at its widest, and 4,101 feet (1,250 meters) at it deepest. Named for Adria, a port that once lay at the mouth of the PO RIVER in Italy. Known for its fishing grounds, but its port facilities are limited, particularly on the eastern coast of Italy. There, the treacherous winter northeasterly winds (*bara*) discourage maritime traffic, even in the major ports of VENICE, TRIESTE, Ancona, and Bari.

Aegean Sea. Island-studded arm of the MEDITERRANEAN SEA. Located between GREECE and TURKEY (Asia Minor), and bounded at the south by the island of CRETE. Estimates of its area range from 69,112 to 82,625 square miles (179,000 to 214,000 sq. km.); about 400 miles (644 km.) long and 249 miles (400 km.) at its widest, and up to 7,500 feet (2,286 meters) deep. Settled as early as 6000 B.C.E., the shores of the Aegean are regarded as the cradle of Western civilization.

Aeolian Islands. See LIPARI ISLANDS.

Åland Islands. Archipelago of numerous islands located off the coast of south-western FINLAND, directly between Finland and SWEDEN. The majority of the 6,500 people there speak Swedish as their mother tongue. Åland Islanders have maintained autonomous rights since 1921 and have their own flag and stamp.

Albania. Country in southeastern Europe. Total area of 11,100 square miles (28,750 sq. km.) with a 1990's population of 3.3 million, mostly Muslim. Capital is TIRANE. Bordered on the north by YUGOSLAVIA, on the east by MACEDONIA, on the south by GREECE, and on the west by the ADRIATIC SEA. Became independent in 1913. Many Albanians live outside of Albania in the KOSOVO region of Yugoslavia or in Macedonia. One of the poorest countries in Europe.

Alföld, Great. Fertile agricultural area in HUNGARY, SERBIA, and ROMANIA. Drained by the DANUBE and TISZA Rivers, known for irrigated grain cultivation. Also called the Great Hungarian Plain.

Alföld, Little. Lowland agricultural area located in HUNGARY and SLOVAKIA. Has many food crops, large-scale dairy farming, orchards, vineyards, and tobacco. Also known for breeding of riding horses. Traditionally, one of the more developed regions of Hungary; it has benefited from its proximity to AUSTRIA and BOHEMIA.

Alps. Major European mountain range. Encompasses almost 80,000 square miles (207,440 sq. km.), sprawling over SWITZERLAND, central eastern and southeastern FRANCE, northern ITALY, southern GERMANY, and western AUSTRIA, and spilling over into SLOVENIA and CROATIA (the DINARIC ALPS). Extends 750 miles (1,200 km.) from west to east; includes the headwaters of the RHINE, RHONE, and PO Rivers. Eleva-

Aberdeen
Page 1374

Aegean Sea
Page 1442

tion varies greatly but averages 6,000 to 8,000 feet (1,800-2,600 meters) above sea level; the peak of Mont Blanc in France marks its highest ascent (15,781 feet/4,810 meters). The summit of the central Alps is permanently covered with glacial ice and snow, the most spectacular of which is Aletsch Glacier in Switzerland. Has both crystalline (ragged, high-peaked) mountains and limestone mountains, and is honeycombed with glacial lakes (particularly in Switzerland), the most important of which are GENEVA, Constance, Neuchatel, Lucerne, Como, and Garda.

Amsterdam Pages 1241, 1373

Amsterdam. Primate city, financial hub, and one of the two capitals of the NETHERLANDS (the other being The HAGUE). Also the seat of North Holland province and the headquarters for the Bank of the Netherlands and the Dutch Stock Exchange. Population of 1 million in the 1990's. Chief industries are shipbuilding, tourism, iron working, and linen, velvet, and porcelain manufacture and export. A dominant railway center and the chief port for the NORTH SEA and North Holland Canals. Founded in the thirteenth century, it became a major trading port and the site of a university (1632).

Andorra. Independent Western European principality in the eastern PYRENEES between FRANCE and SPAIN. Total area of 180 square miles (470 sq. km.). Population in 1999 was 66,900 people, most of whom were Roman Catholic and spoke Catalan. Capital is Andorra la Vella. Theoretically administered jointly by the bishop of Urgel in CATALONIA, Spain, and the president of France; in practice, an elective assembly governs. Dominated by mountains and valleys; economic activity focuses on sheep farming, tourism, tobacco growing, and smuggling.

Antwerp. Major commercial center in BELGIUM. Situated on the River Scheldt, 52 miles (83 km.) from the NORTH SEA coast, it is one of the world's busiest harbors, as well as a railway, highway, and canal nerve center. Chief industries include grain export, diamond cutting, tobacco products, brewing and distilling, shipbuilding, and textile manufacture. Population was 473,000 in the 1990's.

Apennines. Western European mountain range extending the length of the Italian Peninsula, forming an inland "spine" between the TYRRHENIAN and ADRIATIC Seas. Average height is 4,000 feet (1,200 meters); highest peak is Mount Como (9,583 feet/2,920 meters), although the most notorious is the volcanic Mount Vesuvius near NAPLES, whose famous eruption in 79 C.E. buried the cities of Pompeii and Herculaneum.

Apulia. Peninsula and region of extreme southeastern ITALY, making up the "heel" of the Italian "boot." Enclosed by the ADRIATIC and IONIAN Seas, covering 7,468 square miles (19,365 sq. km.). Principal urban centers are Ban (the provincial capital), Brindisi, Lecce, and Taranto. The economy is primarily agricultural, with tobacco, wine, olives, citrus fruit, and cattle the main products. Salt mining is the major nonagricultural activity.

Apuseni Mountains. Large mountain massif in west central ROMANIA. Extends 55 miles (89 km.). Large deposits of iron, manganese, bauxite, and copper; Romania's top producer of precious metals. Some deposits have been worked since Roman times.

Ardennes. Region of wooded hills in Western Europe extending through the Grand Duchy of LUXEMBOURG, the western German Rhineland, southeastern BELGIUM's provinces of Liege and Luxembourg, and the French department of Ardennes. Main industries are pastoral (cattle and sheep raising) and extractive (lumbering and mining for coal, iron, antimony, lead, and manganese). During World War II, the region was a major battleground.

Århus. Second-largest city in DENMARK, northern Europe. Located in eastern JUTLAND, along the Århus Bay, and has an extensive harbor. A busy port and the center of commerce and industry in Jutland, with a population of 215,590 in 1998. Believed to have been founded by the Vikings in the eighth century. Also called Aarhus.

Arno River. Major Italian river; rises in the APENNINES, flows through FLORENCE, empties into the Gulf of GENOA.

Athens. Capital and largest city of GREECE, southeastern Europe. Center of a large metropolitan area that includes the adjoining port of Piraeus. Population of the urban area just over 3 million in the 1990's. Located near the coast of the Saronic Gulf. At its center is a large limestone hill on which rests the Acropolis, or "high city," which contains remains of many of the finest buildings of classical Greece.

Austria. Landlocked republic in Western Europe, bordered by ITALY, SWITZERLAND, LIECHTENSTEIN, GERMANY, SLOVENIA, the CZECH REPUBLIC, SLOVAKIA, and HUNGARY. Total area of 32,375 square miles (83,950 sq. km.). Most of the 1990's population of 8 million were ethnic Germans and Roman Catholics. Capital is VIENNA. Dominated by the ALPS; Gross Glockner, the highest peak in the Austrian Alps, reaches 12,382 feet (3,775 meters). The economy is diversified. Agricultural output in the valley regions includes grains, potatoes, lumber, sheep, sugar beets,

cattle, and wine. Major manufactured products are aluminum, textiles, toys, optical instruments, construction materials, paper, and chemicals. Its winter sports have made tourism and recreation thriving industries. Major urban areas are Vienna, Klagenfurt, Graz, Linz, Salzburg, and Innsbruck. Ethnolinguistic pockets of Croats and Slovenes in Caninthia province are protected by the Austrian State Treaty of 1955.

Arno River Page 1381

Azores. Autonomous region of PORTUGAL. It is an archipelago composed of nine major islands in the North Atlantic Ocean. The islands lie about 1,000 miles (1,600 km.) west of Portugal and reach elevations as high as 7,713 feet

Athens Pages 1310, 1375

Traditional Austrian alpine chalet. (PhotoDisc)

*Balkans
map
Page 1250*

(2,351 meters) on the island of Pico. The Azores have a subtropical climate with high humidity. Their approximately 236,500 (1992) residents are mostly Portuguese.

Azov, Sea of. Inland sea situated off the southern shores of the UKRAINE and RUSSIA. It forms a northern extension of the BLACK SEA, to which it is linked on the south by the Kerch Strait. The Sea of Azov is about 210 miles (340 km.) long and 85 miles (135 km.) wide, and it has a surface area of about 14,500 square miles (37,600 sq. km.).

Balaton, Lake. Largest lake in central-eastern Europe. Covers 230 square miles (596 sq. km.); averages only 10 feet (3 meters) in depth. Located in central HUNGARY at the foot of the Balkony Forest. Known for its rich fish populations. During the communist era, it was a major tourist destination and health resort for East Germans. Overdevelopment and poor environmental management have endangered the lake.

Balearic Islands. Western Mediterranean islands off the east coast of SPAIN that constitute a separate province (Baleares) of Spain. They cover 1,936 square miles (5,010 sq. km.), with a 1998 population of 796,000. The four major islands are MAJORCA, Menorca, Ibiza, and Formentera. The capital, PALMA, is on Majorca, the major island. The balmy climate has made the islands a magnet for tourism. Crops include olives, fruit, and almonds; sheep and pigs are raised. Important exports include cement, salt, fertilizer, and phosphate.

*Barcelona
Page 1375*

Balkan Mountains. Range of folded mountains in northern BULGARIA, southeastern Europe, composed mainly of sandstone and limestone. Harder crystalline rocks form the range's higher peaks. Toward the east, the range becomes lower. Several north-south trans-

portation routes cross these mountains.

Balkan Peninsula. Wide triangular peninsula in southeastern Europe that points south into GREECE; to its west is the ADRIATIC SEA; to its east, the BLACK SEA. Northern extent is usually placed north of the DINARIC ALPS and west of the TRANSYLVANIAN ALPS. Balkan countries are ALBANIA, BOSNIA-HERZEGOVINA, Bulgaria, Macedonia, and YUGOSLAVIA; CROATIA, ROMANIA, SLOVENIA, and the European part of TURKEY are usually regarded as Balkan also.

Baltic Sea. Arm of the Atlantic Ocean in central-eastern Europe. Drains many rivers, including the ODER and VISTULA. Traditionally, an important trading route. A shallow sea—parts of it freeze over in the winter. Amber is found along the coast.

Banat. Low-lying region of central-eastern Europe, between the TRANSYLVANIAN ALPS and the DANUBE, TISZA, and Mures Rivers in ROMANIA, YUGOSLAVIA, and HUNGARY. Originally settled by the Hungarians; held by Slavs, Serbs, and Magyars; later held by the Ottoman Empire; reclaimed by Hungary in 1779. Portions of the Banat were given to Romania and Yugoslavia after World War I.

Barcelona. SPAIN's second-largest city and the center for the CATALONIA region. Population was 1.7 million in the 1990's. Located on the northeastern coast, it is a major seaport and manufacturing area. Primary exports include wines and grapes, olive oil, almonds, peaches, citrus fruit, grains, cork, and fertilizer; principal manufactures are textiles, railway rolling stock, iron products, and heavy machinery.

Barents Sea. Outlying portion of the Arctic Ocean. It is 800 miles (1,300 km.) long and 650 miles (1,050 km.) wide, and it has a surface area of 542,000 square

Munich, the capital of Bavaria. (PhotoDisc)

miles (1,405,000 sq. km.). It is bounded in part by the Norwegian and Russian mainlands. Vikings and medieval Russians knew it as the Murmean Sea.

Bavaria. State of GERMANY covering 27,239 square miles (70,550 sq. km.) in the country's southeastern alpine region. Population was 11.5 million in the early 1990's. Capital is Munich.

Bay of Biscay. See BISCAY, BAY OF.

Belarus. One of the most economically developed of the former republics of the SOVIET UNION. It is located on the western boundary of RUSSIA and has a land area of 80,062 square miles (207,600 sq. km.). Its population in 1999 was estimated as 10,366,719. Ethnically the population is 78 percent Belorussians, or "White" Russians, who are closely related to the ethnic Russians. Capital is MINSK.

Belfast. Main city, port, and capital of NORTHERN IRELAND, part of the UNITED KINGDOM. Population was 295,000 in 1999. Main industries were shipbuilding, aircraft, and textiles; their decline helped fuel violence between Catholic and Protestant gangs.

Bavaria Page 1376

With a cease-fire in the late 1990's, economic confidence and investment began to return.

Belgium. Kingdom in Western Europe, bordered by FRANCE, LUXEMBOURG, GERMANY, the NETHERLANDS, and the NORTH SEA. Total area of 11,783 square miles (30,553 sq. km.) with a population of 10.2 million in 1997. Languages are French, Flemish, and German; Roman Catholicism is the dominant faith. Capital is BRUSSELS; other major urban centers are ANTWERP, Ghent, Bruges, and Liege. Roughly divided between the northern coastal plain and the southern ARDENNES highlands. Chief industries are shipbuilding, coal and iron mining, diamond cutting, and production of steel, textiles, chemicals, lace, glassware, and carpets. Although one of Europe's most intensively industrialized states, Belgium also produces potatoes, sugar beets, cattle, and dairy products.

Belgrade. Capital and largest city of YUGOSLAVIA, southeastern Europe; also capital of the Yugoslav republic of SERBIA. Situated on high limestone bluffs overlooking the junction of the Sava and DANUBE Rivers. Population was 1.5 million in the 1990's. Almost destroyed in World War I and badly damaged in World War II. The name is Serbo-Croatian for "White Fortress."

Belorussia. See BELARUS

Belorussian Ridge. The ridge runs southeast from northeastern POLAND into western BELARUS and then swings northeast. Its total length is 320 miles (520 km.). Its highest point is Dzerzhinskaya Mountain at 1,132 feet (345 meters).

Ben Nevis. Highest mountain of the BRITISH ISLES (4,409 feet/1,344 meters). Located halfway up the rugged, heavily inleted west coast of SCOTLAND, immediately behind Fort William on Loch Linnhe, a sea lake.

Benelux. Acronym originally applied to a customs union among the three LOW COUNTRIES—BELGIUM, the NETHERLANDS, and LUXEMBOURG—begun in 1948. The term is used to describe the region formed by these three states as a whole.

Bergen. Second-largest city in NORWAY, northern Europe. Located in the southwestern part of the country on the NORTH SEA. The most important port on the west coast of Norway, it had a population of 227,280 in 1999. Founded in 1070; Norway's capital in the twelfth and thirteenth centuries.

Berlin. Capital of GERMANY. An inland port surrounded by the Spree River and linked by canals to the ELBE and ODER Rivers and the Baltic seaports. Population was 3.4 million in the 1990's. Important economic activities include production of iron, steel, machinery, chemicals, and chinaware; brewing; printing; and publishing.

Bern. Federal capital of SWITZERLAND. Population was 163,000 in the 1990's. Major products include textiles, scientific and medical instruments, clocks, and machinery. Founded in 1191 and has been part of the Swiss Confederation since 1353.

Beskids. Mountains in the CARPATHIAN Range of central-eastern Europe. Extends 200 miles (320 km.) along the Czech-Slovak and Polish-Slovak borders. Several passes cross the heavily forested range. The Beskids are rich in coal and once had large deposits of iron ore, becoming an iron and steel center in the nineteenth century. Also an area of tourist attractions and winter resorts.

Bessarabia. Region in Eastern Europe that passed successively, from the fifteenth to the twentieth century, to Moldavia, the Ottoman Empire, RUSSIA, ROMANIA, and the SOVIET UNION; now divided between the UKRAINE and MOLDOVA. A large portion of its population is ethnic Romanian.

Birmingham. Second-largest city in ENGLAND. Population was one million in 1995; its extensive conurbation includes the BLACK COUNTRY, Solihull (95,000), and Sutton Coldfield (106,000). Situated in the West MIDLANDS, it has good road and rail links nationwide and is home of the National Exhibition Centre. BRITAIN's rapid industrialization in the early nineteenth century caused it to grow from a small village as a result of nearby coal and iron deposits. It became the center of iron manufactures, particularly machine-making, and is still one of the centers of Britain's auto industry.

Biscay, Bay of. Body of water bordering western FRANCE and northern SPAIN. Depth ranges from 120 to 1,200 feet (37-365 meters); forceful northwesterly winds and currents make it hazardous for shipping. Major ports along its coast are Bilbao, Santander, Gijon, and San Sebastian in Spain; and Bordeaux, Bayonne, La Rochelle, Nantes, and Lorient in France. Also called the Cantabrian Sea.

Black Country. One of the original areas of BRITAIN's nineteenth century industrialization and subsequent prosperity. Situated in the West MIDLANDS, circumscribing the city of BIRMINGHAM. Its largest towns are Dudley (305,000), Walsall (175,000), and West Bromwich (154,000). Named for the industrial soot and grime from countless factories, collieries, and railways. Planned reclamation has resulted in some environmental improvement.

Black Sea. Large inland sea at the south-

eastern extremity of Europe. The UKRAINE to the north, RUSSIA to the northeast, Georgia to the east, TURKEY to the south, and BULGARIA and ROMANIA to the west border it. Its surface area is about 178,000 square miles (461,000 sq. km.), and its maximum depth is more than 7,250 feet (2,210 meters). It is an important shipping artery linking the Ukraine, BULGARIA, Romania, and southwestern Russia with world markets. Several rivers flow into it, including the DANUBE. Has been navigated and its shores colonized for centuries.

Bohemia. Region in the western CZECH REPUBLIC. Home to Slavs by the sixth century, part of the Great Moravian Empire in the ninth century, a kingdom within the Holy Roman Empire, later ruled by the Habsburgs. In 1918 it was incorporated (along with SLOVAKIA and MORAVIA) into an independent nation, CZECHOSLOVAKIA. Fell under German control in World War II. In 1945 Bohemia once again formed part of the republic of Czechoslovakia.

Bay of Biscay Page 1377

Bonn. Capital of West Germany from the end of World War II until shortly after the reunification of GERMANY in 1989.

Bosnia-Herzegovina. Country in southeastern Europe. Total area of 19,900 square miles (51,750 sq. km.) with a 1990's population of 4 million. Capital is SARAJEVO. Bounded on the north and west by CROATIA and on the east and south by YUGOSLAVIA, with a short section of seacoast on the ADRIATIC SEA. From 1918 to 1992, a republic of Yugoslavia. Between 1992 and 1995, the area was torn by a bloody civil war. In 1995 it was established as an independent country, comprising two parts, divided by a complicated, twisting boundary. One part is the Federation of Bosnia and Herzegovina, mainly populated by Muslims and Croats; the other part is Republica Srpska (Serb Republic, not to be confused with the Serb Republic that is part of Yugoslavia), mainly populated by Serbs. The two parts of the country are supposed to cooperate in a common federal government. Also known as Bosnia and Herzegovina.

Bothnia, Gulf of. Northern extension of the BALTIC SEA that separates SWEDEN and FINLAND.

Brasov. Second-largest city, road and rail junction, and a cultural and industrial center in ROMANIA. Population was 350,000 in the early 1990's. Founded by the Teutonic Order in the thirteenth century, it became the center of the Saxon colony and a marketplace for trading cloth, weapons, metalwork, and wax throughout WALACHIA and MOLDAVIA.

Bratislava. National capital of SLOVAKIA. A road and rail center, an important port on the DANUBE RIVER, an industrial center, and a trading center for the surrounding regions. Population was 442,000 in 1991. Originally inhabited by Celts and Romans, was occupied by Slavs in the eighth century. The capital of HUNGARY from 1541-1784.

Bristol. Largest city in the west of ENGLAND. Population was 414,000 in 1999. An ancient port, situated on the River Avon a few miles inland from the SEVERN estuary and the Bristol Channel; harbor area has developed out to Avonmouth. One of the original centers of the Atlantic trade, it became a center of the nation's tobacco industry and food processing.

Britain. Short form of GREAT BRITAIN.

British Isles. Archipelago separated from the west coast of continental Europe by the NORTH SEA, the Strait of DOVER, and the ENGLISH CHANNEL. The archi-

pelago is made up of two large islands, GREAT BRITAIN and IRELAND, and five thousand small islands, including the Isle of MAN and the CHANNEL ISLANDS. The islands' total land area is about 120,880 square miles (314,000 sq. km.).

Brittany. Peninsula making up the extreme northwesterly extension of FRANCE and of continental Europe. The majority of its population are of Celtic origin and culturally distinct from the rest of France; the indigenous Breton language is, along with French, widely spoken. Capital is Rennes. Although the peninsula is predominantly rural, Lorient, Brest, and Nantes are flourishing seaports.

Brno. City in southeast CZECH REPUBLIC. Major city of MORAVIA and second-largest city in Czech Republic. Industrial center known for textile and metal manufacturing; also attracts tourists. Population was 388,300 in 1991. Colonized by Germans in the thirteenth century.

Brussels. Primate city and capital of BELGIUM; headquarters of the European Union and the meeting site for the European Parliament. Population was nearly one million in the 1990's. Major highway, railway, and canal hub, with a small port area at Vilvorde. Economic activity focuses on lace, tapestry, carpets, marble, iron, nails, candles, glass, and sugar beets.

Bucharest. Capital and chief industrial and commercial center of ROMANIA. Population was 2 million in 1992. The city grew up at a crossing place on the Dimbovita River, along a route to Constantinople, about 34 miles (55 km.) north of the DANUBE RIVER on the plain of WALACHIA. The city was founded as a military stronghold in the late fourteenth century. Seat of the patriarch of the Romanian Orthodox Church. Damaged by an earthquake in 1977.

Continued on page 1447

*British Isles
map
Page 1242*

Liechtenstein Castle. A tiny principality located in the Rhine Valley between Austria and Switzer-
land, Liechtenstein has a total area of only 62 square miles (161 sq. km.) and is classified as a
microstate. (PhotoDisc)

Lisbon, the capital and largest city of Portugal. (PhotoDisc)

Scotland. Urquhart Castle on Loch Ness, which is famous as the supposed home of a mysterious aquatic creature, the Loch Ness monster. (R. Kent Rasmussen)

Majorca village. (PhotoDisc)

Marseilles is the main French port on the Mediterranean Sea. (PhotoDisc)

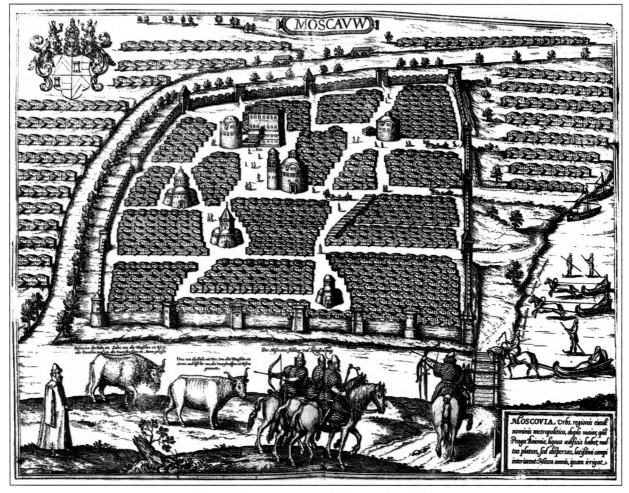

Monaco's Monte Carlo is one of its four administrative districts. The popular Riviera resort is famous for its gambling casino, which opened in 1858. (PhotoDisc)

Sixteenth century map of Moscow. (Corbis)

Moscow, Russia. St. Basil's Cathedral at night. (PhotoDisc)

Switzerland's rugged mountain terrain has required extraordinary engineering efforts to build road and railway systems. (American Stock Photography)

Mykonos, a major tourist attraction in the Cyclades group of islands in the Aegean Sea. (PhotoDisc)

Notre Dame Cathedral on the Seine River in Paris, France. (PhotoDisc)

Po River valley in Italy. (Digital Stock)

A great deal of Portuguese history is tied to the hilltop Castle of St. George in Lisbon's Alfama district. Originally built during the era of Moorish occupation, the castle was later renamed after the patron saint of England to honor Portugal's long alliance with England that began in 1386. (PhotoDisc)

Prague, Czech Republic. (PhotoDisc)

Prague's Old Town on the Vltava River. (PhotoDisc)

The Rhone River in Lyons, France. A major Western European river, the Rhone runs for Switzerland Lyons, where it absorbs the Saone, and proceeds through Avignon and Arles before entering the Mediterranean Sea. (PhotoDisc)

St. Tropez, one of the most popular resorts on the French Riviera. (PhotoDisc)

Better known as the Colosseum, Rome's Flavian Amphitheater was completed in 80 C.E. for gladiatorial games and spectacles. The fifty-thousand-seat stadium originally had a heavy wooden floor, beneath which animals used in the games were kept. (PhotoDisc)

Exterior of the Colosseum. (PhotoDisc)

Santoríni, perhaps the most spectacular of the Cyclades group of Greek islands in the Aegean Sea. (PhotoDisc)

*Split (also known as Spalato) is the second-largest port in Croatia, as well as one of the leading cit-
ies of Dalmatia.* (Charles F. Bahmueller)

St. Petersburg, Russia. Winter palace of the czars. (PhotoDisc)

Stockholm, the capital and largest city of Sweden. (PhotoDisc)

Thanks to the nursery rhyme "London Bridge is Falling Down," that bridge across the Thames River is one of the most famous landmarks in England. In 1970 the bridge was taken apart (pictured) and shipped to Arizona, where it was reassembled over an artificial lake. However, that particular bridge was merely one in a long line of London Bridges, and a new one quickly replaced it over the Thames. (R. Kent Rasmussen)

Tyrrhenian Sea. The Italian town of Cetraro, on the sea's eastern shore, midway between Naples and Sicily. (PhotoDisc)

Venice's Grand Canal. (Digital Stock)

Welsh countryside, showing farmland divided by stone walls. (PhotoDisc)

One of Vienna's most famous sights is its giant ferris wheel, each of whose fourteen gondolas can hold twenty people. (PhotoDisc)

Budapest's House of Parliament stands on the Danube River. (PhotoDisc)

Budapest. Capital and transportation, industrial, and cultural center of HUNGARY. Population was 1.9 million in 1996. Straddles the DANUBE RIVER in the north-central part of the country. Buda, the older part of the city, is located on hilly terrain on the east bank. Pest sits on plains on the west bank at a historically important river-crossing point. Settlement dates to Roman times, but it did not become a unified city until the nineteenth century, when Obuda, Buda, and Pest were combined into a single entity.

Bükk Mountains. Part of the CARPATHIAN chain, located in northeast HUNGARY. Highest peak is Mount Istállósko, which rises to 3,145 feet (959 meters). The heavily forested range contains lignite deposits on its northern slopes. The city of MISKOLC lies to the east of the range, much of which is a national park.

Bukovina. Historic region in northeast ROMANIA and southwest UKRAINE. Thickly wooded area in foothills of the East CARPATHIANS that produces timber, textiles, grain, and livestock. Mineral resources include salt, manganese, iron, and copper. Part of the Roman province of Dacia; invaded after the third century by Huns and other nomadic groups, in the fourth century by eastern Slavic groups, later by the Mongols. Became the center of the Moldavian principality in the fourteenth century.

Bulgaria. Country in southeastern Europe. Total area of 42,823 square miles (110,910 sq. km.) with a 1990's population of 8.5 million. Capital is SOFIA. Bounded on the east by the BLACK SEA, on the south by TURKEY and GREECE, on the west by MACEDONIA and YUGOSLAVIA, and on the north by ROMANIA. Major rivers include the DANUBE, which forms much of Bulgaria's border with Romania, and the Maritsa in the south. Burgas is the chief port on the 235-mile (378-kilometer) Black Sea Coast. Became independent in 1878.

Cagliari. Capital of SARDINIA, a political region of ITALY, in the MEDITERRANEAN SEA. Population was 174,500 in 1995

Calabria. Peninsula in southern ITALY; the "toe" of the Italian "boot." Covers 5,823 square miles (15,100 sq. km.). Largely mountainous and rural; grain, fruit, rice, flax, wine-making, and grazing account for the livelihoods of most Calabrians. The seaport of MESSINA is the largest urban area, followed by Cosenza, Reggo di Calabria, and Catanzaro.

Calais. French town on the ENGLISH CHANNEL, opposite the English port of DOVER. A chief point of entry for passenger traffic from GREAT BRITAIN.

Cambrian Mountains. Generic name of the main mountain massif of WALES. Extends from South Wales to the northern coast, culminating in the peaks of Snowdonia. Main ranges include the Brecon Beacons, the Black Mountains, the Berwyns, the SNOWDON ranges, and the Clwydians. The rocks are geologically some of the oldest in the BRITISH ISLES, being hard old sedimentaries and slates.

Cambridge. Site of the second-oldest university in the BRITISH ISLES. Population was 96,000 in 1999. Located 55 miles north of LONDON on the western limit of EAST ANGLIA. University dates from 1284. Town has retained its academic atmosphere despite being a busy market town and, more recently, the site of large research complexes.

Canea. Capital of CRETE, a political region of GREECE, in the MEDITERRANEAN SEA. Population was 47,450 in 1981.

Cantabrian Sea. See BISCAY, BAY OF.

Capri. Tiny Italian island in the Bay of Naples, in the MEDITERRANEAN SEA. Total area is 4 square miles (10.4 sq. km.). Renowned for its beauty. Its famous Blue Grotto is a cave, largely underwater, that can be entered only by sea.

Cardiff. Port city in south WALES, the capital of Wales, and seat of the new Welsh Assembly. Population was 306,500 in 1994. Located on the northern shore of the Bristol Channel. Grew rapidly in the nineteenth century because of the mas-

sive coal industry in its hinterland and exports and imports through its port. The city is a political, cultural, and administrative center, with modern auto and electronic industries being established.

Carpathian Mountains. Extensive mountain system running in a semicircle from SLOVAKIA to ROMANIA. About 900 miles (1,450 km.) long, with both ends intersecting the DANUBE RIVER. Has several mountain passes that were sites of invasions throughout history. Contain deposits of silver, gold, lead, iron ore, mercury, copper, petroleum, coal, and salt. The Carpathians are divided into several smaller ranges, including the East and West BESKIDS, TRANSYLVANIAN Alps, East Carpathians, HIGH TATRA Range, White Carpathians, and Little Carpathians.

Catalonia. Linguistic-cultural region in northeastern SPAIN that has pressed for autonomy. Comprises BARCELONA, Gerona, Lerida, and Tarragona provinces. Covers 12,323 square miles (31,953 sq. km.). Apart from urban Barcelona, the region is mainly agricultural; livestock, licorice, grains, livestock, citrus fruits, and nuts are the chief products. The Catalan language is derived from Medieval Provencal French.

Channel Islands. Islands in the ENGLISH CHANNEL. Located 14 miles (23 km.) off the French coast, 80 miles (130 km.) south of ENGLAND, but have belonged to the English Crown since 1066. Total area is 75 square miles (194 sq. km.). The only two populous islands are Jersey (85,000 in 1999) and Guernsey (59,000 in 1999). Biggest sources of income are tourism, offshore finance, and market gardening.

Chechnya. Republic within southwestern RUSSIA, situated on the northern flank of the Greater Caucasus range. Total area of 7,400 square miles (19,300 sq. km.) with a 1993 population (including Ingushetia) of 1.3 million. Bordered by Russia proper on the north, Dagestan republic on the east and southeast, Georgia on the southwest, and the Ingushetia Republic on the west. Originally part of the SOVIET UNION as a portion of the Chechen-Ingush autonomous republic. It declared itself independent in 1991 but afterward joined the Russian Federation. Later resistance to Russian authority led to armed conflict and a Russian invasion. The mainstay of its economy is petroleum. Capital is GROZNY.

Chisinau. Sometimes known by its Russian name, Kishinyov, Chisinau is the capital of the independent nation of MOLDOVA. The first documentary reference to Chisinau dates from 1466, when it was under the rule of the Moldovan prince Stefan III. It is the major industrial center of Moldova, and its population was 676,700 in 1991.

Chunnel. Officially known as Eurotunnel, a tunnel beneath the ENGLISH CHANNEL that links GREAT BRITAIN and FRANCE. Completed in 1994, it connects DOVER, ENGLAND, to CALAIS and runs 31 miles (50 km.). Built as a train tunnel, but private cars and trucks are carried through it on trains.

Clydeside. Heavily industrialized area in southern SCOTLAND. Located along the River Clyde, from its mouth to GLASGOW. Clydebank (population 46,000 in 1999), Paisley (44,000), and Greenock (35,000) are its main towns. Known for its shipbuilding and port facilities. With the closing of the shipbuilding yards, it had the highest rate of unemployment in the BRITISH ISLES at the end of the twentieth century.

Commonwealth of Independent States. A free association of sovereign states

formed in 1991. It comprises RUSSIA and eleven other republics that were formerly part of the SOVIET UNION. All of the former Soviet republics with the exceptions of LITHUANIA, LATVIA, and ESTONIA joined the association. The commonwealth's functions are to coordinate its members' policies regarding their economies, foreign relations, defense, immigration policies, environmental protection, and law enforcement.

Copenhagen. Capital, largest city, and seaport of DENMARK, northern Europe. Located on the eastern shore of the island of Zealand, it is only a short distance across a narrows to SWEDEN. Founded as a small fishing village in 1050, it became the capital and royal residence in 1443. Population was 1.3

*Copen-
hagen
Page 1378*

*Chunnel
Page 1369*

Copenhagen's most famous landmark is a simple bronze statue of a mermaid inspired by a Hans Christian Andersen story. (PhotoDisc)

million in 1998. Known for the Tivoli Gardens and the Little Mermaid statue.

Corfu. Second-largest of the IONIAN ISLANDS of GREECE, in the IONIAN SEA. Located off the west coast of the BALKAN PENINSULA opposite the Albanian-Greek border. Area is about 229 square miles (593 sq. km.); highest point is 2,972 feet (908 meters) at Mount Pantokrator. Population was 97,102 in 1981; its chief city is also called Corfu. Celebrated by artists and writers, and a popular vacation destination.

Corinth Canal. Narrow canal in the MEDITERRANEAN connecting the Gulf of Corinth on the northwest with the Saronic Gulf on the southeast. Canal is 4 miles (6.4 km.) long, 72 feet (22 meters) wide, and 26 feet (8 meters) deep. Dug 1881-1893 to enable ships bound to or from the Greek port of Piraeus to avoid sailing around the large peninsula of PELOPONNESOS.

Cork
Page 1376

Cork. Second-largest city of the Republic of IRELAND. Located along Ireland's south coast; population was 127,000 in 1999, plus a larger metropolitan area. An important Atlantic port, it serves the whole southern part of the country; large numbers of cattle are exported through it.

Land's End
Page 1379

Cornwall. Southwestern promontory of ENGLAND, covering about 1,355 square miles (3,513 sq. km.). Contains both the southernmost (Lizard Point) and westernmost (Land's End) points in GREAT BRITAIN. The region was historically the home of a Gaelic-speaking people who became culturally integrated into the rest of England; it later became a primarily agricultural region. Major ports include Falmouth, Penzance, and Hayle.

Corsica. Large, mountainous French island; fourth-largest island in the MEDITERRANEAN SEA. Located about 99 miles (160 km.) southeast of FRANCE, 60 miles (97 km.) west of ITALY, and 7.5 miles (12 km.) north of SARDINIA. Total area is about 3,350 square miles (8,600 sq. km.); about 115 miles (185 km.) long and 52 miles (84 km.) across at its widest. Highest point is 8,892 feet (2,710 meters) at Monte Cinto. Population was 250,600 in 1991. An active independence movement has been in existence for decades. The island is an administrative department of France that has manifested some separatist activity.

Cracow. City in southern POLAND. Population was 751,000 in 1994. Straddles the VISTULA RIVER. An important rail junction and a center of culture and commerce. The Jagellonian University, attended by Nicholas Copernicus, is among Europe's oldest (1364). City was founded about 700 and was the residence of Polish kings in the fourteenth century. A fire in 1595 caused the capital to move to WARSAW in 1609, but kings continued to be crowned and buried in Cracow. Pope John Paul II was born and served as archbishop here. Also called Kraków.

Crete. Large, mountainous island in the MEDITERRANEAN SEA. Located about 60 miles (97 km.) south of the Greek mainland. Total area is about 3,189 square miles (8,260 sq. km.); is 152 miles (245 km.) long and 35 miles (56 km.) at its widest. Highest point is 8,058 feet (2,456 meters) at Mount Ida. Population was 536,980 in 1991. Together with some smaller islands, forms a Greek political region of the same name with its capital at CANEA.

Crimea. An autonomous republic within the UKRAINE. It is coterminous with the Crimean Peninsula. Primarily Tartars populated it until they were dispersed in 1945 for alleged collaboration with the Germans during World War II. The

Crimea has extensive agriculture, mining, and industrial operations. Its area is 10,400 square miles (27,000 sq. km.), and its population was 2,549,800 in 1991.

Croatia. Country in southeastern Europe. Total area of 21,829 square miles (56,537 sq. km.) with a 1990's population of 4.2 million. Capital is ZAGREB. From 1918 to 1991, was part of YUGOSLAVIA. Declared independence in 1991, bringing on extensive fighting between Serbs and Croats inside of Croatia.

Cyclades. Group of some two hundred islands, twenty-four of them inhabited, in the southern AEGEAN SEA. Have a total area of 1,000 square miles (2,590 sq. km.). Population was 95,000 in 1991. Group is a political department of GREECE; the largest island is NAXOS. Name derives from the fact that they form a circle ("kyklos") around the island of Delos, once regarded as sacred. A popular tourist destination.

Cyprus. Large island in the northeastern corner of the MEDITERRANEAN SEA. Located about 40 miles (65 km.) south of TURKEY (Asia Minor) and 59 miles (95 km.) west of Syria. Covers 3,586 square miles (9,287 sq. km.); is about 139 miles (223 km.) long from east to west. Population was 875,000 in 1999. Highest point is 6,405 feet (1,952 meters) at Mount Olympus (not to be confused with the more famous mountain of the same name in GREECE's mainland). Once a British colony, was divided in 1975 between the Republic of Cyprus and a smaller, ethnically Turkish region, known as the Turkish Republic of Northern Cyprus. The capital of the Republic of Cyprus is NICOSIA. Largely ethnic Greek in population; recognized as the legitimate government of the island by all nations of the world except Turkey. The Turkish Republic of

Northern Cyprus occupies almost half the island. It is recognized as a legitimate government only by the nation of Turkey. Population was 200,587 in 1996; capital is Lefkosa (known to Greek Cypriots as Nicosia).

Czech Republic. Central European nation created in 1993 by the peaceful breakup of CZECHOSLOVAKIA, from which it took the larger, western portion. Borders GERMANY on the west and north, POLAND on the northeast, AUSTRIA on the south, and SLOVAKIA on the southeast; area is 30,352 square miles (78,703 sq. km.); population in 1999 was 10,272,179. The country has large coal and iron ore reserves and is highly industrialized. In 1999 it joined the North Atlantic Treaty Organization and was being considered for membership in the European Union. Capital is PRAGUE.

Czechoslovakia. Central European nation created in 1919 by settlement of World War I. After World War II, was dominated by SOVIET UNION; Capital was PRAGUE. In 1993 broke up; western part became CZECH REPUBLIC; eastern portion became SLOVAKIA.

Dalmatian Islands. Archipelago of eight hundred islands in the ADRIATIC SEA. Located off the coast of Dalmatia, a region of CROATIA. Renowned for their austere beauty, they were important tourist destinations until the disintegration of YUGOSLAVIA brought fighting to the region in the late twentieth century.

Danube River. Second-longest river in Europe and one of its principal transportation routes. Unique among major European rivers, it flows from west to east, about 1,776 miles (2,859 km.) from its headwaters in southern GERMANY to the BLACK SEA, passing through AUSTRIA, SLOVAKIA, HUNGARY, YUGOSLAVIA, CROATIA, BOSNIA-HERZEGOVINA, SLOVENIA, BULGARIA, ROMANIA, and

Cyclades
Page 1442

Dalmatia
Page 1442

UKRAINE. In northern Yugoslavia, three important tributaries join the Danube: the TISZA, which drains the CARPATHIAN MOUNTAINS; the Drava, which drains northern Yugoslavia; and the Sava, which drains Croatia and northern Yugoslavia. Passes through the IRON GATE, then forms most of the boundary between Romania and Bulgaria. Before entering the Black Sea, it breaks up into several branches, the northernmost of which forms the boundary between Romania and the Ukraine. Drains a basin of 315,444 square miles (817,000 sq. km.). Several countries have built dams and hydroelectric power plants along its length. Pollution has diminished once-rich fishing grounds and water for drinking and irrigation.

Danzig. See GDÁNSK.

Debrecen. Second-largest city, transportation hub, administrative center, and industrial city in eastern HUNGARY. Economic and cultural center of Great ALFÖLD east of TISZA RIVER. Population was 213,900 in 1991. Grew as marketplace for cattle and grain. Under Ottoman Turkish occupation, was a stronghold of Hungarian Protestantism in sixteenth century. Became center of Hungarian resistance against Austrian rule in the nineteenth century.

Denmark. The most southern of the Scandinavian countries. Bounded on the north by the SKAGERRAK STRAIT and NORWAY beyond, the NORTH SEA on the west, GERMANY on the south, and the KATTEGAT STRAIT, SWEDEN, and the BALTIC SEA on the east. Total area of 16,639 square miles (43,094 sq. km.), half the size of Maine, with a population of 5.3 million in 1999. Capital is COPENHAGEN (Kobenhavn). Largely made up of the JUTLAND Peninsula (11,497 square miles) and the islands of Zealand (2,876 square miles) and Fyn (1,152 square miles). A low-lying region with little hilly terrain, well known for its agriculture and dairy industry. Until 1979, the world's largest island, Greenland, was part of the Danish Kingdom.

Derry. Second-largest town of NORTHERN IRELAND. Located at the base of Lough Foyle, 70 miles (113 km.) east of BELFAST; population was 72,000 in 1999. Its political past has been bitterly divisive between Catholic and Protestant communities. Called Londonderry by the Protestant community.

Dinaric Alps. Mountain range along the eastern shore of the ADRIATIC SEA in southeastern Europe. An extension of the Eastern ALPS, these limestone mountains follow the Adriatic coast from SLOVENIA to ALBANIA and greatly restrict access from the Adriatic Sea to the interior of the BALKAN PENINSULA.

Dnieper River. The fourth longest river of Europe, 1,420 miles (2,286 km.), after the VOLGA, DANUBE, and URAL Rivers. More than three hundred hydroelectric plants operate in the Dnieper Basin, supplying water to the Donets Basin and Kryvyy Rih industrial regions, and for irrigation to the arid lands of the southern UKRAINE and the CRIMEA.

Dniester River. River of the southwestern UKRAINE and of MOLDOVA. In Moldova it is called the Nistru river. It starts on the north side of the CARPATHIAN MOUNTAINS and flow south and east for 877 miles (1,412 km.) to the BLACK SEA near ODESSA. The river is used for carrying logs, which are brought together at the mouths of the Carpathian tributaries and rafted downstream.

Dobruja. Agricultural region in central-eastern Europe, located in southeast ROMANIA and northeast BULGARIA between the lower DANUBE RIVER and the BLACK SEA. A low, dry coastal strip with a hilly and forested upland. Supports cereal grains, vineyards, sheep herding, some industry, and tourism. Original inhabitants were conquered in sixth century by Greeks. As part of Roman and Byzantine Empires, was frequently invaded. In 1878 given to Romania and Bulgaria.

Dodecanese Islands. Group of Greek islands lying off the coast of Asia Minor (TURKEY) in the AEGEAN SEA. Total area is 1,048 square miles (2,714 sq. km.); population was 163,476 in 1991. Name is derived from the Greek word for twelve ("dodeka"), but there are fourteen major islands, the largest being RHODES. Sometimes included in the Southern SPORADES group.

Don River. Russian river that rises in the small reservoir of Shat near the city of Novomoskovsk, south of MOSCOW in the central Russian uplands. It flows for 1,224 miles (1,971 km.) in a southerly direction and empties into the Gulf of Taganrog in the Sea of AZOV. The lower portion of the river is a major transportation artery.

Dover. English port on the ENGLISH CHANNEL opposite the French port of CALAIS. Long the chief port of entry for passenger traffic from the Continent, it has become a terminus of the undersea CHUNNEL.

Dover, Strait of. Narrow channel between GREAT BRITAIN and FRANCE that connects the NORTH SEA and ENGLISH CHANNEL.

Dublin. Ancient and current capital and leading city of IRELAND. Population was 860,000 in 1999, with 55,000 more in Dun Laoghaire, its passenger port. Has a sheltered harbor facing the IRISH SEA on Ireland's east coast, through which the bulk of the country's imports and exports go. Its center was laid out in its eighteenth century Anglo-Irish prime.

Has prospered through Ireland's membership in the European Union. Has one-third of the Republic of Ireland's population and is the center of its road and rail networks.

Duero River. Major river on the IBERIAN PENINSULA of Western Europe. Flowing east to west for 485 miles (780 km.), it originates near Soria, SPAIN, and runs through Valladollid before entering PORTUGAL to Oporto, and thence to the Atlantic. Navigation past Oporto is hampered by rapids. It runs through the Paiz do Vinho, one of Portugal's most prolific wine-producing regions.

Dundee. City on the east coast of SCOTLAND at the mouth of the Firth of Tay. Population was 148,900 in 1997. Main industry traditionally has been jute manufacturing, followed by confectionery and preserves, fishing, and docking.

Dvina River. Sometimes referred to as the Northern Dvina. It is formed by the junction of the Sukhona and Yug rivers at the city of Velikiy Ustyug, in the Vologod province of RUSSIA. The Dvina flows 462 miles (744 km.) in a northwesterly direction and drains into the Dvina inlet of the WHITE SEA below the city of Arkhangelsk.

East Anglia. Eastern projection of ENGLAND between the THAMES estuary and the WASH. Population was 2.1 million in 1995; chief cities are Norwich (171,000), Ipswich (130,000), and CAMBRIDGE. Flat, fertile land formed the basis of England's medieval prosperity with sheep-raising and wheat-growing. Still agriculturally significant, its coastal areas and shallow lakes also attract tourists.

Ebro River. Major Spanish river originating in the Cantabrian Mountains of northeastern SPAIN and flowing west to east past Zaragoza, 465 miles (750 km.), to feed into the MEDITERRANEAN at

Edinburgh
Page 1380

Cabo de Tortosa. Only navigable to ocean traffic as far as Tortosa, 20 miles (32 km.) inland.

Edinburgh. Ancient capital, cultural and religious center of SCOTLAND, and seat of the Scottish Parliament. Located a few miles inland from the Firth of Forth on Scotland's southeast coast; population of 420,000 in the 1990's. Has one of BRITAIN's oldest universities and a royal palace. Its famous festival attracts many visitors.

Elba. Small Italian island of the Tuscan Archipelago in the MEDITERRANEAN SEA. Located less than 6 miles (10 km.) off the northwestern coast of ITALY. Total area is about 86 square miles (223 sq. km.). French ruler Napoleon Bonaparte was exiled there from May, 1814, to February, 1815.

Elbe River. Major river in Western Europe. Rises in the CZECH REPUBLIC but flows through GERMANY for most of its 724 miles (1,186 km.). With canals linking it to the Spree and Oder, the Elbe runs through Magdeburg, Dessau, and Hamburg before joining the NORTH SEA at Cuxhaven.

England. Historical kingdom that makes up the major part of the island of GREAT BRITAIN and the UNITED KINGDOM. Borders SCOTLAND on the north and WALES on the west. CORNWALL, historically a separate realm to England's southwest, is now considered a part of England.

Mt. Etna
Page 1380

English Channel. Body of water separating FRANCE from GREAT BRITAIN. Runs for roughly 350 miles (560 km.), stretching from the Atlantic Ocean in the west to the Strait of DOVER in the east, where it is only 21 miles wide (34 km.) wide. The channel washes ENGLAND's south coast, along which are situated several major ports, including Southampton (population of 211,000 in the 1990's) and

Poole (213,000); and naval dockyards, such as Portsmouth (174,000) and Devonport, part of Plymouth (245,295), the second-largest town in the west of England. Many resorts and retirement communities are here also: Brighton, also a LONDON commuter town; Bournemouth; Torquay; and Paignton. Its main continental ports are Le Havre, Cherbourg, and CALAIS in France. The channel is a major highway for container, oil tanker, and hovercraft traffic. Completion of the Eurotunnel (also called the CHUNNEL), linking DOVER and Calais, opened steady rail and automobile transportation between Britain and the continent beneath the channel.

Estonia. Former Soviet republic which became independent in 1991. ESTONIA had been part of Imperial RUSSIA, then independent from 1918 to 1940, then incorporated into the SOVIET UNION in 1940. It is located on the western rim of the former Soviet Union, on the eastern coast of the BALTIC SEA and just south of FINLAND on the southern shores of the Gulf of Finland. The people ethnically are Finnish and their language is very similar to Finnish. Estonia's land area is 17,442 miles (45,226 sq. km.). Its population in 1999 was 1,431,471. Estonians comprise 65 percent of the population and ethnic Russians 28 percent. Capital is TALLINN.

Etna, Mount. Europe's largest volcano and one of its most active. Located on the Italian island of SICILY, at 37°45′ north latitude, longitude 15° east. Rises to 10,959 feet (3,340 meters). Its eruptions have been documented from about 1500 B.C.E.

Euskadi. Linguistic and cultural region in western FRANCE (Gascony) and Vizcaya, Guipuzcoa, and San Sebastian provinces in northern SPAIN, where the majority of the population is Basque. The Basque language, Euskara, is unrelated to any other language, and the Basques have been extremely tenacious, to the point of separatism, in maintaining their cultural identity. The Basque way of life is largely pastoral; Euskadi remains predominantly rural, although the city of Bilbao is becoming a notable industrial and business center.

Finland. Easternmost country of northern Europe, bounded by RUSSIA on the east, the Gulf of FINLAND on the south, the Gulf of BOTHNIA and SWEDEN on the west, and NORWAY on the far north and northwest. Total area of 130,560 square miles (338,145 sq. km.), three times the size of Ohio, with a population of 5.1 million in 1999. Capital is HELSINKI. Independent since 1917, its history includes Swedish and Russian domination since the thirteenth century. Called Suomi by the Finns.

Florence. Capital of central ITALY's Florence province, located on the ARNO RIVER. Famous for its art treasures, Florence was a major center of the Italian Renaissance and was capital of much of Italy through the early nineteenth century. A major tourist destination and the center of a prosperous agricultural region.

Florence Page 1381

France. Largest state in Western Europe with an area of 210,964 square miles (547,030 sq. km.) and a 1999 population of 59,329,691. Capital is PARIS. Bounded on the south by the PYRENEES range, the Spanish border, and the MEDITERRANEAN coast (the RIVIERA); on the west by the Bay of BISCAY and Atlantic Ocean; on the north by the ENGLISH CHANNEL; and on the east by BELGIUM, LUXEMBOURG, GERMANY, SWITZERLAND, and ITALY. France divides into the French Plain running in a crescent from Gascony to the Belgian

Florence, Italy. (PhotoDisc)

Gdánsk, Poland. (PhotoDisc)

border, and the central uplands (Massif Central), culminating in the French ALPS. French is the official language, but Breton is also spoken in BRITTANY, Euskara in Gascony, and Italian in Savoy and Nice. Although Roman Catholicism is the leading religious denomination, there are significant Jewish and Muslim communities in Paris and other urban areas and Protestants (Huguenots) in the south. Major cities include Paris, MARSEILLES, Lyons, Bordeaux, Toulouse, Lille, Saint-Etienne, Toulon, Le Havre, Nancy, Le Mans, and Strasbourg. The island of CORSICA is considered to be part of metropolitan France.

Fyn. See DENMARK.

Garonne River. Major river of FRANCE. Rises in the eastern PYRENEES and runs through Foix and Toulouse, where it becomes navigable and takes in the Lot and Tarn as tributaries; continues to Bordeaux, where it links with the Dordogne to form the Gironde estuary, and empties into the Bay of BISCAY. Length is 355 miles (570 km.).

Gdánsk. One of chief ports and an industrial and communications center in Po-

LAND. Located on BALTIC SEA at the Gulf of Gdánsk. Population was 466,700 in 1993. Its shipyards are among the world's largest. Originally a Slavic settlement, many German merchants subsequently arrived. Joined the Hanseatic League (thirteenth century); conquered by the Teutonic Order in 1308. Returned to Poland in 1466, later became a free city, then belonged to Prussia; became a free city again. Hitler's demand that the city be returned to GERMANY was the principal excuse for German invasion of Poland leading to World War II. Annexed to Germany from 1939 to 1945. Labor unrest in Gdánsk shipyards led to formation of the Solidarity Union in 1980. Also known as Danzig.

Geneva. City in a canon of the same name, located at the southern tip of Lake Geneva in southwestern SWITZERLAND; population 170,000 in the early 1990's. An important center of manufacturing as well as the site of many world organizations—including the League of Nations (1919-1946)—and international conferences.

Genoa. Major port and commercial center in northwestern ITALY, on the LIGURIAN SEA. Historically a major shipbuilding center and the boyhood home of explorer Christopher Columbus.

Germany. Federal republic; formed on October 3, 1990, by the reunification of the former German Federal (West) and German Democratic (East) Republics. Total area of 137,803 square miles (357,323 sq. km.) with a 1990's population of eighty-four million. Capital is BERLIN as of January 1, 2000; major cities are Hamburg, Munich, and Cologne. The north consists of the German extension of the Great European Plain, while the center and south are mountainous; the highest elevations are found in the Bavarian ALPS. Official language is German, although in the eastern region of Lusatia, large numbers of the local Sorbs speak a Slavic language. Roman Catholicism is the main denomination in the country's southern states, and Protestantism (mainly Lutheran) in the north. Primary industries include machinery, motor vehicles, iron, brewing, shipbuilding, livestock, coal mining, petroleum products, aluminum, textiles, wood products, and rubber.

Gibraltar. British crown colony, consisting of a promontory (the Rock of Gibraltar) in southern SPAIN commanding the Strait of GIBRALTAR. Covers 2.5 square miles (4 sq. km.); population of 29,000 in the 1990's. Held by GREAT BRITAIN since 1713. Administered by an appointed governor, assisted by executive and legislative councils. English and Spanish are spoken.

Gibraltar, Strait of. Strait linking the Atlantic Ocean and MEDITERRANEAN SEA; 8 miles (12.8 km.) wide at its narrowest. Located between the IBERIAN PENINSULA and the northwestern tip of Africa; named for the Rock of Gibraltar, a large headland on the southern coast of SPAIN. Is the site of the Pillars of Hercules—Gibraltar and Mount Acho (in some traditions, Jebel Musa) in Africa—which the ancient Greeks regarded as the limits of the known world.

Glasgow. Most populous city in SCOTLAND. Located on the River Clyde; population was 611,660 in 1997. Site of Scotland's first wave of industrialization, especially its engineering works, and much of the ensuing commercial development. A densely populated city, it has had tre-

mendous social problems with slums. Great efforts at urban renewal made in the 1990's.

Gorky. See NIZHNY NOVGOROD

Göteborg. Second-largest city in SWEDEN, northern Europe, with a population of 459,600 in 1998. Located on the southwestern edge of the country, along the KATTEGAT STRAIT. An important seaport, shipbuilding, and industrial center. Founded in 1619 by King Gustavus Adolphus.

Great Alföld. See ALFÖLD, GREAT.

Great Britain. Island off the coast of Western Europe that includes ENGLAND, Scotland, and WALES. Together with NORTHERN IRELAND and the Isle of MAN, makes up the the UNITED KINGDOM—with which it is not synonymous.

Great Hungarian Plain. See ALFÖLD, GREAT.

Greece. Country in southeastern Europe. Total area of 50,950 square miles (131,945 sq. km.) with a 1990's population of 10.3 million. Capital is ATHENS. Located on the southern tip of the BALKAN PENINSULA, bounded on the north by ALBANIA, MACEDONIA, and BULGARIA, and on the east by TURKEY. Its territory includes many islands in the adjoining seas. Much of Greece is dominated by the rugged Pindus Mountains. Only one-third of the land in Greece is capable of cultivating crops. Modern Greece gained its independence in 1829 and reached its present size in the twentieth century. The only Balkan country that is a member of the European Union.

Grozny. City and capital of the Republic of CHECHNYA. It lies along the Sunzha River at the foot of the Sunzha Range of the Caucasus. The Grozny area is a significant oil-producing region. It has been partially destroyed by heavy fighting between Russian troops and Che-

Hadrian's Wall Page 1382

chen independent fighters in the 1990's. Its population was 364,000 in 1993.

Guadalquivir River. Major river in SPAIN, Western Europe. Rises in the eastern hills of Jaen Province and flows through Cordoba and Seville (the point up to which it is navigable to ocean traffic) and into the Gulf of Cadiz at Sanlucar de Barrameda in the Las Marismas marshlands. Total length is 408 miles (656 km.). Name derives from the Moorish *Wadi el Kebir* (Great River).

Guadiana River. Important Iberian river in Western Europe. Rises in the Cuenca Mountains of southeastern SPAIN and turns westward into the arid Badajoz Province, where it has been dammed to water the region by a vast irrigation system and provide power from hydroelectricity. From Badajoz it turns south, winding for a total of 483 miles (777 km.) before merging into the Gulf of Cadiz at Tavira, PORTUGAL.

Hadrian's Wall. Roman structure built in northern England in the early second century C.E. to protect the northern limit of Roman occupation in Britain. The wall is 73 miles (118 km.) long.

Hague, The. Administrative capital of the NETHERLANDS and of South Holland Province. Contains the official residence of the royal family, the Netherlands high court, the Council of State, and the International Court of Justice. Printing, distilling, jewelry, and furniture manufacturing are the principal economic activities. Population was 683,000 in the 1990's. Also called S'Gravenhage.

Hammerfest. Northernmost town in Europe. Located in northwestern NORWAY, on the shores of the Arctic Ocean, with a population of 9,150 in 1999. Tourism, fish-oil processing, and livestock are its economic mainstays. Despite its location, its excellent harbor is ice-free year-round.

Like many Dutch cities, The Hague is built on canals. (PhotoDisc)

Hebrides. Group of islands stretching along the west coast of Scotland. Population was 29,000 in 1995. The Inner Hebrides lie adjacent to the coast, entwined in its convolutions. The largest are Skye, Mull, and Islay; includes Iona, the first Christian settlement in Scotland. The Outer Hebrides, comprising the islands of Lewis and Uist, are 36 miles (54 km.) off the mainland. Also known as the Western Isles.

Hekla, Mount. Active volcano in southern ICELAND. Located 70 miles (110 km.) east of REYKJAVIK, at 63.53 degrees north latitude, longitude 19.37 degrees west. Stands 4,892 feet (1,491 meters) above sea level. Known in early times as the Mountain of Hell, it erupted fourteen times between 1104 and 1970. A volcanic eruption in 1766 caused great loss of life.

Helsinki. Capital of FINLAND. Located on the south central coast of the country along the Gulf of Finland. Founded in 1550; became the capital in 1812, after Russians gained the territory of Finland from the Swedish Kingdom in 1809. Had a population of 546,300 in 1999. The 1952 Summer Olympic Games were held there.

High Tatra Mountains. Highest part of the CARPATHIAN MOUNTAIN chain in central-eastern Europe. Located along border between POLAND and SLOVAKIA. Extends 37 miles (60 km.); highest peak is Slovakia's Gerlachovský Stit at 8,711 feet (2,655 meters). Glaciated mountains with lakes, moraines, and hanging valleys. Year-round resort area with excellent ski slopes. National parks were established in 1948 on both sides of the international border.

Highlands, Scottish. See LOWLANDS AND HIGHLANDS.

Holland. Historic kingdom that formed the core region of modern NETHER-LANDS, which is often called by the same name.

Home Counties. Counties in the southeast of ENGLAND, contiguous to LONDON. Once rural, the region has become largely suburban with the movement of population into London. Towns within a 15-mile radius (24 km.) of London have been absorbed into London, including Watford (113,000) and Epsom (65,000). Many of the remaining open spaces are used for recreational purposes, protected by greenbelt zoning laws.

Hull. Port on the east coast of ENGLAND, part of Humberside. Located on the estuarial River Humber; population was 332,000 in 1995, with a population for Humberside of 890,000. Used by the NORTH SEA fishing and oil industries, and for trade with the NETHER-LANDS and GERMANY, especially from the industrial areas of the north of England and the MIDLANDS. Also called Kingston-upon-Hull.

Helsinki
Page 1369

Hungary. Central European country bordered on the north by SLOVAKIA, on the east by UKRAINE and ROMANIA, on the south by CROATIA and YUGOSLAVIA, and on the west by AUSTRIA; area is 35,919 square miles (93,030 sq. km.); population was 10,138,844 in 1999. Capital is Budapest. Before World War I was part of the Austro-Hungarian Empire but lost much of its territory in the postwar settlement. Dominated by the SOVIET UNION from 1945 to 1989, when it cast off communist rule and began to democratize. Joined the North Atlantic Treaty Organization in 1999.

Iberian Peninsula. Western European land mass containing SPAIN and POR-TUGAL that separates the MEDITERRA-NEAN SEA from the Atlantic Ocean. It is separated from FRANCE and the rest of the Continent by the PYRENEES; mostly composed of uplands and plateaus. GI-BRALTAR, near the southern tip of the peninsula, is owned by Great Britain.

Iceland. Island country located in the North Atlantic Ocean; considered to be part of northern Europe. Bounded by the Greenland Sea on the north, the NORWEGIAN SEA on the east, the Atlantic Ocean on the south and west, and the Denmark Strait. on the northwest. Total area of 39,768 square miles (103,000 sq. km.) with a population of 278,700 in 1999, almost entirely of Scandinavian origin. Capital is REYKJA-VIK. The nearest land neighbor is GREENLAND, 200 miles (320 km.) to the northwest. Situated on top of the northern part of the Atlantic Mid-Oceanic Ridge, it is characterized by major volcanic activities, geothermal springs, and glaciers. About one-tenth of the land is covered by glaciers and cooled lava beds. Settled more than 1,000 years ago during the Viking Age of exploration.

Inverness. Chief town and center of the HIGHLANDS of Scotland. Population was 62,000 in 1999. Strategically positioned on the Moray Firth, between it and the northern tip of Loch Ness, between the mountains and the flatter coastal strip of northeast Scotland. All road and rail communications to the far north must pass through it. Area of outstanding natural beauty, covering most of the north and west of Scotland. Has a thriving tourist industry.

Ionian Islands. Series of four major and several minor Greek islands in the IONIAN SEA. Located off the west and southwest coast of GREECE. The largest islands are Cephalonia and CORFU. Total area is about 891 square miles (2,307 sq. km.). Population was 193,700 in 1991, more than half of whom lived on Corfu.

Ionian Sea. Arm of the MEDITERRANEAN SEA between southern ITALY and GREECE. About 420 miles (676 km.) at its widest; descends to a depth of 16,897 feet (5,150 meters) in the Hellenic Trough, the deepest point in the Mediterranean Sea. The name is derived from the Ionians, an Indo-European tribe which invaded Greece c. 1450 B.C.E.

Ireland. Second largest of the BRITISH ISLES; separated from GREAT BRITAIN by the IRISH SEA. Historically dominated by Britain; most of the island became independent as the Irish Free State in 1922; later became the Republic of Ireland. Area of the republic is 27,135 square miles (70,280 sq. km.); population was 3,797,257 in 1999. Largely rural, having few mineral resources to exploit. Many areas of outstanding natural beauty form the basis of a thriving tourist industry. DUBLIN is the capital and only major city. When the Irish Free State was created, Great Britain kept the island's industrial base in NORTHERN IRELAND.

Irish Sea. Sea that separates IRELAND and GREAT BRITAIN. Covers 40,000 square miles (103,600 sq. km.); 143 miles (230 km.) across at its widest. Connected to the Atlantic Ocean in the north by the North Channel and to the Celtic Sea in the south by Saint George's Channel. Its fishing resources have become limited, but oil and natural gas deposits have been found in Morecombe and Liverpool Bays off the English coast.

Iron Gate. Narrowest part of the 80-mile (128-kilometer) Kazan Gorge where the DANUBE RIVER passes between the BALKAN MOUNTAINS and the TRANSYLVANIAN ALPS. YUGOSLAVIA is located on the south side of the gorge and ROMANIA on the north side. Once a major barrier to transportation along the Danube River, it was cleared of rock ob-

*Ireland
Pages
1376, 1382*

*Loch Ness
Page 1310*

structions in the 1860's. Now the site of one of Europe's largest hydroelectric power dams, a joint Yugoslav-Romanian project opened in 1971. The dam improved river navigation by creating a large lake and has large electricity-generating capacity. On the Serbian side of the gorge is a national park.

Isle of Man. See MAN, ISLE OF.

Italy. Republic in southern Europe. Located below the ALPS and bordered on the north by FRANCE, SWITZERLAND, AUSTRIA, and SLOVENIA. Total area of 116,195 square miles (301,293 sq. km.) including SICILY, SARDINIA, and smaller isles; had a 1990's population of fifty-eight million. Capital and primate city is ROME; other major urban centers are Milan, NAPLES, and Turin. The Italian Peninsula runs north-south for 846 miles (1,360 km.), averaging 150 miles (240 km.) in width. Much of the interior is taken up by the APENNINES Mountain chain, which begins just below the Lombard Plain (PO RIVER Valley) and continues through to Messina in the south. Italy is seismically quite active: Earthquakes occur periodically and there are three active volcanoes—Mount Vesuvius, STROMBOLI Isle, and Mount ETNA in Sicily. Production of wine is second only to France; of olive oil, second to SPAIN. Other major products include grains, cheese, potatoes, and sugar beets. Major industries are automobile and heavy machinery production, tourism, food processing, and sugar refining. Roman Catholicism is the major religion.

Jutland. Peninsula jutting north from mainland Europe, where DENMARK is connected to GERMANY along a land border 42 miles (68 km.) long. This is the largest land area in Denmark, covering 11,497 square miles (29,812 sq. km.). Its highest point is in the east cen-

tral region, and is only 568 feet (173 meters) above sea level.

Kama River. Rivers that rises in the Upper Kama Upland of Udmurtia in west-central RUSSIA. It flows north, then east, south, and southwest for about 1,261 miles (2,030 km.) until it enters the VOLGA RIVER below Kazan, in the Samara Reservoir.

Kattegat Strait. Strait between SWEDEN and DENMARK that connects the NORTH Sea with the BALTIC SEA, through the ØRESUND STRAIT.

Kingston-upon-Hull. See HULL.

Kiruna. City in northern SWEDEN, north of the Arctic Circle, recognized as having the world's largest area. Since incorporating nearby areas in 1948, the city limits include more than 7,800 square miles (20,669 sq. km.), slightly larger than the state of New Jersey. Population was 26,000 in 1995. Founded in 1899. Mining is the principal industry.

Knossos. Ruined city near the northern coast of the Greek island of CRETE. Settled as early as 6000 B.C.E. and regarded as the center of the ancient Minoan civilization.

Kosovo. Region of SERBIA in YUGOSLAVIA. Most of the population is Albanian-speaking. Much of the land is hilly and used for grazing livestock. In 1998-1999, Serb forces drove out most of the Albanian population. Forces from the North Atlantic Treaty Organization (NATO) entered Kosovo and permitted the refugees to return.

Kraków. See CRACOW.

Ladoga, Lake. Largest lake in Europe; located in northwestern RUSSIA, about 25 miles (40 km.) east of ST. PETERSBURG. Its surface covers about 6,700 square miles (17,600 sq. km.) and is 136 miles (219 km.) long. It has an average width of 50 miles (80 km.) and an average depth of 167 feet (51 meters).

Its greatest depth is 754 feet (230 meters).

Lake District. Area in the Cumbrian mountains of northwest ENGLAND. Formerly remote, it was made famous by the Romantic poets of the nineteenth century and has become a popular tourist area, particularly for hikers and mountaineers. Includes the Lake District National Park.

Lapland. Region in northern Europe, above the Arctic Circle. Located in the mountains of northern SCANDINAVIA in FINLAND, SWEDEN, NORWAY, and the Kola Peninsula of northwestern RUSSIA. Total area of 150,000 square miles (388,000 sq. km.) is slightly larger than Montana. It is home to about 55,000 Saami people, nomadic reindeer herdsmen.

Latvia. Former Soviet republic which became an independent nation in 1991. Latvia had been part of Imperial RUSSIA, then independent from 1918 to 1940, then incorporated into the SOVIET UNION in 1940. Industry accounts for more than 40 percent of the country's gross domestic product. Its land area is 24,720 square miles (64,100 sq. km.). Its population in 1999 was 2,404,926, of whom 55 percent were Latvian and 33 percent ethnic Russian.

Leeds. Largest city in the county of Yorkshire in northern ENGLAND. Its population was 430,000 in the 1990's. The surrounding West Yorkshire conurbation, covering 480 square miles (778 sq. km.), had a 1995 population of 2.1 million, including the cities of Bradford (290,000), Huddersfield (144,000), Halifax (91,000), and Wakefield (74,000). Grew rapidly during the Industrial Revolution, as a center for woolen manufactures and clothing. Most important cultural center of northeast England.

Lefkosa. See NICOSIA.

Leningrad. Name for RUSSIA's ST. PETERSBURG from 1924 until 1991, during the period of the SOVIET UNION.

Liechtenstein. Principality in Western Europe. Located in the RHINE RIVER Valley between AUSTRIA and SWITZERLAND. Total area of 62 square miles (161 sq. km.) with a 1990's population of thirty-one thousand. Capital is Vaduz. Self-governing since 1713, Liechtenstein is closely linked to Switzerland through a 1923 customs union. Major economic activities are postage stamps, tourism, banking, and finance.

Ligurian Sea. Western European sea bordering to the north on the French and Italian RIVIERAS and to south, as a branch of the MEDITERRANEAN SEA, by the island of CORSICA. Its major ports are Nice in FRANCE, and GENOA, La Spezia, Pisa, and Livorno in ITALY.

Lillehammer. Site of the 1994 Winter Olympics. Located north of OSLO in the southeastern part of NORWAY. Industries include textiles, lumber, paper and food processing, and tourism. Population was 24,530 in 1999. Chartered in 1827.

Lipari Islands. Group of small, volcanic Italian islands off the coast of SICILY in the southeastern corner of the TYRRHENIAN SEA. STROMBOLI is the most famous. Total area is about 45 square miles (117 sq. km.). Believed by the ancient Greeks to be the home of the wind god Aeolus; also known as the Aeolian Islands.

Lisbon. Capital, primate city, and leading port of PORTUGAL. Located on the TAGUS RIVER estuary. Population was 807,000 in the 1990's. Major manufacturing center for cement, ceramics, textiles, cork, plastics, glassware, food processing (particularly fish), and soap products. The center, Cidade Baixa, re-

Liechten-stein
Page 1431

Lisbon
Page 1432

tains the broad boulevards and squares that were built after Lisbon's devastating 1755 earthquake.

Lithuania. A former Soviet republic which became independent in 1991. Lithuania had been part of Imperial RUSSIA, then independent from 1918 to 1940, then incorporated into the SOVIET UNION in 1940. Like neighboring LATVIA, Lithuania is very industrialized. Its land area is 25,210 square miles (65,040 sq. km.). Its population in 1999 was 3,620,756, 81 percent of whom were Lithuanian and 9 percent ethnic Russian. Capital is VILNIUS.

Little Alföld. See ALFÖLD, LITTLE.

Liverpool. Most important port on the west coast of BRITAIN. Located on the estuary of the River Mersey, which opens into Liverpool Bay and thence the IRISH SEA. Population was just over half a million in the late 1990's. Since the eighteenth century, has traded across the Atlantic and with West Africa; heavily involved with the slave trade until 1820. The main port of transit for IRELAND; many Irish and Welsh migrant workers helped the city's rapid but problematic growth in the mid-nineteenth century. In the late twentieth century, the city's fortunes declined with loss of trade, industrial unrest, and social problems, but it retains a strong sense of identity.

Ljubljana. Capital, largest city, and industrial and commercial center of SLOVENIA. Located on Ljubljana River, a tributary of the Sava River. An imposing castle dominates the center of the town. Until 1918, controlled by AUSTRIA and known as Laibach.

London's House of Parliament and Big Ben clock tower. London was long famous for its thick "pea-soup" fogs; however, the use of cleaner-burning coal has made them largely a thing of the past. (PhotoDisc)

Lódz. Second-largest city and major industrial center in POLAND. Population was 833,700 in 1994. Center of the Polish textile industry; developed as a food processing and textile center after 1850. Chartered in 1423; became a Prussian center in 1793; given to RUSSIA in 1815; reverted to Poland in 1919; incorporated into GERMANY during World War II.

Loire River. Important river in FRANCE. Has its source in the Cevennes Hills and travels to the west for 634 miles (1,021 km.) into the Bay of BISCAY near Saint Nazaire. Passes through Orleans, Tours, Angers, Nantes, and the Chateaux Country that is one of France's main historic tourist regions.

London. Largest city of the BRITISH ISLES; capital of the UNITED KINGDOM and a major world cultural and financial center. Located on the River THAMES near its estuary in southeast ENGLAND. Its immediate population is 7.5 million; the Greater London area of 720 square miles (1,168 sq. km.) has 25 percent of the English population. Originally, the City of London (the City) was fortified. The adjacent City of Westminster became the area of royalty and government. In the eighteenth and nineteenth centuries, London expanded eastward along newly built dock areas along the estuary and then in all directions. In the twentieth century, Greater London swallowed up the former County of London, the County of Middlesex, and large parts of the other HOME COUNTIES. Immigrants have continued to swell its numbers. The center of BRITAIN's road and rail network, with thirteen railroad termini, and of air and sea communications worldwide, with three international airports and extensive port facilities.

Londonderry. See DERRY.

Low Countries. Collective term for BELGIUM, LUXEMBOURG, and the NETHERLANDS. See also BENELUX.

Lowlands and Highlands. The two geographic and cultural areas of SCOTLAND. The lowland areas include the central valley running between GLASGOW and EDINBURGH and the northeast coastal strip round ABERDEEN. Most of Scotland's population and industry are concentrated there. Most of the rest of the country makes up the highlands.

Luxembourg. Grand duchy in Western Europe. Borders on FRANCE, BELGIUM, and GERMANY. Total area of 999 square miles (2,590 sq. km.) with a 1990's population of 422,000. Capital is Luxembourg City, which is the site of the Court of the European Communities, the European Investment Bank, and the European Parliament Secretariat. French, German, and the local Letzeburgisch language are spoken; Roman Catholicism is the major religion. Chief industries include iron and steel, chemicals,

*Majorca
Page 1433*

plastics, banking, and finance. Independent since 1867.

Macedonia. Country in southeastern Europe. Total area of 9,928 square miles (25,174 sq. km.) with a 1990's population of 2 million. Capital is SKOPJE. Was a republic of YUGOSLAVIA until independence in 1991; now the poorest of Yugoslavia's former republics. Its diverse population includes people who speak Serbo-Croatian, Bulgarian, Albanian, and Greek. GREECE objects to the use of the name Macedonia by this country, because they consider Macedonia to be a Greek term.

Madrid. Capital and primate city of SPAIN. Located on a 2,130-foot (650-meter) plateau near the Guadarrama Mountains; 1990's population was 3.2 million. Major commercial, industrial, and administrative center. Major industries include machinery, engineering, electronics, printing and publishing, food processing, finance, chemicals, building materials, and tobacco products.

Majorca. Largest of the BALEARIC ISLANDS in the western MEDITERRANEAN SEA. Located at 39°30′ north latitude, longitude 3° east. Covers 1,410 square miles (3,653 sq. km.); highest point is 4,738 feet (1,444 meters), in the Puig Major. Site of the Balearic's capital, PALMA, and a popular tourist destination. Also known as Mallorca.

Mallorca. See MAJORCA.

Malmö. Third-largest city in SWEDEN, northern Europe, with a population of 254,900 in 1998. Located across the ØRESUND STRAIT from COPENHAGEN, DENMARK, in the most southwestern corner of the country. A commercial and industrial city, blessed with a mild, pleasant climate. Founded in the twelfth century.

Malta. Island nation in the MEDITERRANEAN SEA. Located 58 miles (93 km.)

south of SICILY. Total area is 122 square miles (317 sq. km.); population was about 380,000 in 1999. Comprises the island of Malta and several smaller islands; member of the British Commonwealth. Strategically located at the crossroads of the Mediterranean, they have played a pivotal role throughout history. A famous modern siege occurred when Malta was unsuccessfully attacked by German and Italian forces during World War II.

Man, Isle of. British island in the northern section of the IRISH SEA. Located midway between SCOTLAND, IRELAND, and ENGLAND. Has a landmass of only 227 square miles (572 sq. km.) with a 1990's population of 72,000. Originally settled by the Vikings, but its original language, Manx, is Celtic. Like the CHANNEL ISLANDS, a territory of the UNITED KINGDOM but has its own parliament. Income derived from tourism and offshore finance. Popularly known as the original home of Manx cats.

Manchester. Most important cultural and financial center in the north of ENGLAND; considered to be England's third city. Population was 450,000 in 1995. The Greater Manchester area covers 380 square miles (984 sq. km.), including Stockport (133,000), Bolton (140,000), Oldham (104,000), and Rochdale (95,000); its total population was 2.6 million in 1995. Has BRITAIN's largest international airport outside LONDON. The Manchester Ship Canal enables ships to dock in the heart of the city. Its growth began with cotton manufacturing at the beginning of the Industrial Revolution.

Marseilles. Seaport of southeastern FRANCE on the MEDITERANNEAN SEA; population 810,000 in the early 1990's. A major center of manufacturing and trade.

Mediterranean Sea. Large sea between Europe to the north and Africa to the south, and bounded by Asia to the east. Covers about 969,100 square miles (2.5 million sq. km.); 2,200 miles (3,540 km.) at its longest and 1,000 miles (1,600 km.) at its widest; its greatest depth is 16,897 feet (5,150 meters) in the Hellenic Trough. Studded with islands, it is the birthplace of many ancient civilizations, including EGYPT, GREECE, and ROME. Has a mild climate and often spectacular scenery, and is popular with tourists. Name is derived from Latin words meaning "in the middle of land"—a reference to its nearly land-locked nature.

Merseyside. Urban area along the banks of the River Mersey in northwest ENGLAND. Population was 1.4 million in 1995. Largest concentration is in LIVERPOOL, on the north bank; Southport (90,000), a once-popular resort, is also on the north side. To the south lies the Wirral Peninsula with the dock and shipbuilding town of Birkenhead (93,000), and the town of Ellesmere Port (64,500). The area's biggest industries are chemical works, including soap and glass manufacture, and automaking.

Messina, Strait of. Part of the MEDITERRANEAN SEA that separates SICILY from the Italian Peninsula.

Midlands. Relatively low-lying central area of ENGLAND. BRITAIN's industrial heartland, with plentiful resources of coal, iron, and steel. The soil is fertile and supports cattle, cereals, and market gardening. The center of auto-making, machine tools, and more recently, electronics. The West Midlands urban area, centered around BIRMINGHAM, is largely industrialized. It had a 1995 population of 5.3 million; the largest cities are Wolverhampton (258,000)

Mediterranean map Page 1247

Marseilles Page 1433

*Monaco
Page 1434*

and Coventry (300,000). Some rural areas remain toward the Welsh border and in Oxfordshire. The East Midlands, with a 1995 population of 4.1 million, has more distinct borders between town and country. Its largest cities are Nottingham (273,000), Leicester (319,000), Derby (224,000), and Northampton (180,000). Pharmaceuticals, clothing, hosiery, and shoes have been major industries.

Minsk. Capital of BELARUS and administrative center of the Minsk *oblast* (province). First mentioned in 1067, it became the seat of a principality in 1101. Minsk passed to LITHUANIA in the fourteenth century and later to POLAND, being regained by RUSSIA in 1793. It is the major industrial center of Belarus. Its population in 1991 was 1,633,600.

Miskolc. Third-largest city and a major industrial center in HUNGARY. Population was 180,000 in 1996. Located in a valley below the BÜKK MOUNTAINS. Settled by Germanic tribes and prospered because of a nearby iron field from about the tenth century. Invaded by Mongols in the thirteenth century, Ottoman Turks in the sixteenth century, and Habsburgs in the seventeenth and eighteenth centuries. Local limestone caves are used as cellars by winemakers.

Moldau River. See VLTAVA RIVER.

Moldavia. See MOLDOVA

Moldova. Former republic of the SOVIET UNION which became independent in 1991. Closely linked to ROMANIA by language, history, and customs, Moldova (formerly Moldavia) became a part of the Russian Empire in 1812. Partially russified under the reign of Nicholas I, Moldova was reincorporated into Romania after World War I. It was reincorporated into the Soviet Union in 1940. It covers an area of 12,997 square miles (33,700 sq. km.). Its population in 1999

was 4,430,654, of whom 65 percent were ethnic Moldovan/Romanian.

Monaco. Principality in Western Europe. Located on the French RIVIERA between Nice and Menton, surrounded by FRANCE. Total area of 0.7 square mile (1.8 sq. km.) with a 1990's population of thirty-two thousand. Capital is Monaco-Ville. Economic mainstays are tourism, casino gambling, banking, and finance.

Montenegro. One of the two republics that make up the country of YUGOSLAVIA. Independent from 1878 to 1918, then became part of Yugoslavia. Capital is Podgorica, known as Titograd 1946-1992. Population of 600,000 in the early 1990's, most of whom speak Serbo-Croatian.

Morava River. River in CZECH REPUBLIC. Flows from the SUDETES Mountains south into the DANUBE RIVER and west of BRATISLAVA. An important north-south transportation route over its 242 miles (390 km.). Sugar beets, grains, grapes, and tobacco are grown in the fertile river valley.

Moravia. Historic region of the CZECH REPUBLIC located between BOHEMIA and SLOVAKIA. Central Moravia is a fertile agricultural area drained by the MORAVA RIVER and its tributaries. Mineral resources include lignite, coal, iron, oil, copper, lead, and silver. Occupied since at least the first century by a succession of Celtic, Germanic, and Slavic peoples. Incorporated into an independent CZECHOSLOVAKIA in 1919.

Moravian Gate. Mountain pass in the CZECH REPUBLIC. It is a wide pass between the eastern end of the SUDETES Mountains and the western end of the CARPATHIAN MOUNTAINS in northern MORAVIA and has been a natural communication channel and important trade route since pre-Roman times.

Moscow. Capital of RUSSIA. It is located in the western part of the country, about 400 miles (640 km.) southeast of ST. PETERSBURG and 600 miles (970 km.) east of the Polish border. It was first mentioned in 1147 and for more than six hundred years it has been the spiritual center of the Russian Orthodox Church. The city covers about 386 square miles (1,000 sq. km.). Its population in 1991 was 8,801,500.

Moskva River. River flowing through Moscow *oblast* (province) and part of Smolensk *oblast*, in western RUSSIA. Starting in the Smolensk-Moscow Upland, the river flows 312 miles (500 km.) in a southeasterly direction. It is an important source of Moscow's water supply.

Mykonos. Island of the CYCLADES group of Greek islands in the AEGEAN SEA. Located at 37°27′ north latitude, longitude 25°23′ east. Total area is 35 square miles (91 sq. km.). A major tourist destination.

Naples. Historic seaport and modern commercial and cultural center on the southwestern coast of ITALY, near the active volcano Mount Vesuvius. Population in the early 1990's was 1,055,000.

Naxos. Largest of the CYCLADES group of Greek islands in the AEGEAN SEA. Located at 37° north latitude, longitude 25°35′ east. Covers 169 square miles (438 sq. km.); highest point is 3,284 feet (1,001 meters) at Mount Dryos.

Neglina River. One of two rivers at whose junction the city of MOSCOW is located.

Netherlands. Kingdom in Western Europe. Total area of 14,143 square miles (36,673 sq. km.) with a 1990's population of 15.6 million people. Has two capital cities: AMSTERDAM and The HAGUE. Other major cities include Rotterdam, Utrecht, and Leiden. Forty percent of the Netherlands' land area

lies below sea level and must be protected a system of dunes, dikes, and water-pumping. Massive pumping has reclaimed areas called polders from the sea for resettlement of the population. Major enterprises are shipbuilding, iron and steel, chemicals, food processing, textiles, fishing, and diamond cutting. Also known as HOLLAND.

Newport. Town on the River Usk in south Wales, near its confluence with the SEVERN estuary. Population was 137,400 in 1994. Originally a fortified border town, it is now Wales's third city. After the demise of the Welsh coal industry, its main industry is consumer electronics.

Nicosia. City on the island of CYPRUS, the capital of both the Republic of Cyprus and the Turkish Republic of Northern Cyprus. Population was 177,450 in 1992. Also called Lefkosa.

Nistru River. See DNIESTER RIVER.

Nizhny Novgorod. City, also known as Gorky, that is the administrative center of Nizhegorod *oblast* (province) in western RUSSIA, at the junction of the VOLGA and Oka rivers, 260 miles (420 km.) east of MOSCOW. The well-known writer Maxim Gorky was born in Nizhny Novgorod in 1868, and in 1932, the town was renamed in his honor by the SOVIET UNION regime. Its original name was restored in 1990. Its population was 1,382,500 in 1995.

North Cape. Northernmost point in Europe. Located at the tip of NORWAY, at 71.15 degrees north latitude and longitude 25.80 degrees east. Although well beyond the Arctic Circle, where winter and darkness remain for six months, its maritime climate is moderated by the Gulf Stream that flows past the region.

North Sea. Sea that separates GREAT BRITAIN from northern Europe. Covers 220,000 square miles (572,000 sq. km.).

Moscow Pages 1252, 1434, 1435

Mykonos Page 1437

Subject to storms and changing tidal patterns, it has often caused disastrous coastal flooding. Once a rich fishing area, being relatively shallow, but over-fishing and strict quotas have made serious inroads into the British fishing industry. Large reserves of oil and natural gas were found in the British sectors of the North Sea in the 1970's. Britain's natural gas supply comes exclusively from these fields

Northern Ireland. Northeastern portion of IRELAND; an integral part of the UNITED KINGDOM of Great Britain and Northern Ireland. Area of 5,242 square miles (14,000 sq. km.) comprises six original Irish counties; population was about 1,663,300 in 1996. Long the site of English invasion and control of Ireland, territory is home to a Protestant majority introduced in the seventeenth century. Separated from the rest of Ireland in 1921; since 1969 has been focus of sectarian violence pitting Protestants against native Roman Catholic minority. Also known as Ulster.

Norway
Pages
1246, 1247

Norway. Country in the western half of SCANDINAVIAN PENINSULA. Bordered by SWEDEN on the east, FINLAND on the far northeast, the Arctic and NORTH Seas on the north and west, and on the south by SKAGERRAK STRAIT and DENMARK beyond. Total area of 125,050 square miles (323,880 sq. km.), slightly larger than New Mexico, with a population of 4.4 million in 1999. Capital is OSLO. The traditional home of the Vikings, the elongated country is characterized by hundreds of fjords, rugged mountains throughout, and relatively mild winters as a result of the Gulf Stream on the Atlantic. A number of islands high in the Arctic Ocean also belong to Norway. Called Norge in Norwegian.

Norwegian Sea. Section of the North Atlantic Ocean. NORWAY borders it on the east and ICELAND on the west. A submarine ridge linking Greenland, Iceland, the Faroe Islands, and northern Scotland separates the Norwegian Sea from the open Atlantic. Cut by the Arctic Circle, the sea is often associated with the Arctic Ocean to the north. Reaches a maximum depth of about 13,020 feet (3,970 meters).

Nowa Huta. City in southern POLAND. A suburb of CRACOW, built from the ground up in 1949 as an example of the triumph of communism. It housed one of the region's largest iron and steel plants and the laborers who were to work there. Since the fall of the SOVIET UNION, the steel works have fallen on hard times.

Odense. Seaport and third-largest city in DENMARK. Located on northern Funen Island, with a population of 145,300 in 1998. Industries include manufacturing, shipbuilding, and meat and fish canneries. Also the home of author Hans Christian Andersen. Named after Odin, the Norse god of war, it is one of the oldest settlements in Denmark.

Oder River. Major river in central Europe. Begins in the Oder Mountains of the CZECH REPUBLIC, flows north into POLAND, through WROCLAW, and, absorbing the Neisse River, continues as part of the German-Polish border; reaches the BALTIC SEA just north of Szczecin (Stettin). Length is about 550 miles (885 km.). The Oder-Havel Canal is a vital link to the Baltic for BERLIN. Power dams have been built in its headwaters. The Oder connects the industrial region of SILESIA with the Baltic Sea. Iron, coal, and coke are transported along the river.

Odessa. Seaport and administrative center of Odessa *oblast* (province) in the southwestern UKRAINE. It is the largest port in the Ukraine and an important industrial center. It has many research establishments that are headed by the Filatov Institute of Eye Diseases. Its population in 1991 was 1,100,700.

Onega, Lake. It is located in northwestern European RUSSIA between Lake LADOGA and the WHITE SEA. Its area is 3,753 square miles (9,720 sq. km.); it is about 150 miles (250 km.) in length, with a greatest width of 50 miles (80 km.) and a maximum depth of about 380 feet (115 meters). Lake Onega is connected with the BALTIC and White Seas by the White Sea-Baltic Canal and with the basin of the VOLGA RIVER by the Volga-Baltic Waterway, which enable Lake Onega to play an important part in both internal and international transportation.

Ore Mountains. Mountain chain on the border separating the CZECH REPUBLIC from GERMANY. Extending 93 miles (150 km.), they are named for their rich mineral deposits. Silver and iron were mined extensively from the fourteenth to nineteenth centuries; in the twentieth century, uranium, lead, and zinc were more commonly mined. A densely populated industrial area.

Øresund Strait. Strait that separates DEN-MARK and SWEDEN.

Oslo. NORWAY's capital and largest city. Located in the southeastern corner of the country, with a population of 502,870 in 1999. The center of Norwegian trade, banking, industry, and shipping; its harbor is the largest and busiest in the country. Founded by King Harald Hardraade about 1050.

Oxford. Site of BRITAIN's oldest university, dating from 1214. Located on the River THAMES, 56 miles (90 km.) west of LONDON; population was 119,000 in 1999. It has not retained its country-town appearance, becoming industrialized at the beginning of the auto-making era.

Palermo. Capital of the Italian region of SICILY; located on the island of the same name. Population was 689,300 in 1995.

Palma. Capital of the Spanish province of BALEARES. Located on the island of MAJORCA. Population was 323,138 in 1995.

Pannonian Basin. Basin enclosed by the CARPATHIAN MOUNTAINS, Eastern ALPS and DINARIC Ranges in central-eastern Europe. Covers more than 110,000 square miles (284,900 sq. km.). Includes the Little ALFÖLD, Great ALFÖLD, and Transylvanian Basin. Named for Roman province of Pannonia.

Paris. Capital and primate city of FRANCE. Population was nearly ten million in

*Paris
Page 1437*

Oslo, Norway. (PhotoDisc)

In its Eiffel Tower, Paris has the world's most widely recognized landmark; however, the tower was originally built for an exposition and was intended to be torn down. (PhotoDisc)

Po River
Page 1438

the 1990's. Striding the banks of the River SEINE, it is the hub of France's railways, roads, air transport, and communications. It also enjoys a long-standing status as an international cultural, educational, tourist, and entertainment center. Finance, government, services, and the manufacture of pharmaceuticals, automobiles, luxury items, and electronics are its economic mainstays. The main avenue for intra-city commuter transport in the extensive Metro subway.

Peloponnesos. The southern region of the country of GREECE. Except for a small land bridge, the Gulf of Corinth separates the Peloponnesos from the remainder of Greece. A rugged area of small, poor farms. Climate is hot and dry in the summer, warm with some rain in the winter. Products include wheat, wine, and olives.

Pennines. Range of hills that divides northern ENGLAND into east and west. Running south from the Scottish border, it culminates in the Peak District, one of BRITAIN's national parks. The Pennine Way is the most popular long-distance hiking trail in the BRITISH ISLES. The Yorkshire Dales form another national park area halfway along.

Po River. River in northern ITALY. Runs for 417 miles (671 km.) from its source near Monte Viso in the Italian ALPS eastward into the ADRIATIC SEA. Farmlands along the Po Valley are fertile, but periodic flooding can create major problems. The Po runs through or near the urban centers of Turin, Piacenza, Cremona, Mantua, and Ferrara.

Poland. Central European country on the BALTIC SEA; surrounded by GERMANY, CZECH REPUBLIC, SLOVAKIA, UKRAINE, BELARUS, LITHUANIA, and RUSSIA.

Area is 120,727 square miles (312,683 sq. km.); population was 38,646,023 in 1999. WARSAW is the capital. Historically overrun and partitioned by its more powerful neighbors; dominated by the SOVIET UNION before 1989, when it began to democratize. Joined the North Atlantic Treaty Organization in 1999.

Pomerania. Historic region of central-eastern Europe, extending along the BALTIC SEA from GERMANY to the VISTULA RIVER in POLAND. Part of the North European Plain, primarily agricultural lowland. Main crops are cereals, sugar beets, and potatoes. Area has numerous lakes and forests. Other important economic activities include livestock raising, forestry, and industry. Region was inhabited by Slavic tribes in sixth century. Through history, the area, or parts of it, have been ruled by Poland, the Holy Roman Empire, SWEDEN, and Prussia.

Portugal. Republic in Western Europe. Bordered by the Atlantic Ocean on the west and encircled in other directions by SPAIN. Total area of 35,552 square miles (92,186 sq. km.) with a 1990's population of ten million. Capital is LISBON; other large urban areas are Oporto, Coimbra, Braga, Setobal, and Funchal. Although shipbuilding and the apparel industry are significant, Portugal is predominantly rural; wheat and other cereal grains, livestock, tomatoes, and cork are the primary products. Roman Catholicism is the major religion.

Poznán. City in west central POLAND. A port on the WARTA RIVER, important railroad center, and major trade center. Population was 590,000 in 1993. Founded before the tenth century. Poznán has been part of RUSSIA, Prussia, GERMANY, and Poland. Destroyed

by the Germans in 1939. After World War II, textile mills and chemical and metal plants were built.

Prague. Capital, transportation hub, and a leading commercial and industrial center of the CZECH REPUBLIC. Has a long, distinguished tradition as a center of music, art, and literature. The location of one of the oldest universities in Europe (1348) and the oldest remaining synagogue in Europe (thirteenth century). Located at the intersection of numerous ancient trade routes, it was an important trading center by the tenth century. Later, the capital of BOHEMIA.

Prague
Page 1439

Pyrenees. Western European mountain range running about 270 miles (435 km.) along the border separating FRANCE and SPAIN, from the Bay of BISCAY to the Golfe du Lion. Highest point is Aneto Peak (11,169 feet/3,404 meters). Economy is mainly pastoral and agricultural. The eastern Pyrenees receive rainfall from the Atlantic Ocean; main products are potatoes and corn. The western sector has a more Mediterranean climate where fruit, leafy vegetables, and grapes are widely cultivated.

Portugal
Page 1438

Reykjavik. Capital, largest city, chief seaport, and commercial center of ICELAND. Located on the southwestern coast of the island, with a population of 109,800 in 1999. The name means "Smoking Bay" and refers to the many hot streams that let off steam in the area. Founded by Vikings in 874 and became the island's first permanent settlement.

Ruins near
Coimbra
Page 1240

Rhine River. Western Europe's longest river. Meanders for about 820 miles (1,320km.) from its source near Chur, SWITZERLAND, into the NORTH SEA. Forming Lake Constance, the Rhine winds roughly along the Swiss-German border to Basel, where it turns northward, forming a valley between the Vosges and Schwartzwald along the

The city of Nice on the French Riviera. (PhotoDisc)

*Rhone
River
Page 1440*

Franco-German border. Running into GERMANY, it goes through Mainz, Coblenz, BONN, and Cologne, taking in the Main, Neckar, and Moselle as tributary rivers. In the NETHERLANDS, it divides into a delta, its largest branch passing the Europoort at Rotterdam and entering the sea at Hoek van Holland.

Rhodes. Largest of the DODECANESE group of Greek islands in the AEGEAN SEA. Located at 36°10′ north latitude, longitude 28° east. Total area is 540 square miles (1,400 sq. km.); highest point is 3,986 feet (1,215 meters) at Mount Attavyros. Population was 87,831 in 1981. In the third century B.C.E., was the site of the Colossus of Rhodes, an enormous bronze statue that stood at the entrance to its harbor and that was celebrated as one of the Seven Wonders of the World. A popular tourist destination.

Rhodope Mountains. Mountain range in southern BULGARIA. The highest mountains in the BALKANS, with peaks reaching 9,595 feet (2,925 meters). Mainly made up of hard crystalline rocks that are resistant to erosion. With no major valleys crossing the Rhodope, they are a major barrier to transportation. The mountains become wider toward the southeast. The Maritsa River begins in the Rhodope Mountains.

Rhone River. Major Western European river. Runs for about 505 miles (810 km.) from the Rhone Glacier in SWITZERLAND through GENEVA, absorbing the Saone River at Lyons, FRANCE, and proceeding through Valence, the vineyards of the Côte du Rhone, Avignon, and Arles before forming the Camargue Delta and entering the MEDITERRANEAN SEA.

Riga. Capital of LATVIA located on both banks of the Western DVINA RIVER, 9 miles (15 km.) above its mouth on the Gulf of Riga. Bishop Albert I of Livonia founded Riga in 1201. He made Riga the seat of his bishopric and founded there the Brothers of the Sword (1201), which attached as a branch unit to the Teutonic Knights in 1237. Modern Riga is a major administrative, cultural, and industrial center. Its population in 1993 was 867,000.

Riviera. Coastal region of southeastern FRANCE and northwestern ITALY on the MEDITERRANEAN SEA. Both the French and Italian Rivieras contain popular tourist resorts, including the principality of MONACO.

Romania. Country in southeastern Europe. Total area of 91,700 square miles (237,500 sq. km.) with a 1990's population of 22.5 million. Capital is BUCHAREST. Bordered on the north by MOLDOVA and the UKRAINE, on the west by HUNGARY and YUGOSLAVIA, and on the south by BULGARIA. Came into existence in 1862, with the union of WALACHIA and Moldavia. Major mountain ranges are the CARPATHIANS and the TRANSYLVANIAN ALPS.

Rome. Capital and primate city of ITALY. Population was 3 million in the 1990's. Once the axis of the Roman Empire, its multilayered architectural heritage (especially the Colosseum forum and the Pantheon) remains a significant cultural, services, and tourist center. Government is the major employer; Rome is Italy's principal road, railway, and air transport center. Other important activities are food processing, electronics, chemicals, and textiles.

Rovaniemi. World's most northern large city. Located directly on the Arctic Circle in northern FINLAND. Had a population of nearly 40,000 in 1999. A major attraction for foreign tourists, many of whom travel there to visit Santa Claus or experience the Northern Lights in the winter.

Rumania. See ROMANIA.

Russia. The world's largest country, with a land area of 6.6 million square miles (17.03 million sq. km.), Russia extends from Eastern Europe through Asia to the north Pacific Ocean. European Russia is the portion that lies west of the URAL MOUNTAINS. About 240,000,000 people—most of the country's population—live in the European portion. European Russia is part of the Russian Federation, which includes most of SIBERIA and which still has autonomous republics and regions with occasionally restive minorities. The Russian Federation was the core and the driving force of the old SOVIET UNION that dissolved in 1991. Due to its control of Siberia,

*Riviera
Page 1440*

*Rome
Pages
1305, 1441*

The Roman Forum. (PhotoDisc)

Russia is still the largest country in the world. It annually produces approximately 18 percent of the world's crude oil, 30 percent of the world's natural gas, and 15 percent of the world's metals. Its mineral resources include a near-monopoly on industrially critical metals such as platinum. European Russia is composed of glacier-created plains with low hills which rise to the Ural Mountains. The ethnic makeup of European Russia is overwhelmingly ethnic Russian, with other small ethnic groups scattered throughout. It is one of the most industrialized nations in the world.

Russian Plain. Also known as the East European Plain. Plain and series of broad river basins in Eastern Europe including western RUSSIA. It extends over nearly 1,500,000 square miles (4 million sq. km.) and averages about 560 feet (170 meters) in elevation.

Saimaa, Lake. Largest lake in FINLAND. Located in the eastern part of the country; covers 443 square miles (1,147 sq. km.). Thousands of cottages and saunas surround this and other lakes in Finland.

St. Petersburg. The second largest city in RUSSIA (after MOSCOW). It was for two centuries the capital of the Russian Empire (1712-1918). The modern city is important as a cultural center and as the nation's largest seaport. In 1924 it was renamed for the SOVIET UNION leader Vladimir Lenin, but it reverted to its original name in 1991. It is located on the delta of the Neva River where it empties into the Gulf of Finland, about 100 miles (160 km.) from the Finnish border. Its land area is 521 square miles (1,355 sq. km.), and its population was 4,387,400 in 1993

Samos. Mountainous but fertile Greek island lying off the coast of TURKEY in the

*Santoríni
Page 1442*

*St.
Petersburg
Pages
1250, 1443*

AEGEAN SEA. Located at 37°45′ north latitude, longitude 26°48′ east. Total area is 172 square miles (445 sq. km.); highest point is 4,725 feet (1,440 meters) at Mount Kerki. Population was 40,520 in 1981.

San Marino. Independent republic in Western Europe, completely encircled by ITALY. Total area of 23.4 square miles (60 sq. km.) with a 1990's population of twenty-five thousand. Capital is San Marino City. Dominated by three castles atop Mount Titano. Economy is dominated by ceramics, the sale of postage stamps, tourism, and wheat and dairy farming. According to legend, founded by the Christian refugee Saint Marinus in the fourth century.

Santoríni. Most spectacular of the CYCLADES group of Greek islands in the AEGEAN SEA. Located at 36°24′ north latitude, longitude 25°26′ east. Covers 30 square miles (78 sq. km.). Santoríni is the rim of an extinct volcano whose explosive eruption may be the basis for the legend of Atlantis. Also called Thera.

Sarajevo. Capital, largest city, and major industrial and commercial center of BOSNIA-HERZEGOVINA. Population about 380,000 in the 1990's. Located on the Miljacka River, at the center of a fertile agricultural region. The assassination of Francis Ferdinand in Sarajevo, on June 28, 1914, triggered World War I. Badly damaged in a bloody siege during the Bosnian civil war, 1992-1995. The population is mainly Muslim. Many Serb-speaking non-Muslims moved out after the end of the civil war.

Sardinia. Second-largest island in the MEDITERRANEAN SEA. Located about 7.5 miles (12 km.) south of CORSICA and 99 miles (160 km.) west of ITALY, of which it is a part. Covers 9,301 square miles (24,090 sq. km.); about 166 miles

(267 km.) long from north to south. About 90 percent of the island is mountainous; highest point is 6,017 feet (1,834 meters) at Mount Gennargentu. Together with some smaller nearby islands, it is an Italian political region of the same name with a population of 1.7 million in 1995. Its capital is CAGLIARI.

Scandinavia. Scandinavia proper is a large northern European peninsula extending to the southwest from the northwestern corner of RUSSIA; includes the countries of SWEDEN and NORWAY. As a region, Scandinavia also includes DENMARK, ICELAND, and FINLAND. The term Norden is sometimes used to refer to all five countries.

Scotland. Northern portion of Great Britain and its offshore islands; its 29,797 square miles (77,174 sq. km.) constitute almost exactly a third of Britain's total area. Originally an independent kingdom, Scotland was often at war with England, it's larger southern neighbor, until the Scottish king James VI inherited the English throne in 1603 and became King James I of England. Scotland formally united with England in 1707 to form legal systems and regained its own parliament, with limited power of taxation, in 2000. Largest cities are GLASGOW and EDINBURGH.

Seine River. Major river in FRANCE. Rises in the Langres Plateau of eastern France and, augmented by its tributaries (the Aube, Yonne, Oise, and Maine), runs through PARIS and winds tortuously past Rouen into the ENGLISH CHANNEL near Le Havre. Length is 485 miles (780 km.).

Paris on the Seine. (PhotoDisc)

Serbia. One of two republics that make up the country of YUGOSLAVIA. Capital and largest city is BELGRADE. Most of the population is Serb-speaking, but there are many Albanian-speakers in the south (Kosovo) and Magyar (Hungarian) speakers in the north (VOIVODINA). Was independent 1878-1918.

Sevastopol. City and seaport in the CRIMEA in the southern UKRAINE. West of the modern town there existed the ancient Greek colony of Chersonesus founded in 421 B.C. The city sits on the southern shore of the long, narrow Akhtiarskaya Bay, which forms a magnificent harbor. Its population was 366,200 in 1991.

Severn, River. Longest river in GREAT BRITAIN, at 220 miles (350 km.). Rises in mid-WALES at an elevation of 2,000 feet (610 meters), flows northeast to the English border, then turns southward. Its estuary reaches a width of 12.5

Scandinavia map Page 1245

Scotland Pages 1242, 1432

Seine River Page 1437

miles (20 km.) before entering the Bristol Channel. A rail tunnel and two road suspension bridges connect South Wales with ENGLAND over the estuary.

Shannon, River. Longest river in the BRITISH ISLES, at 250 miles (402 km.); the mouth is 50 miles (80 km.) long. Rises in the upper Leinster region of IRELAND, flowing southwest into the Atlantic Ocean. Has historically divided the west of Ireland from the rest of the island. Many lakes lie along its length; a hydroelectric plant near Limerick provides much of the Republic of Ireland's power.

Sheffield. Second-largest city in Yorkshire, ENGLAND. Located in the southwest of the county, running up into the PENNINES. Population was 432,000 in 1999; the overall South Yorkshire conurbation has 1.3 million inhabitants. Known for steel manufacturing, cutlery, and silverware. Nearby coal mines were exhausted by the 1970's, causing widespread economic depression.

Siberia. Vast region of RUSSIA and northern Kazakhstan. It constitutes all of northern Asia. Siberia extends from the URAL MOUNTAINS on the west to the Pacific Ocean on the east and southward from the Arctic Ocean to the hills of north-central Kazakshtan and the borders of Mongolia and China. Siberia in the wider sense, including the areas outside Russia, has an area of 5.2 million square miles (13.5 million sq. km.).

Sicily
Page 1380

Sicily. Largest island in the MEDITERRANEAN SEA. Located south of the Italian Peninsula, from which it is separated by the Strait of MESSINA. Covers 9,926 square miles (25,708 sq. km.). Predominantly mountainous; highest point is Mount ETNA, an active volcano 10,959 feet (3,340 meters) high. Together with some smaller islands, Sicily is an Italian

political region of the same name whose population was 5 million in 1995. Region's capital is PALERMO. Other large urban areas are Messina and Catania. One of ITALY's less-developed regions, the economy is predominantly rural; olives, grapes, citrus fruit, and grain are widely cultivated. Chief industries include petroleum products, food processing, and chemicals.

Silesia. Historic region of southwest POLAND, portions of the CZECH REPUBLIC, and eastern GERMANY. Located in the wide valley of the upper ODER RIVER. Silesia houses one of the largest industrial concentrations of Europe. The major city of the region is WROCLAW, Poland. Upper Silesia, in Poland, has extensive deposits of coal and lignite as well as zinc, iron, lead, and other ore deposits. Silesia has been occupied since the third century B.C.E. Has been ruled by various Polish and German powers.

Skagerrak Strait. Arm of the NORTH SEA that separates NORWAY and DENMARK and meets the KATTEGAT STRAIT.

Skopje. Capital and largest city of MACEDONIA. Population of about 444,500 in the 1990's. Located on the VARDAR RIVER. An earthquake destroyed much of the town in 1963. A center for trade in agricultural products, including livestock, grain, and cotton, and for manufacturing. In Roman times there was a fort there called Scupi.

Slovakia. Central European nation created in 1993 by the peaceful breakup of CZECHOSLOVAKIA, from which it took the smaller, eastern portion. Borders CZECH REPUBLIC on the northwest, POLAND on the north, AUSTRIA on the west, HUNGARY on the south, and UKRAINE on the east; area is 18,923 square miles (49,010 sq. km.); population in 1999 was 5,407,000 in 1999. Capital is BRATISLAVA.

Slovenia. Country in southeastern Europe. Total area of 18,923 square miles (49,011 sq. km.) with a 1990's population of 2 million. Capital is LJUBLJANA. Bounded on the north by AUSTRIA, on the east and south by CROATIA, and on the west by ITALY. Has a short coastline on the ADRIATIC SEA. Part of YUGOSLAVIA 1918-1991. The Republic of Slovenia declared its independence from Yugoslavia on June 25, 1991. By 2000 it was the wealthiest of the former republics of Yugoslavia.

Snowdon, Mount. Highest peak in WALES, at 3,559 feet (1,085 meters). Located in northwest Wales; part of the CAMBRIAN MOUNTAINS. Snowdonia National Park is one of the most popular climbing areas in the BRITISH ISLES.

Sofia. Capital, largest city, and major manufacturing and administrative center of BULGARIA. Population was 1.1 million in the 1990's. Located in western Bulgaria, in an upland basin drained by the river Isker. Site was the crossroads of many ancient trade routs linking Istanbul with the Danube valley. There was a Roman city at this location.

Southern Carpathian Mountains. See TRANSYLVANIAN ALPS.

Soviet Union. Former northern Eurasian empire (1917-1991) stretching from the BALTIC and BLACK Seas to the Pacific Ocean and, in its final years, consisting of fifteen Soviet Socialist Republics—Armenia, Azerbaijan, Belorussia (now BELARUS), ESTONIA, Georgia, Kazakhstan, Kirgiziya (now Kyrgyzstan), LATVIA, LITHUANIA, Moldavia (now MOLDOVA), RUSSIA, Tajikistan, Turkmenistan, UKRAINE, and Uzbekistan. With the exception of Estonia, Latvia, and Lithuania, all these nations are members of the COMMONWEALTH OF INDEPENDENT STATES.

Spain. Kingdom in Western Europe. Total area of 194,884 square miles (505,334 sq. km.) with a 1990's population of thirty-nine million. Capital is MADRID; other major cities are BARCELONA, Valladolid, Zaragoza, Malaga, Valencia, and Bilbao. Bordered on the north by FRANCE and ANDORRA, and on the west by PORTUGAL. The central plateau dominates the country, causing greater extremes of hot and cold temperatures than in other areas of Western Europe. With exception of the northwestern Atlantic coastal province of Galicia, rainfall is light, and drought can be a problem in many midlands areas. Mountain ranges (sierras) alternate with large river valleys to punctuate the landscape. The chief economic activities are tourism, services, lumber, Mediterranean agriculture and viticulture, livestock, mining, and food processing.

Sporades. Two groups of Greek islands, the Northern Sporades and the Southern Sporades (also referred to as the DODECANESE), stretching from the northern to the southeastern AEGEAN SEA. Principal islands include SAMOS and (in some groupings) Chios. Name means "scattered."

Stockholm. Capital and largest city of SWEDEN. Located on the eastern coastal area of Sweden, with a population of 736,100 in 1998. Founded in the late twelfth century. One of the most important centers in northern Europe, its old part—Gamla Stan—has been the seat of power for the Swedish Kingdom for centuries.

Straits. See under individual names.

Stromboli. One of Europe's most active volcanoes. Located on an island of the same name in the LIPARI ISLANDS in the TYRRHENIAN SEA at 38°48′ north latitude, longitude 15°15′ east. The volcano is 3,041 feet (927 meters) high.

Spain Pages 1248, 1249

Stockholm Page 1443

Sudetenland. Historic region in the SUDETES Mountains in BOHEMIA and MORAVIA, of the CZECH REPUBLIC. Before World War II, these areas had large German populations. Annexed by GERMANY in 1939; restored to CZECHOSLOVAKIA after the war. Most of the German population was expelled as a result of the Potsdam Conference at the close of World War II.

Sudetes. Mountain system extending roughly from the ODER RIVER to the ELBE RIVER, along the border between the CZECH REPUBLIC and POLAND. The range is about 183 miles (298 km.) long. Its highest peak is Snezka (5,256 feet/1,602 meters). Contains coal and iron ore deposits, forests, pasture, agricultural land, mineral springs, and resorts.

Swansea. Second city of WALES. Located 37 miles (60 km.) west of CARDIFF. Population was 231,000 in 1994. Its fortunes have paralleled those of Cardiff closely. Steelworks at nearby Port Talbot are important to Swansea's economy.

Sweden. Country in northern Europe, bounded on the east by FINLAND and the Gulf of BOTHNIA, on the north and west by NORWAY, and on the south by DENMARK and the BALTIC SEA. Total area of 173,732 square miles (445,000 sq. km.) with a population of 8.8 million in 1999. Capital is STOCKHOLM. Long and narrow, it is the largest of the Scandinavian countries, somewhat larger than the U.S. state of California. Rich in resources, varied in its physical geography, and most populated of all surrounding countries. The Swedish name is Sverige.

Switzerland. Land-locked confederation in Western Europe. Total area of 15,943 square miles (41,340 sq. km.) with a 1990's population of 7.2 million. Fed-

Switzerland Page 1436

Thames River Pages 1318, 1367, 1444

eral capital is BERN; largest cities are Zurich, Lausanne, and Basel. Situated in the heart of the ALPS, Switzerland is Europe's most mountainous country. Economic mainstays are tourism and recreation, finance, crafts, jewelry, and watches.

Tagus River. Longest river on the IBERIAN PENINSULA in Western Europe. Begins in the Sierra Albarracui hills of SPAIN, east of MADRID, and takes a westerly course past Toledo and Alcantara, reaching the Atlantic Ocean just beyond LISBON, PORTUGAL. Length is 566 miles (910 km.).

Tallinn. Capital of ESTONIA and located on Tallinn Bay of the Gulf of Finland. The site has been continuously settled since the late first millennium B.C. In 1285 Tallinn joined the Hanseatic League. Peter I the Great captured Tallinn in 1710 and it remained a Russian city until it became the capital of independent ESTONIA from 1918 to 1940. It then fell under SOVIET UNION control until 1991. Modern Tallinn is a major commercial and industrial center and a fishing port. The population was 481,500 in 1991. Estonians comprise 56 percent of the population. Much of the rest is ethnic Russian.

Tampere. Third-largest city in FINLAND, in northern Europe, with a population of 191,250 in 1999. Located in the southwestern part of the country, at the shores of Lakes Pyhäjärvi and Näsijärvi. A major textile manufacturing center of Finland. The neighboring city of Nokia, at the city's western outskirts, is the home of Nokia cellular phones.

Tatra Mountains. See HIGH TATRA MOUNTAINS.

Thames River. Most famous river in GREAT BRITAIN. LONDON spreads many miles along its banks near its estuary. Higher up are Windsor, seat of a royal castle;

Sunrise over the Thames in London. (PhotoDisc)

Reading (pop 214,000), a town involved in food manufacture; and OXFORD. Rises in Gloucestershire in the Cotswold Hills; length is 200 miles (354 km.). It is tidal right through London.

Thera. See SANTORÍNI.

Tiber River. Historic river in ITALY. Originates in the Tuscan Mountains of the APPENINE Range near Arezzo and empties into the TYRRHENIAN SEA near the ruins of the Roman port of Ostia. Length is 244 miles (392 km.). ROME was founded on the Seven Hills along its banks.

Tirane. Capital and largest city of ALBANIA. Population was 240,000 in the 1990's. Located inland, but linked by railroad to the ADRIATIC SEA.

Tiraspol. City in eastern MOLDOVA. It lies along the DNIESTER (Nistru) River and the ODESSA-CHISINAU railway. It is very industrialized and the center of an agricultural area. It has a large restive Russian population in an ethnically Romanian country. Its population was 186,000 in 1991.

Tisza River. River in central-eastern Europe with headwaters in the UKRAINE, flowing through ROMANIA, HUNGARY, and into SERBIA. Longest tributary of the DANUBE, at 621 miles (1,000 km.). Controlled by a series of dikes, it is prone to spring and summer flooding. Known for its fisheries; also used for irrigation in the Great ALFÖLD.

Transdniester Moldovan Soviet Socialist Republic. It was present-day MOLDOVA when it was a Soviet Socialist republic after 1940 when the SOVIET UNION annexed it from ROMANIA. It became independent as Moldova in 1991. The region's name means "across the DNIESTER River."

Transylvania. Historic region of western and central ROMANIA. Located between the CARPATHIAN MOUNTAINS and the TRANSYLVANIAN ALPS, it has low hills and a harsh climate. Cluj is the largest city. Most of the population speaks Romanian, but there is a large minority of Magyar (Hungarian-speakers called Szeklers). It is rich in mineral resources, including lignite, iron, lead, manganese, gold, copper, natural gas, salt, and sulfur. Originally a part of the Roman province of Dacia; later, a center of Hungarian culture. Ruled by the Ottoman Turks in the sixteenth and seventeenth centuries; became part of the Austro-Hungarian Empire at the end of the seventeenth century. Given to Romania after World War I, although a large Hungarian minority remains in the region. Ancestral home of the legendary Count Dracula.

Transylvanian Alps. Part of the CARPATHIAN MOUNTAIN chain in central-eastern Europe. Consists of three parallel ridges extending from the Carpathian Mountains in the east to BALKAN MOUNTAINS in the west. The highest peaks exceed 6,800 feet (2,100 meters) in elevation. To their south is the Danube plain, and to their north is the plateau of TRANSYLVANIA. They are rugged and consist mainly of sedimentary rocks. Densely forested and a famous hunting ground; meadows are used to graze sheep; mountains contain coal, iron, and lignite deposits. Also called the Southern Carpathians.

Trieste. Commercial seaport and industrial center of northeastern ITALY near the northern tip of the ADRIATIC SEA, on the border with SLOVENIA; population 230,000 in the early 1990's.

Trondheim. Historic port and third-largest city of NORWAY. Located in central Norway on the NORWEGIAN SEA. A major land and sea transport link of Norway, connecting the more densely settled south with the far-northern regions. Population was 147,190 in 1999. Founded in 997 by King Olaf I Tryggvason of Norway.

Turkey. Secular Middle East state located at the eastern end of the MEDITERRANEAN SEA, which it separates from the BLACK SEA. The western portion of Turkey is considered to be in Europe, while its larger eastern portion is considered part of Asia. The country's total area is 301,303 square miles (780,580 sq. km.), and it had a population of about 69 million in 2000.

Turku. Historic first capital (until 1812) and oldest city in FINLAND. Located at the southwestern coast of Finland. Founded in the thirteenth century and incorporated in 1525. Major attractions include Turku Castle and Turku Cathedral. The fifth-largest city in Finland, with a population of 170,930 in 1999.

Tuscany. Mountainous region of north central ITALY; regional capital is FLORENCE.

Tyne and Wear. Metropolitan area between the River Tyne and the River Wear in northeast ENGLAND. Its 1995 population was 1.1 million. Newcastle-upon-Tyne is the largest city (199,000), the oldest coal-producing area in BRITAIN, and an important NORTH SEA port. Other large towns include Gateshead (83,000) and seaside Whitley Bay (33,000). Wallsend lies at the eastern end of HADRIAN'S WALL. Sunderland (195,000), at the mouth of the Wear, was famous for its ship-building. Japanese auto and electronic factories have replaced this, but the area was in serious recession in the late 1990's.

Tyrrhenian Sea. Triangular arm of the MEDITERRANEAN SEA west of ITALY, east of CORSICA and SARDINIA, and north of SICILY. Total area is about 60,000 square miles (155,400 sq. km.); about 472 miles (760 km.) in length from north to south and 300 miles (483 km.) across at its widest. Its waters contain the Tuscan Archipelago (the largest island of which is ELBA) and the LIPARI (including the volcanic isle of STROMBOLI). Major ports along its coast include NAPLES, Italy; PALERMO, Sicily; and Bastia, Corsica.

Ukraine. One of the largest countries in Europe. The Ukraine became independent of the SOVIET UNION in 1991. It has long striven for independence. Ukrainians have historically resented Russian domination. At the end of World War I there was a short-lived Ukrainian Republic. During World War II Ukrainians collaborated with GERMANY in the hope of gaining independence from the Soviet Union. Armed Ukrainian resistance to the Soviets continued well into the 1950's. The Ukraine is very industrialized and a rich agricultural region to the point of being the breadbasket of Eastern Europe. It is also rich in iron ore and coal. The land consists mostly of rolling plains, hills, and plateaus. Its land area is 240,000 square miles (619,200 sq. km.). Its population was 52,130,000 in the early 1990's. Its populace includes 72 percent Ukrainians and 22 percent ethnic Russians. Its large Russian population has presented occasional problems. For example, there is an ongoing dispute with RUSSIA and the Russian inhabitants of the CRIMEA over sovereignty.

Ulster. See NORTHERN IRELAND.

Union of Soviet Socialist Republics. See SOVIET UNION

United Kingdom. Short form of the United Kingdom of GREAT BRITAIN and NORTHERN IRELAND, the sovereign nation that includes ENGLAND, WALES, SCOTLAND, Northern Ireland, the CHANNEL ISLANDS, and the Isle of MAN. Formed in 1707, when Scotland and England were united under one crown.

Ural Mountains. Mountain range in west-central RUSSIA extending for about 1,300 miles (2,100 km.) from the Kara Sea in the north to the URAL RIVER in the south. The Urals' eastern slopes form part of the traditional physiographic boundary between Europe and Asia. The Urals are one of the richest mineral-bearing areas in the world.

Ural River. River in RUSSIA and Kazakhstan. About 1,575 miles (2,536 km.) long, the Ural drains an area of about 91,500 square miles (237,000 sq. km.). It starts in the URAL MOUNTAINS near Mount Kruglaya and flows south along their eastern side past Magnitogorsk. At Orsk it cuts westward across the southern end of the Urals, past Orenburg, and turns south again across a lowland of semidesert to enter the Caspian Sea at Atyrau.

Valletta. Capital of the MEDITERRANEAN SEA nation of MALTA. Population was about 9,130 in 1994.

Vänern, Lake. Largest lake in southwestern SWEDEN. Located at 58.52 degrees north latitude, longitude 13.17 degrees east. Covers 2,156 square miles (5,585 sq. km.). Numerous rivers feed the lake, which drains westward into the KATTEGAT STRAIT through the Göta River, which flows through the city of GÖTEBORG.

Vardar River. River in southeastern Europe. Begins in MACEDONIA and flows south through GREECE into the AEGEAN SEA. Its headwaters are near those of the Serbian MORAVA RIVER, and

Tyrrhenian Sea Page 1444

their combined valleys form the easiest route from the ocean into the interior of the BALKAN PENINSULA. A railroad from the Greek port of Thessaloniki follows the Vardar valley through Macedonia to BELGRADE.

Vatican City. Sovereign state in Western Europe; worldwide administrative center for the Roman Catholic Church. Its head of state is the pope. With an area of 0.17 square mile (0.44 sq. km.) and a population of 830, it is the world's smallest independent state by either measure. A magnet for pilgrims and tourists, who come mainly to view Saint Peter's Basilica and the Sistine Chapel.

Venice. ADRIATIC seaport on northeastern coast of ITALY; capital of Veneto province; population was 310,000 during the early 1990's. Built on more than 100 islands in a lagoon covering 160 square miles (260 sq. km.); noted for its picturesque canals and gondola transport. Major industrial and tourist center.

Vestmannaeyjar. Important fishing village in southern ICELAND. Located on Heima Island (Heimaey) at 63 degrees north latitude, longitude 20 degrees west. One of the older Icelandic settlements, it had a population of 4,585 in 1999. Major volcanic activity has caused disasters such as the 1973 eruption of Helgafell Volcano, which buried the town under a rain of ash and cinder, forcing most residents to evacuate.

Vienna. Capital, largest city, and cultural, commercial, and industrial center of AUSTRIA; population was 1.6 million in the late 1990's. Located on the DANUBE RIVER in the northeastern part of the country.

Vilnius. Capital of LITHUANIA at the junction of the Neris and Vilnia Rivers. The first reference to it dates from 1128. It is

St. Peter's Basilica Page 1313

Venice Pages 1313, 1370, 1445

Vienna Page 1446

Venice, Italy. (PhotoDisc)

an important industrial center producing such items as machine tools, agricultural machinery, and electronic equipment. The population was 593,000 in 1990 and was about 50 percent Lithuanian, 18 percent Polish, and the rest mostly Russian.

Visla River. See VISTULA RIVER.

Vistula River. Longest river and principal waterway of POLAND. Headwaters are in the CARPATHIAN MOUNTAINS; it empties into the BALTIC SEA after flowing 665 miles (1,070 km.) through several major Polish cities. Connected by canals with the ODER, DNIEPER, Neman, and Pregel Rivers. Along the river, coal and lumber are transported by barges. Also called the Visla.

Vltava River. Longest river in the CZECH REPUBLIC. Rises in the Bohemian Forest, flows through PRAGUE, and empties into the ELBE RIVER 270 miles (435 km.) away. Has several large dams and hydroelectric stations. Also called the Moldau River.

Voivodina. Region of the SERB REPUBLIC in YUGOSLAVIA. Most of the land is flat, rich, and densely populated. Serbo-Croatian speakers are the majority of the population, but there is a large Magyar-speaking (Hungarian) minority. Important rivers in the region are the DANUBE and the TISZA. Wheat and maize (corn) are the major agricultural products.

Volga River. Longest river in Europe and the principal waterway of western RUSSIA. The Volga rises in the Valdai Hills northwest of MOSCOW and flows 2,293 miles (3,692 km.) generally southeastward to empty into the Caspian Sea.

Walachia. Part of southern ROMANIA. Bounded by the TRANSYLVANIAN ALPS and the DANUBE RIVER. Economically, the most developed region of Romania. The capital, BUCHAREST, is located

there. Has rich oil fields and agricultural areas, and is a manufacturing center for the nation. Originally part of the Roman province of Dacia; later came under the control of the Hungarians and the Ottoman Turks.

Wales. Politically integral, but culturally and historically distinct, region of GREAT BRITAIN that forms an 8,016-square-mile (20,761 sq. km.) peninsula on Britain's IRISH SEA coast. Capital is CARDIFF.

Wallachian Plain. Lowland area in ROMANIA, between the TRANSYLVANIAN ALPS and DOBRUJA. Bounded on the south by the DANUBE RIVER. BUCHAREST is located in this region. Was a gulf of the BLACK SEA, but has been filled by river deposits from the Transylvanian Alps.

Warsaw. Capital, commercial and cultural center, and transportation hub of POLAND. Straddles the VISTULA RIVER in the central part of the country. Population was 1.7 million in 1993. Dates to the thirteenth century; became the capital after the destruction of CRACOW in 1596. Despite frequent invasions, wars, occupations, and destruction, it continued to thrive. Almost completely destroyed in World War II, but the Old Town, dating from medieval times, was rebuilt according to the original plan.

Warta River. River in POLAND. Rises in southern Poland and flows north and west 475 miles (764 km.) to the ODER RIVER. Connected with the VISTULA RIVER by a tributary and a canal.

Wash, The. Shallow bay on ENGLAND's east coast that appears on maps as a distinct notch. Several rivers feed into the NORTH SEA through this inlet.

Wear. See TYNE AND WEAR.

West Country. The southwest of ENGLAND, especially the peninsula comprising the counties of Devon and CORNWALL; the counties southeast of the Bristol

*Wales
Pages
1245, 1445*

Channel (Somerset, Gloucestershire, and Wiltshire); and the county of Dorset on the south coast. Sometimes referred to as "Wessex," although the ancient Saxon kingdom of that name extended further east. Largely rural, containing the Exmoor and Dartmoor National Parks. Agriculture and tourism are the main industries; the old tin, china, clay, and fishing industries have seriously declined. Only the BRISTOL area is industrialized to any degree, with small areas around Plymouth in south Devon, and Swindon (pop. 155,000) in Wiltshire, formerly a rail repair center and now an overspill town with new industries. Many resort towns lie on its south coast.

Western Isles. See HEBRIDES.

White Sea. An almost landlocked extension of the Arctic Ocean indenting the shores of northwestern RUSSIA. A long, narrow strait known as the Gorlo (throat) connects it to the more northerly BARENTS SEA. The surface area of the White Sea is about 35,000 square miles (93,000 sq. km.). It has an average depth of 200 feet (60 meters) and a maximum depth of 1,115 feet (340 meters).

Wroclaw. City, river port, rail center, and industrial hub in southwest POLAND. Located on the ODER RIVER. Population was 644,000 in 1993. Originated on trade route between the Roman Empire and the BALTIC SEA. In 1163, Wroclaw became the capital of SILESIA. Sacked by the Mongols in 1241; rebuilt by German settlers as a trade center. In 1335 it became part of BOHEMIA and a member of the Hanseatic League. Ceded to the Habsburg Empire in 1526; to Prussia in 1742. Damaged by Russian and German sieges in 1945, it was rebuilt and experienced major industrialization in the 1950's and 1960's.

Yalta. City in the CRIMEA in the southern UKRAINE. It is a popular holiday and health resort. Yalta became famous because in February, 1945, the three key Allied leaders of World War II met at Yalta in the Livadiya Palace in what became known as the Yalta Conference. Its population was 89,300 in 1991.

Yugoslavia. Balkan country in southeastern Europe. Total area of 39,450 square miles (102,173 sq. km.) with a 1990's population of 10.6 million. Capital is BELGRADE. Bounded on the north by CROATIA and HUNGARY, on the east by ROMANIA and BULGARIA, on the south by MACEDONIA and ALBANIA, and on the west by BOSNIA-HERZEGOVINA. Originally created in 1918 as a much larger federal state consisting of six republics: Bosnia-Herzegovina, Croatia, Macedonia, MONTENEGRO, SERBIA, and SLOVENIA. Beginning in 1991, all but Serbia and Montenegro broke away to form independent countries. Most of the population speaks Serbo-Croatian, but large minorities speak Albanian and Magyar (Hungarian).

Zagreb. Capital and largest city of CROATIA. Population was about 700,000 in the 1990's. Located at the eastern end of Slovene ALPS on the northern bank of the Sava River. Surrounding region is fertile and densely populated. Industries include flour milling, food processing, paper and textile manufacturing, and the production of electrical goods; a university is also located here. Was the site of a Roman city.

Zealand. See DENMARK.

David Barratt; Michelle Behr; William A. Dando; Raymond Pierre Hylton; William D. Walters, Jr.; Grove Koger; Dana P. McDermott; Mika Roinila

1484

INDEX TO VOLUME 5

See volume 8 for a comprehensive index to all eight volumes in set.

F L A G S   O F   T H E   W O R L D

Lebanon

Lesotho

Liberia

Libya

Liechtenstein

Lithuania

Luxembourg

Macedonia

Madagascar

Malawi

Malaysia

Maldives

Mali

Malta

Marshall Islands

Mauritania

Mauritius

Mexico

Micronesia

Moldova

Monaco

Mongolia

Morocco

Mozambique

Myanmar

Namibia

Nauru

Nepal

Netherlands

New Zealand

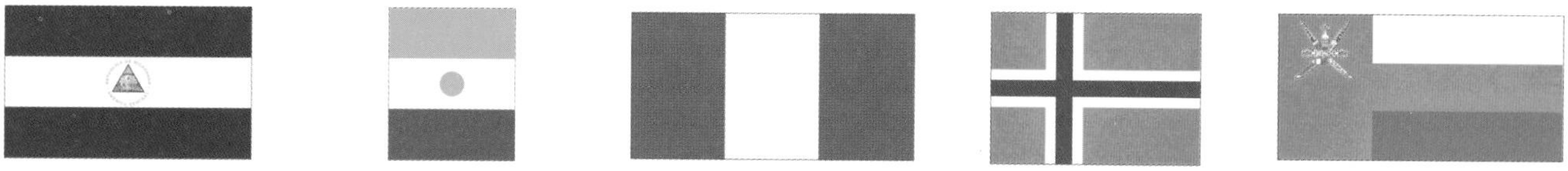

Nicaragua

Niger

Nigeria

Norway

Oman

Pakistan

Palau

Palestine

Panama

Papua New Guinea

Paraguay

Peru

Philippines

Poland

Portugal

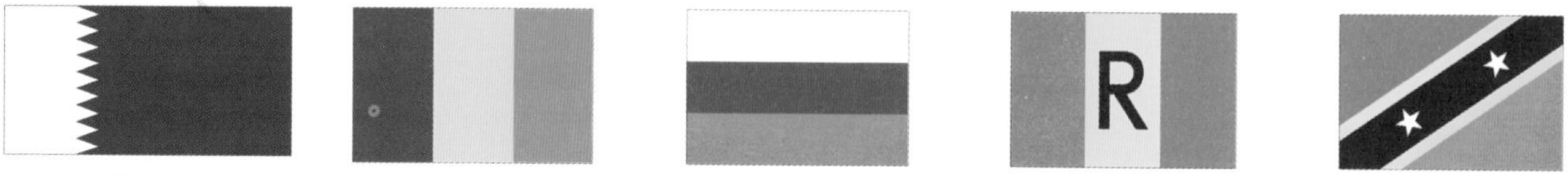

Qatar

Romania

Russia

Rwanda

St. Kitts & Nevis